Stuart McCabe

Let the WOlves DevoUr

War, religion and espionage during
the minority of Mary Queen of Scots, 1542-1560

Stuart McCabe

Let the WOLVES DEVOUR

War, religion and espionage during
the minority of Mary Queen of Scots, 1542-1560

MEREO
Cirencester

Mereo Books

1A The Wool Market Dyer Street Cirencester Gloucestershire GL7 2PR
An imprint of Memoirs Publishing www.mereobooks.com

Let the Wolves Devour: 978-1-86151-542-1

First published in Great Britain in 2015
by Mereo Books, an imprint of Memoirs Publishing

Copyright ©2015

Stuart McCabe has asserted his right under the Copyright Designs and
Patents Act 1988 to be identified as the author of this work.

A CIP catalogue record for this book is available from the British Library.

This book is sold subject to the condition that it shall not by way of trade or
otherwise be lent, resold, hired out or otherwise circulated without the publisher's
prior consent in any form of binding or cover, other than that in which it is
published and without a similar condition, including this condition being imposed
on the subsequent purchaser.

The address for Memoirs Publishing Group Limited can be found at
www.memoirspublishing.com

The Memoirs Publishing Group Ltd Reg. No. 7834348

The Memoirs Publishing Group supports both The Forest Stewardship Council®
(FSC®) and the PEFC® leading international forest-certification organisations. Our
books carrying both the FSC label and the PEFC® and are printed on FSC®-certified
paper. FSC® is the only forest-certification scheme supported by the leading
environmental organisations including Greenpeace. Our paper procurement policy
can be found at www.memoirspublishing.com/environment

Typeset in 9/14pt Century Schoolbook
by Wiltshire Associates Publisher Services Ltd. Printed and bound in Great Britain
by Printondemand-Worldwide, Peterborough PE2 6XD

Contents

Introduction

1. The Scotland of James V	P.1
2. The stones will rise	P.26
3. Effusion of blood	P.93
4. Not with painted words	P.148
5. To pardon the unpardonable deed	P.179
6. The Frenchman's grave	P.218
7. Dangerous elevation	P.249
8. The rascal multitude	P.285
Epilogue	P.339
Bibliography	P.346
Index	P.350

Introduction

———◆———

This book is a narrative of the events that shaped Scottish history during the period 1542-1560. On December 14th, 1542 King James V of Scotland died and left a Queen, Mary of Guise, as well as an infant daughter, Mary, born several days before his death. The nation was beset by powerful forces from within and without, all seeking to gain control of the infant Queen. These forces were feudalistic, religious and political. Powerful families such as the Hamiltons, Douglases, Lennox-Stewarts, Campbell's and others took sides and fought to either retain their power or increase it.

The people of Scotland during that period were also becoming influenced by the Reformation in Europe and the Church settlement of Henry VIII of England. New ideas and questions about religion were flowing in from the Continent, whether Calvinist Geneva or Lutheran Germany, inspiring evangelistic preaching to spread within Scotland. The Catholic faith was represented by Cardinal David Beaton, who fought vigorously and ruthlessly against the religious reformers, and also to preserve the strategically important Scottish/French alliance.

The nations of England and France circled around Scotland seeking to dominant the wounded and leaderless nation, and whilst a Protestant faction would seek favour with Henry VIII, the French patriot Queen Mary de Guise fought, conspired for and succeeded in retaining strong French support against England, whilst using diplomacy and duplicity to protect her daughter from the ambitions of kings and nobles.

During this period not only was Scotland beset by warfare with England, there was a brutal economic naval conflict with England's ally, the Habsburg Empire. The Emperor Charles V also supplied experienced and professional soldiers from the Continent to fight in Scotland, introducing new forms of warfare and weaponry into the bloody border campaigns. In retaliation the Scots employed privateers with letters of marque to make the sea lanes unsafe for imperial shipping. There were also dangers from the Highlands and Isles, as England and Scotland fought a proxy war using Gaelic clans. From Dublin and Carrickfergus, Irish mercenaries threatened the Scottish coasts and fought on Scottish soil alongside foreign mercenaries from Germany, Spain, Italy and across Europe.

The lifeblood of this multi-layered conflict was espionage and treachery in which spies and double agents were used to report and undermine powerful men and sabotage their agendas. Intricate spy networks were stretched across Scotland, spreading disinformation and propaganda, and a campaign could be lost or won on the effectiveness of an act of betrayal. English money and power found ways to buy allegiance. On the borders was created a system of 'assurance', whereby in return for not being attacked or having their lands wasted a Scot would become 'assured' and fight for England. Whilst this system would cause divisions and uncertainty amongst Scots, it would in time backfire when French money competed with English coin and a band of assured Scots could turn on former English allies.

The wars and politics of the period 1542-1560 heralded in a new determination of the Scots not to be dominated by the English, and equally not by the French. By 1559 a new Scottish identity began to emerge which combined a fierce independent will with a reformed religion shaped by Calvinism. The following work examines how an ancient nation with a long association with the Church of Rome turned into the first nation in Europe to successfully revolt against the established church and a constitutional monarchy, and legislate into life a new form of church worship, the Kirk. It was this new Scotland that awaited Queen Mary of Scots when she returned from Catholic France in 1561 to claim her crown.

Chapter One

The Scotland of James V

When James IV of Scotland, with a large number of nobles, churchmen, soldiery and commons to the number of 9,000, died at the Battle of Flodden, September 9th, 1513, Scotland was left politically and militarily weakened. Fear of English invasion caused the rushed coronation at Linlithgow of the infant James V, on September 21st, 1513. James IV had written a will in which his queen Margaret Tudor, sister of Henry VIII, King of England, was to act as regent of Scotland and tutor to James V. The King of England would have believed that through his sister's influential position he would be better able to influence Scotland politically. About this he would be proved wrong.

Margaret had married James in 1502 as part of a negotiated settlement known as the Treaty of Perpetual

Peace, where Scotland and England would become friends and allies, and each would support the other in the event of war. With Pope Alexander VI confirming a papal bull, either party that broke the treaty would be subject to excommunication.[1] It was a remarkable treaty, considering the previous two centuries of war and hostility between Scotland and England. However, in 1512 James decided to renew the Scottish-French treaties in 1512 just as hostilities were ensuing between Henry VIII and Louis XII, King of France. Once he received 50,000 francs from France he invaded England in 1513.[2] Margaret begged him not to wage war against her brother, but James ignored her, and died a heroic if pointless death on the battlefield.[3] He left his queen and young son, born on April 10th, 1512, to the mercies and intrigues of differing rival factions.

Within Scotland there were interlinking power structures. There was a feudal system introduced by David I (1124-53), whereby the crown owned all the land, and the nobility were granted land and title from the King in return for payment of taxes and military service. Succession was through primogeniture, through the line of oldest son. The next layer of power below the King were the earls, who in turn would parcel out lands to lords, barons, and knights. And below them were farmers, tenants, and householders.[4]

Many of the great earls had power equivalent to mini-kings. To put a check on this power, David had introduced sheriffs, who were to administer crown-owned regions in the name of the King. They were responsible for collecting taxes and rents, and for acting as magistrates by trying civil and criminal cases. They were also responsible for calling men to military duty. There would be rivalry between sheriffs and feudal lords in respect to judicial authority, with the latter having their own barony courts which could rule on certain criminal cases. Supervising the sheriffs were the Justiciars. Historically there were two, one commanding the regions north of the Firth of Forth, the other the south. They were expected to tour the sheriffdoms twice a year, with powers to investigate serious crimes, investigate illegal land seizures and hear appeals from the sheriff courts.[5] There were other positions created by royal writ, such as the chancellor, responsible for the great seal and checking all charters, documents and treaties before authorizing them with the King's seal. There were also constables, chamberlains and others with various important roles to play. [6]

The King would also have a council of selected advisers, a mechanism that would evolve over the years into what historians call the Privy Council, made up of nobles and churchmen. The numbers could range from ten to twenty, depending on circumstances. He also had permanent officials, such as a lord treasurer, comptroller, justice clerk, clerk of council, advocate and secretary.[7] The priority of this council was to ensure stability in the realm, and consider matters of national and international importance. It would act on issues such as treaties, war, peace, trade, criminality, economics and religion. It would also consider judicial and civil disputes,[8] if that dispute was potentially a danger to national security.

Representing the economic arm of Scottish were the burghs, towns built on crown land and confirmed by charter. They did not pay taxes to feudal lords, and were allowed to establish their own markets. They produced goods that were traded or sold with other burghs, or exchanged with

European merchandise as traders from England or across the seas brought in goods. They were virtually autonomous entities, and could form police forces, elect magistrates called baillies, and form their own assemblies. The burghs developed into powerful mercantile townships and formed strong economic ties and treaties with Scandinavian, Baltic, German, Netherland, Flemish and French townships.[9]

The Scottish church was another hierarchical power structure. At the top end were the Archbishoprics of St Andrews and of Glasgow, below them bishops, and then abbots and parish priests. The pope had the power to appoint bishops and all church appointments, until Innocent VIII conceded the right for the monarch of Scotland to recommend a candidate, and would wait eight months to consider all arguments until making a decision. In time the Scottish rulers would effectively pick appointees.[10]

The Scottish Church was powerful and wealthy; owning nearly a half of the land rents,[11] and from the agricultural produce of each parish, a tenth or tithe was granted for the functioning of the parish church.[12] The church also had political influence, with 53 seats in parliament by 1544, as well as a number of political posts in government.[13]

The Scottish Parliament would become known as the Three Estates, as it was made up of nobility, clerics and burgesses. In order to introduce legislation the monarch needed the votes of the majority within parliament. However as a parliament would take time to call, the Privy Council, also known as Lords of the Council, would effectively become the government. Within this political structure during 1513 there was a body of magnates, such as James Beaton, the Bishop of Glasgow, and the Lord

Chamberlain, Hume, who were setting themselves as opposition to Margaret. They and their supporters were keen to renew the alliance with France and to invite John Stewart, Duke of Albany as regent.

Albany was a Frenchman of Scots descent. Being a nephew of James III, he was also heir apparent to the throne of Scotland after James V. The divisions within Scotland would sharpen when in August 1514 Margaret married Archibald, the sixth Earl of Angus, and leader of the powerful Red Douglas faction. At a council in Edinburgh Margaret was deprived of regency powers and these were to be passed to Albany.

Angus's father had died at Flodden, and the new Earl inherited vast estates and titles, such as Crawford and Douglas in Lanarkshire, Tantallon in Haddingtonshire, the regalities of Jedburgh Forest and Selkirk and the governorship of Abernethy collegiate church in Perthshire, to mention only a few. He maintained a persistent claim to Coldingham Priory, Berwickshire, important both for its potential wealth and for its position near the border, though here he faced competition from the Humes. He had powerful allies with the earls of Glencairn, the earls of Montrose, the Hays of Yester and the Lyons of Glamis. He could call on vast wealth and a vast retinue of armed men, which made him powerful. Margaret also possessed lands and wealth in Dunbar, Methven and Crawford, and most importantly the strategically important castle of Stirling.[14]

The Duke of Albany arrived in Scotland in May 1515, bringing with him French support, aid and manpower. His terms of governorship when in Scotland were May 1515-June 1517, November 1521-October 1522 and September

1523–May 1524. He brought political unity and stabilized justice during these periods. Once he was gone the differing factions would form up and each fight against the others. In the parliament of July 1515 he was appointed guardian of Lord James and his younger brother Alexander, Duke of Rothesay. Margaret's reluctance to hand over the young king compelled Albany to raise an army of 7,000 and march to Stirling. Margaret surrendered the King on August 1st, 1515 and left for England with Angus and his brother, Sir George Douglas.

Angus would later leave Margaret and reconcile himself with Albany, much to his wife's disgust. Henry would prove supportive of this separation, as he hoped that Angus would front a pro-English party within Scotland. When Albany left for France in June 1517, Angus entered into a dangerous dispute with the Earl of Arran representing the powerful Hamilton clan, and himself an heir to the throne after Albany. During one street fight in Edinburgh called 'Clean the Causeway', on April 30th, 1520, Angus had Arran and his followers chased out of the town. When Albany returned from France on March 1522 he had Angus forfeit his estates and banished him from Scotland. Angus went to France.[15]

During Albany's visit to France he had signed the Treaty of Rouen, a renewal of political alliance between Scotland and France, which also included a promise for James to marry a French bride of the highest nobility, and in the first instance, under certain conditions, a daughter of the King of France. There was also agreement to support each other in event of war against England.[16]

Margaret would return to Scotland and reconcile herself to Albany. When he left once more for France on May 1524, she arranged with Arran's compliance to have her son taken from Stirling and brought to Edinburgh. She then had him proclaimed king of Scotland at the age of 12. A pro-English party was forming in Scotland, headed by Margaret. Henry paid for a royal guard of 200, and supplied pensions to supporters.[17]

Angus returned to Scotland in 1524/25, visiting England on the way. In England he met with Henry VIII in London and reached some kind of arrangement with Henry in which he would support James V on the throne and retain friendly relations with England. Due to this understanding Angus and Margaret publicly reconciled their differences. At a parliament of February 1525 he was restored of his titles, estates and possessions, and was allowed his place in council. He would also be appointed Warden of the East and Middle Marches.[18]

In January 1526, parliament approved a rotating list of lords to provide guardianship of the young King for three months each. Angus was the first appointee, a move not popular with Queen Margaret. She joined with the Earls of Moray and Arran and mustered an army at Linlithgow during January 1526. When Angus's army showed with James at the head the rival army dispersed, nobody wishing to fight against the King. James was declared to have 'Royal Authority' on June 14th, 1526; however he was practically kept a prisoner by Angus and the Red Douglas faction for nearly two years.

On July 20th 1526 at Melrose, and on September 4th 1526 at Linlithgow, Angus won two battles. In the latter the Earl of Lennox was slain.

On April 1528 it was announced in Scotland that

Margaret's divorce had been granted in Rome in March 1527. She now married Henry Stewart. On May 20th, James escaped from Angus whilst at Falkland and found refuge in Stirling Castle, which his mother occupied. Taking control of government, he purged it of the Douglas faction and supporters. He ordered Angus and his followers to ward themselves, and when this was refused, he summons Angus to parliament to face charges of treason. With another refusal a war broke out between the King and Angus, an inconclusive conflict in which Henry intervened and granted Angus and his follower's exile in England. James allowed this.[19] Angus, Sir George Douglas and the rest of his close family would have their estates forfeited. Angus would now be an exile receiving a pension from the English crown.[10]

King James attempted to impose royal authority by bringing law to the Borders, Highlands and Isles. A peace was agreed between Scotland and England at Berwick in December 1528 to last five years. James began to fall out with powerful magnates of Scotland, such as the Earl of Argyll, who was imprisoned because the King fears his power. He also wards Patrick Hepburn, third Earl of Bothwell, Lord Hume, the lairds Maxwell, Johnstone and Buccleuch and others because he believes they are secretly supporting raids against England and threatening the treaty. His treatment would cause Bothwell in December 1531 to enter into treasonous correspondence with the Earl of Northumberland, offering 7,000 men to any English campaign against James. And he adds that other nobles are of that mind.[21] Even the King's half-brother, the Earl of Moray is subject to James's style of rule when he loses lands over a technicality.

With King James alienating many of the nobles and gentry, he began to turn more to the clergy for favour and financial support, in return for waging war against heresy and Lutherism. Martin Luther, the reformer, was excommunicated in 1520, and by 1525 his works were reaching the east coast of Scotland through merchants and mariners, and finding footholds in Leith and Perth.[22] The threat of this spread of heretic literature compelled Parliament to effect an Act prohibiting the importation by sea of the 'books and works of the said Luther, his disciples or servants', and permission was given for ships to be searched. If works of heresy were found the owners were to be imprisoned.[23]

This Act did not halt Patrick Hamilton, a nobleman turned preacher who had studied in Paris as a student. He attended lectures by Erasmus and Reuchlin and his curiosity took him to Wittenburg and Marburg University to become influenced by the works of Luther, Melanchthon and Lambert. He returned to Scotland and began to spread his catechism called *Patrick's Place*, based on the doctrine of justification by faith. His preaching was openly defiant of church authority and doctrine. In 1528 Hamilton was captured by the Archbishop of St Andrews' men and taken to the castle. After a hurried trial Hamilton was convicted of being an 'obstinate heretic' and burned at the stake outside St Salvador's college.[24] Archbishop James Beaton was advised that burning Hamilton had been counter-productive since now more people were curious as to why he had been burned and were actively seeking out his works, reflecting how 'the reek of Master Patrick Hamilton has infected as many as it blew upon!' Within a few years individuals belonging to either the grey or black friars began to question the errors of the church.[25]

The archbishops and bishops openly displayed a wealth that was at odds with the poverty of the country. The tithe which was meant to pay parish priests and support him in bring religion and education to his flock was being diverted to the religious houses and allowing those churchmen at the top of the hierarchy to enjoy a lifestyle unbecoming a follower of Christ.[26] In the 1540s the provincial council of the clergy noted the moral decay of the church through the 'profane lewdness' of the churchmen,[27] and James Beaton, Archbishop of St Andrews, Patrick Hepburn, Bishop of Moray and Cardinal David Beaton were all alleged to have several mistresses, as well as illegitimate children.[28]

In this they had something in common with the King. James would have several mistresses, and several illegitimate children.[29] Providing for his offspring would cause widespread discontent due to policy decisions of James V, such as the granting of the abbey kirks of Kelso, Melrose, Holyroodhouse and St Andrews to his natural sons.[30] He was also prone to having affairs with other men's wives 'or taking them as mistresses, possessing a reputation as a man with loose morals'.[31] Before his death he had been with a mistress at Tantallon Castle.[32] With the commoners it was said he was popular because he brought order and justice. He would however prove an unpopular king amongst the nobility. Those that lost his favour could find themselves deprived of property, rights, liberty or life.[33]

King James would profit from his relationship with the church. In 1532 Pope Clement VIII granted him the power to tax monastic incomes, which allowed him to fund the

College of Justice, made up of seven lay and seven spiritual judges and one president. It was a court to pass judgment on civil actions; however Buchanan states that in his time it was an 'instrument of tyrannical injustice'.[34] This relationship with the clergy would coincide with events in England, where Henry VIII was seeking to divorce Catherine of Aragon, leading to a break with Rome and the English parliament dissolving papal authority. Henry would appoint himself head of the Church of England and enrich the crown with the dissolution of monasteries. The Scottish treaty with England was to expire in 1533 and before that date border raiding had returned on a large scale. With French intervention the truce was extended to May 1534, and after that a truce was agreed until one of the kings died.

Henry tried to get James to convert to the reformed faith. English commentators considered James a servant of the clergy, and during August 1534 he had three 'heretics' burned to death. James declined any invitation to meet with Henry to discuss religion and politics. James would also find time to torment the Douglas clan by having Angus's sister Jane, the Lady Glamis, burned at the stake on Castle Hill, Edinburgh, in 1537, on being found guilty of planning to poison him and charges of witchcraft. Angus's brother-in-law Forbes was also executed, having been found guilty of planning a royal assassination.

James further widened the divide between himself and his uncle Henry by travelling to France in 1536 and choosing as a bride Madeleine, third daughter of the French king. In January 1st, 1537 they married at the Church of Notre Dame in Paris. In February 25th he received at Compiègne gifts from Pope Paul III, a blessed sword and hat, to strengthen his faith against the heretics of England.[35] Returning to Scotland on July 7th 1537, James would suffer misfortune when Queen Madeline died a few months later. He sent David Beaton, the forty-three year old nephew of the Archbishop of St Andrews, to choose a new bride. Beaton had enjoyed the patronage of Albany in 1515-1524. Having spent some time in France it was Albany who had introduced Beaton to King James.

Beaton was well thought of as a diplomat, visiting England in 1522 in that capacity, and he took part in Royal marriage negotiations in France in 1524. He became Abbot of Arbroath, and this allowed him a seat in parliament, and in 1529 he became Keeper of the Royal Seal. Whilst he was clearly for the clergy there was a growing movement in Scotland towards reform of the church, and this became linked with moves towards better relations with England. Beaton had to learn to tread carefully in the dangerous political environment of Scotland. Beaton's knowledge of French politics compelled James to send him across the water to pick a new bride, returning with his choice of Mary of Lorraine. James and Mary married at St Andrews on June 17th, 1538.[36]

Born at the castle of Bar-le-Duc in November 1515, Mary of Lorraine was a member of the de Guise family, eldest daughter of Claude, first Duke of Guise and Antoinette de Bourbon. She was initially to be educated in a nunnery, but after a few years she was released from this service and visited the court of the French King, Francis I. She married Louis Duke of Longueville in 1534 at Paris, followed by sixteen days of celebration. She had two sons, Francis and Louie, but her husband died in 1537 at Rouen of a fever just before Louie was born. A few months later Louie also died. Although she had planned to retire to her vast estates at Châteaudun, the King of France wanted to arrange a marriage with James V so as to keep solid the alliance between the two countries.[37] With marriage to Mary, James V would become related to a family that would become powerful and formidable in French and European politics.

Mary's father Claude, the first Duke of Guise, was the son of Rene, King of Sicily, who owned the Duchy of Lorraine and vast estates in France. Whilst Anthony, the first son, inherited Lorraine and the foreign lands, Claude would become Count of Guise, later Duke, and gain the French possessions. He was sent to the French court to become a naturalized Frenchman.

Claude became good friends with Francis, the son of King Louis XII. When Francis became King on January 1st 1515, Claude's career turned military. He took part in warfare in Italy, Spain and Northern France, being awarded vice-regal powers in his own French lands. In 1525, when Francis once more invaded Italy, this time disastrously with the capture of the King by imperial forces at the Battle of Pavia, Claude remained in France to act as Regent. At the same time German Lutherans invaded Lorraine. Claude and his brother Duke Anthony marched into Lorraine and defeated the Protestants. In Paris he was treated as a returning Christian hero, and the Pope sent congratulations. When Francis was released he rewarded Claude by making him Duke of Guise. Mary had eight brothers and three sisters, and marriage alliances and crown and church patronage would ensure that Guise influence and power would grow. Her younger brothers Francis and Charles would respectively become Duke of Guise and Cardinal of Lorraine and would be rising men in the French court earning Europe-wide reputations.[38]

Out of the two French marriages James received dowries amounting to £168, 750.[39] Mary, a devout Catholic, encouraged James in applying a harder line against reformists and heretics. Also of significance was the appointment of David Beaton as Archbishop of St Andrews in September 1539.[40] This was considered a papal appointment influenced by the French King Francis, who had also nominated Beaton as Cardinal and as Bishop of Mirepoix in 1538. Whilst holding clerical offices in both nations, Beaton embodied the religious and political importance of the Scottish-French alliance.[41] Beaton was also emboldened by this increase in religious prestige, and there would be the beginning of a campaign to locate and drive out heretics. Those believed to be sympathetic to reformist ideas were barred from public or royal office. Money was offered for uncovering heretics, and it was prohibited for anyone to communicate with them. As the restriction grew, the proscribed teachings began to spread across Scotland. Violence and oppression did not appear to put a halt of the new form of worship.[42] Even in Fife and Angus there were nobles and professional people who whilst having reformist ideas and attitude were too powerful to be intimidated by Beaton's inquisition.[43]

In April 1541 the royal household suffered tragedy when James's two sons, Prince James and Prince Robert, Duke of Albany, died in infancy, and were buried in Holyrood Abbey.[44] Scott claims the Queen and the clergy blamed this misfortune on James's slowness in prosecuting heresy.[45] Allegations that the infants had been poisoned were reported to the King of England, and such unfounded and malicious rumours would not have helped the balance of James's mind. Prior to the deaths the Queen had been sending to France for drugs to counter the deteriorating physical and mental health of King James.[46]

As a diversion from the loss, and to reassure his subjects, James and Mary, escorted by leading nobles, travelled across the country, to Perth, Aberdeen, then Dundee, Falkland and finally Edinburgh. They were greeted by crowds of people and provided with entertainment by the universities and towns.[47]

Whilst Cardinal Beaton visited France, Henry sent his envoy Ralph Sadler to Scotland to once more try and persuade James to convert, and suggested laying possession of the revenues of the church as an incentive. Whilst James may have been tempted, the result of such a change would have been alienation with France, the papacy and the Holy Roman Empire, and in return friendship with an uncle who had sheltered James's mortal enemies, the Red Douglas clan.[48] Nevertheless he agreed to meet Henry, who invited him to York for September, 1541. The clergy were fearful that such a meeting could result in a Scottish/English understanding, and that James might follow Henry's example in overturning the Catholic faith in Scotland. There were many Scottish nobles and gentry supporting the reformed faith, which would prove a significant opposition to Catholic survival.

The clergy offered bribes to tempt James to spurn the meeting and provided a list of nobles and gentry across the country that were suspected heretics. The vast clerical information network provided hundreds of names, and any that were found guilty of heresy would have land and property forfeited to the crown. Kirkcaldy, the Laird of Grange and Lord Treasurer, advised against this course, as it could cause great strife within the country. The clergy however countered by offering 50,000 crowns towards raising an army, and accused Grange of being a heretic. Oliver Sinclair, a pensioner of the clergy, and close associate of James, supported this position. James agreed not to meet Henry.[49] The King of England went to York expecting to meet with his nephew, and had a house especially built for him. His hospitality turned to anger upon finally realising that James had snubbed him. Henry VIII returned to London by September 29th, and although he wanted to teach the Scots a lesson for making a fool of him, he could do nothing at that time.

Margaret Tudor, Henry's sister and James's mother, died in October 1541 at Methven. It was said that she pleaded for her son to visit her before she passed on, and she wanted the King to reconcile himself with Angus, yet he arrived too late. Despite the reported sentiments of conciliation from his mother, James would not hold back in his feud with the Red Douglas.[50] Leaving no will, James set out to settle her affairs;[51] it was the last tie of kinship between the House of Stuart and House of Tudor.[52] With his English neighbor the relationship would further worsen as Henry in late 1541 would enter into a mutual military alliance against France with the Emperor Charles V and the Holy Roman Empire. Despite the religious differences between the two, France was seen as a mutual threat to both the new allies. In an attempt to claim suzerainty over Scotland, Henry sent the Archbishop of York to find documents that might claim this. As troops were being mobilized on the borders James tried to defuse the situation by sending delegates for talks at Windsor, but Henry was not in the mood for conciliation or stalling, and nothing came out of the meetings.[53]

In May 1542, Queen Mary was pregnant again, and expecting delivery of a child in the winter.[54] At the same time the clouds of war were looming on the borders. Early in 1542 the English Warden, Sir Thomas Wharton, had offered a proposal, which Henry VIII rejected, to capture James when another appointment for a meeting was discussed for January. Nothing came of this.

Along the borders the Scots were raiding the English.[55] On 24th August, Sir Robert Bowes, Captain of Norham castle, with 3,000 men including Angus and Sir George Douglas, pensioners of the English crown, launched a raid into Scotland by the East March. Near Kelso they set out to devastate the surrounding countryside. They were ambushed by the Earl of Huntley at Hadden Rigg. Bowes, his brother, and Sir William Mowbray were captured. Hundreds were killed and hundreds made prisoner.

Later that year Henry gave the Duke of Norfolk the order to raise an army at Newcastle for the purpose of another invasion. In October 1542, ignoring James's attempts to open negotiations, Henry declared war on Scotland, and the army of Norfolk crossed the border. However his campaign was a failure. Marching along the north bank of the Tweed the Scottish forces shadowed the English, which made raiding ineffective. Norfolk's army was slowed by wet and cold weather conditions, and having to bring heavy artillery across ground not suited for that type of transport. Supplies were also short and when Norfolk fell ill the army was effectively leaderless. It soon returned south, a humiliation for Henry and a moral boast for the Scots.[56]

James decided that he wanted to follow up with an invasion of England, despite the month being November with harsh weather. A muster was called at Fala Muir near the Lammermuir Hills. There was a reluctance in the army to this invasion, and the King was reminded that he had lost his two sons,[57] and that although Queen Mary was pregnant, an invasion of England would put James's at risk, with the added risk of Scotland being once more governed by a minority. As James, Earl of Moray, and the King's half-brother explained, the English had lost this latest campaign and many of the magnates within the army were unwilling to risk their men in any further campaigning that was unnecessary. James had no choice but to disband the army.[58]

Scottish kings did not have standing or contracted armies, although they had the power to call a muster if the country was under threat after approval by council or parliament. Men were obliged to serve free for forty days, and bring their own supplies and equipment and outfit themselves depending on status. Each gentleman would be expected to show with helmet, armour, sword, dagger and pike, while those without adequate resources or land could be supplied equipment by sheriffs and baillies. Yeomen between 16 and 60 years of age were to bring bows and arrows, or axes, swords, pikes and shields.[59] The pike was the most important weapon for the infantry, where men stood side by side, shoulder to shoulder, presenting to an enemy a thick array of pikes in a formation called a schiltron. The infantry received training at wappenshaws (weapon shows), held four times a year, where drills and maneuvers were practiced, especially on how to effectively form up a troop of archers or a division of pikes. Unless used for carriages, the footmen were not allowed to take horses, due to the damage and confusion that could be caused if they were panicked.[60]

The nobility and burgesses contributed to the cavalry arms of an army, and would outfit themselves depending on wealth and status. The most destructive arm of the Scottish army was not the heavy horse of the upper ranks but the light horsemen of the border clans. Besides being great horsemen and fierce fighters, they were also experts at wasting the economic resources of a town or district by stealing livestock, burning towns, villages, farms and homes, burning crops and terrorizing whole communities. They also employed skirmishing as an effective military tactic, to harry and annoy an approaching or withdrawing army. They were an independent minded people who did not have an agricultural economy to encourage farming. The rearing of livestock and the stealing of it were widespread activities which drove the economies of the borders.

The well-equipped borderers and light horsemen usually wore steel bonnets and quilted leather coats covered with metal or horn plates. Leather boots and breeches were also worn. For weapons they would carry lances, swords, daggers and possibly handguns.[61] James V had tried to impose peace on the borders through violence and executions, which subdued some clans, while it forced others to consider their national loyalty. In the wars between Scotland and England, the Scottish borderers would be subject to a system called 'assurance', where in return for switching sides to England they would be assured that their lands and possessions, as well as those of friends, would be safe from raids.

The Scots did not keep up with the latest European military innovations. Very few firearms were present in the Scottish armies, except when they joined with French allies.[62] The Earl of Sussex considered the archer more effective than the harquebusier,[63] although Henry would be an enthusiastic hirer of highly-trained and experienced Spanish, Italian, German and other continental mercenaries. The harquebusiers would become a vital component in the English armies during the 1540s, where the rapid fire of piercing iron balls had the added psychological effect of noise and smoke. A bullet could pierce light armour and quilted jackets and the wounds were hard to treat; afflictions like lead poisoning were still not fully understood. Artillery was used by the Scots, the most powerful cannon being in castles, such as Edinburgh and manned by expert gunners.[64] In general the field artillery was not up to continental standard, and would be proved inadequate, especially against strong castles, such as during the siege of St Andrews.[65]

After forty days of service the Scottish levies would be paid by the King, or as a substitute for payment the soldiers could keep whatever spoils they took from the enemy. Under these terms it is understandable why some armies were reluctant to invade, especially during winter where the spoils would be small and the risks of ill-health through cold or wet weather much higher. The lords would have to take into consideration the opinions of their own adherents and servants.

James however was determined to march against England, and the church was willing to fund it. Instead of a general muster James sent out privy letters to individual magnates asking them to come to a designated place with their retinue. Through this method two armies were mustered, one at Haddington under Beaton and the Earl of Moray, the second on the West March and commanded by the King. This latter army was meant to march towards Carlisle, but at Lochmaben James took ill and the army continued without him. It crossed the Sark river and entered the debatable land by the 23rd of November. The army of Moray and Cardinal Beaton disbanded upon hearing of the King's illness.

It was expected that Lord Maxwell, the Warden of the West March, would have been the official commander of this expedition, which had 18,000 men. It seems that Oliver Sinclair, the King's companion as well as pensioner of the clergy, was declared commander of the army through a proclamation of the King. As this was made whilst crossing the Sark it seems to have led to crisis and confusion in command, especially as prior to this Maxwell seems to have been commanding.[66]

The army was initially divided into two divisions, the horse led by Maxwell as the vanguard whilst the rear was made up of foot. Lord Wharton, the captain of Carlisle, Lord Darce and Sir William Musgrave mobilized a force estimated at 1,300. Wharton sent out horsemen to skirmish with the Scots. The Scots, on restricted and narrow ground, began to fragment under these attacks, whilst there was a lack of accurate communication between vanguard and rear. Scots began to withdraw, and the continued attacks began to turn retreat into rout. Many fell into the marsh and waters of Solway Moss. The army totally disintegrated, with hundreds captured or offering themselves up as prisoners, and hundreds more drowned in the rivers and bogs. It is said only 20 Scots died in the actual fighting, which suggests the attacks had a psychological effect.[67] When Oliver Sinclair was proclaimed Lord-Lieutenant of the army, many were said to have refused to fight and allowed themselves to be taken prisoner.[68]

Musgrave accounts how the Scots drove down the West March, burning out the Graham clan. As the Scots advanced, the English horse was sent out to harass the flanks, whilst the remainder dismounted and arrayed themselves with 'bill and bow'. As they approached, the Scots horsemen galloped away, whilst the 'multiple' at the rear began to withdraw in disorder. Although reports of the encounter do not give precise details, it appears that an apparent retreat by Scots horsemen from the vanguard could have caused the more general retreat.[69]

One of the more controversial accusations leveled at Maxwell and his associates were that they deliberately caused the rout at Solway Moss. There is no satisfactory explanation for why the Scots in the rear of the army retreated as they did, and it is difficult to comprehend how an experienced commander like Maxwell allowed the army to be outplayed by the light horsemen of Wharton, especially as they were smaller in number compared to the Scots. What the horsemen were doing was skirmishing as an attempt to harass and slow down a much larger army.

The Venetian secretary in England would provide an opinion around the time of the battle which he claims came from a reliable source of secret intelligence. Lord Maxwell was in the vanguard when the English army began attacking. In an attempt to organize the rear he galloped towards them, an action which the rear perceived as being a retreat, which in turn caused panic and a general rout. The writer states that such an act in approaching the rear whilst deserting the vanguard could be considered military incompetence, or 'devious' in that he aimed to give the impression of a rout so that the army would be defeated. The writer does not suggest that Maxwell was in the pay of England. He mentions that he is of the Lutheran faith and an enemy of Beaton, and the engineering of the defeat may have been to embarrass and weaken James V, Beaton and the clergy. As it happened, Maxwell would be captured.[70]

According to Calderwood, Lord Maxwell had said that he would rather remain and take his chances against the English, stating that he believed he would be hanged in Scotland. Despite ordering an array, Sinclair apparently could not control the army, and there seems to have been a counter-order to the rear division to retreat covered by the horse, although Calderwood does not specify how the order came about. If Maxwell did ride to the rear it may have been he that made this order, or his advance to the rear may have given the impression that the army was in retreat, which spread panic through the army. Blame then could have been leveled at him, which explains his returning to the vanguard to allowing himself to be captured.[71]

With news of the defeat James seems to have fallen into a deep depression, not helped by his being ill at

Caerlaverock castle. He briefly visited his Queen at Linlithgow who was heavily pregnant, before leaving her side to go to Falkland Castle. He would learn that on the 8th December his Queen had given birth to a daughter, who would also be named Mary. Despite this joyous news King James lapsed into states of mental confusion and excitement, supposedly crying out for his companion Oliver Sinclair, whilst wailing about the defeat at Solway. On 14th December James died, reportedly of "regret, sorrow and rage".[72]

References: (1) (SHD, p.93). (2) (MacDougall, pp.115-117). (3) (ODNB, vol. 29, pp.619-620). (4) (Somerset Fry, P & F. (1982). (5) (Grant, pp.150-151). (6) (Somerset Fry, pp.71-72). (7) (RPCS, vol 1, June 5th, 1546, (24)). (8) (RPCS, vol 1, x-xii). (9) (Somerset Fry, pp.70-71). (10) (SHD, 89-90). (11) (Thomson, vol 3, pp.225-226). (12) (Somerset-Fry, p.64). (13) (Thomson, vol 3, pp.225-226). (14) (ODNB, vol 16, pp.616-620). (15) (SP, vol.1, pp.190-191). (16) (SHD, pp.98-100). (17) (Hume-Brown, vol.1, pp.303-304). (18) (SP, vol.1, p.191). (19) (Hume-Brown, vol.1, pp.304-305). (20) (SP, vol.1, pp.191-192). (21) (Hume-Brown, vol.1, pp. 303-304). (22) (McCulloch,pp.202-204. Knox, pp.16-19). (23) (SHD, pp.102-103). (24) (Knox, pp.3-8. Luckoch, pp.114-117). (25) (Knox, pp.7-10). (26) (Thomson, pp. 225-226). (27) (Somerset-Fry, pp.131-132). (28) (Thomson, vol.3, pp.228-229). (29) (Marshall, p.32). (30) (HP, vol.1 (272), pp.357-359, Lisle and Tunstall to Henry VIII, Jan 5th 1543). (31) (Calderwood, pp.150-154). (32) (Marshall, p.44). (33) (Hume-Brown, pp.317-321). (34) (Hume-Brown, p.318). (35) (Hume-Brown, pp.306-308. MacDougall, pp.130-132). (36) (ODNB, vol.4, pp.551-556). (37) (ODNB, vol.37, pp.71-77). (38) (Marshall, pp.7-14). (39) (MacDougall, pp131-132). (40) (Scott, pp.402-403). (41) (ODNB, vol.4, pp.551-556). (42) (Scott, pp.402-403). (43) (ODNB, vol.4, pp.551-556). (44) (Marshall, pp.39-40). (45) (Scott, pp.401-403). (46) (Fraser, p.258. Marshal, p.38-40). (47) (Hume-Brown, pp.312-313. Marshall, pp.39-41). (48) (Scott, pp. 402-403). (49) (Melville, pp.1-5). (50) (Fraser, pp.258-260). (51) (Marshal, p.41). (52) (Hume-Brown, vol 1, p.313). (53) (Paterson, pp. 163-164). (54) (Marshal, pp.42-43). (55) (Fraser, p.247-248). (56) (Paterson, pp.164-165). (57) (Lesley, pp.163-164). (58) (Paterson, pp.165-166). (59) (Thomson, vol 3, pp.28-29). (60) (Thomson, vol 3, pp.260-261). (61) (MacDonald Fraser, p.86-89). (62) (Thomson, p.260). (63) (MacDonald Fraser, pp,88-89). (64) (Merriman, pp.145-149). (65) (RPCS, vol.1, pp.58-59). (66) (Paterson, pp.166-168). (67) (Paterson, pp. 167-168). (68) (Melville). (69) (Hamilton Papers, Vol.1, 1532-1543, Bain, J (ed.) (1890), H.M. General Register House, Edinburgh) (HP, vol.1, (240), pp.307-309. Report of Battle of Solway Moss. Sir William Musgrave to Sir Anthony Brown, Nov 24th, 1542). (70) (CSPV, Venice, Hironimo Zucculo, Venetian secretary in England to the Church of the Ten, 16th Dec, 1542). (71) (Calderwood, pp.150-154). (72) (CSPS, Eustace to Queen of Hungary, Dec 23rd 1542. Holinshed, pp.529-530. Marshal, p.45).

Chapter Two

The stones will rise

The King's servant, Simon Penningham, who was also in the employ of Sir George Douglas, arranged to meet Douglas at Berwick.[1] Once informed of the details of James's death during late December 1542, Sir George passed this news on to the English Privy Council, informing them that the Scots nobles intended to keep the death a secret so as to keep receiving the subsidies from the French King. Cardinal Beaton, the Earls of Moray, Argyll and Huntley, were to act as joint governors of the realm.[2] A rumour was also spread that James had been poisoned,[3] and whilst John Knox makes no mention of this, later writers would repeat this allegation, with Mary of Guise being a suspect and Cardinal Beaton an accomplice.[4] Melville points the finger at the clergy, fearing that King James was going to blame them for the advice that led to the disastrous war. They feared James would use the defeat to instigate an English-type revolution with papal authority being usurped.[5]

For the royal funeral in early January, the body of James V was taken from Falkland to Edinburgh, escorted by nobles, prelates and adherents. In the Dolorous Chapel of the abbey at Holyrood, the coffin was placed on a bier covered with a cloth with a white cross on a black background. A life-sized effigy of James lay across the coffin, with replica crown, robe and scepter. A carver called Andrew Mansioun designed a figure of a lion set above the crown, and engraved a superscription measuring 18 feet in Roman letters across the tomb. Cardinal Beaton conducted the funeral and the Earl of Arran was principle mourner. James was placed in the vault next to Queen Madeleine and his two sons.[6]

For the Red Douglas faction the death of the hated James V was an opportunity. Prior to learning of the death of his nephew Henry VIII had decided to have the prisoners of Solway Moss humiliated by being marched through the streets of London, and then lodged under close confinement in the Tower. With Queen Mary, baby daughter of James V, Scotland was now faced with the prospect of another minority, and the possibility of more faction fighting between powerful nobles. The Queen Mother would obviously be concerned that her daughter and herself could be captured, and south of the border King Henry VIII was concocting plans to possess the young Queen. When he and his council learned of the death of James they proposed a plan in which a union between Scotland and England could be forged through a marriage between Mary and Edward, son of Henry VIII.

The Scottish prisoners were to be offered conciliation.[7] These prisoners would prove to be political weapons that both the exiled Earl of Angus and Sir George Douglas would use in a plan to regain power and prestige in Scotland. First there needed to be some kind of understanding reached between Henry and the Scottish prisoners, and we can assume that Sir Angus and Sir George used their influence to ensure better treatment for their compatriots. Due to his diplomatic abilities, Sir George was tasked as lead negotiator in marriage talks. He enjoyed the confidence of King Henry and he used this to ensure a common purpose for all key parties. The Scottish prisoners wanted freedom and a return to Scotland, and Henry wanted Scotland on a lease. The prisoners, along with the Red Douglas faction, could offer political, diplomatic and military means for Henry to gain rule over his northern neighbour.[8]

Henry ordered them to be taken from the Tower and brought to Westminster on the 20th December. They made a commitment to use their resources to support the idea of political union through marriage.[9] This union also entailed conditions in which Scotland was to acknowledge Henry as lord superior, and the strongest Scottish fortress was to be handed over into English possession. The young Queen Mary was to be sent immediately to England. The Scottish prisoners, known as 'assured Scots', offered solemn pledges, as well as hostages, to ensure their bond and service to Henry VIII.[10] If they failed in their mission they were to return to England and prison, although if war ensued they would have the choice to fight for Henry.[11] They were also to attempt to bribe any tutors appointed to look after the Princess Mary.[12] Enthusiasm for these agreements was reported by the Spanish Ambassador. The Scottish prisoners at Henry's court on 24th December 1542 were encouraging him to conquer Scotland. In their opinion there would not be a better chance. Before allowing them to go home to Scotland, Henry gifted them Christmas presents, and gave them gold chains according to rank. The Earl of Angus and Sir George Douglas were also quick to act, both entering Scotland to reclaim those landed possessions forfeited to the Scottish crown.[13]

It is easy to judge these individuals from a narrow patriotic point of view, but their choices were prison or freedom. There is also the religious context to consider; many were influenced by the reformation and believed they had more in common with English Protestants than they did with the perceived corruption and immorality of Cardinal Beaton and the Scottish clergy. As Calderwood states, 'many hated the cardinal, and distained to be ruled by a priest'. The prisoners had also been victims of the Scottish crown's adherence to the French alliance, which like Flodden had led to disaster. Possibly they believed a marriage alliance would lead to political transformations that would bind Scotland and England closer together, although Henry's idea of union was not one based on equality and respect for sovereignty but the type of arrangement where Scotland is turned into a province of England.[14]

The Scottish parliament needed a figurehead to govern. However, within Scotland there were two political groupings, one dominated by Cardinal Beaton, who was also Chancellor. His group comprised the Queen Mother and the Earls of Argyll, Moray and Huntley, who were all supportive of a continuation of the French alliance.[15] Beaton would produce a will, which he claimed James V made at his deathbed, appointing himself, Huntley, Moray and Argyll as joint governors of Scotland and tutors to the infant Queen Mary.[16] The Cardinal had a copy of the will posted on the Market Cross, Edinburgh, announcing to the world the supposed legitimacy of his power.[17] The accusation that the will was forged, supposedly produced by a priest called Henry Balfour, was widely reported.[18] James Kirkcaldy, Laird of Grange, encouraged James Hamilton, the Earl of Arran, to assemble the nobles and claim the government.[19]

Arran had a powerful claim to the governorship, being recognised as second person of the realm and heir presumptive after the infant Queen Mary. His grandfather, James Hamilton, had married Mary Stewart, sister of James III of Scotland. Arran was born in 1519, the son of James, the first earl, who had died in 1529, and Jane Beaton, who died in 1522. The heir to vast estates in Lanarkshire, Linlithgowshire, Renfrewshire and Ayrshire, the Isle of Arran and the castle of Brodick, and interests in Kirkcudbrightshire and Roxburghshire, he was placed under the guardianship of his half-brother Sir James Hamilton Finnart until July 1539. There was definitely bitterness against Finnart, for when James V had this former favourite tried and convicted for treason in 16th August 1540, Arran was one of the lords on the assize. In the following month he was confirmed by the Great Seal as Earl of Arran with all the landed possessions and titles and privileges that entailed. He was a young man of twenty-three when Grange asked him to take the leadership in opposition to Beaton.[20] He was also said to possess a 'gentle nature', which is meant to explain the supposed indecisiveness of his character,[21] yet he would display a dogged ability to survive that would balance out his youth and inexperience.

The party that would be led by Arran was made of individuals influenced generally by reformation doctrines and fearful of the extremities of the Catholic church. Arran himself had an interest in the ideas of the reformation. Whilst those commoners critical of church corruption were open to a re-interpretation of the bible, especially translated bibles which could be read in Scots or English, they had little say in parliament or government. The burgesses and merchant classes did participate in parliamentary politics, and this influential class would cultivate contacts with the Continent, becoming exposed to the ideas of church reform, whether these were the preaching's of Luther, Calvin, or the translated bible of the Welsh scholar William Tyndale.[22] They would also be cynical of the church's adherence to the Franco-Scot military alliance that often led to wars. They may also have looked over the border to England, which was Protestant, and here hoped that through religion a better relationship could develop between the two nations.

At an Edinburgh Parliament of December 2nd, Beaton had challenged Arran's right, opposing the idea of one man who was not a king taking control of government. He also attacked the family of Hamilton, called them 'murderers' and 'thieves'. Arran would remind the nobles that he was heir apparent after Queen Mary, and thereby second person of the realm. He would ask them 'not to defraud of my just title, before yee have experience of my government'.[23] Arran would also challenge the authenticity of James V's will and produce a scroll, supposedly found in the late king's pocket, which displayed a list of 360 people, with Arran at the top. It was claimed that Beaton and the King had intended to prosecute the names on the list as heretics.[24] It appears that Arran was being ably advised by his entourage of supporters.

The clergy could not sit in judgment in criminal cases, so it had no judicial authority over the nobility. The list compiled by the clergy had offered the opportunity to target that nobility with suspect loyalties to Pope or King. And if accused and convicted of heresy or treason they would have properties and titles confiscated, bringing wealth to crown and clergy.[25] The list had reportedly been shown to James V after the campaign of 1542, when the Scottish muster refused to cross the English border. Despite Beaton's prompting that the list could be used to intimidate or punish those that would trouble the King's authority, James had concluded that the clergy were trying to stir up mischief between monarch and nobility. After Solway Moss, James may have been more encouraged to use the scroll to punish the nobility for the failure of the campaign, especially those Protestant-minded lords captured by the English. This may explain why, if true, the scroll was found on his person.[26]

This revelation was enough to ensure that the Edinburgh Parliament would choose James Hamilton, Earl of Arran, as Lord Governor of the realm on December 22nd, and again on January 3rd. He would also be appointed tutor to Queen Mary. This would give him power over Great and Privy Seals, and the mechanisms of fiscal policy. He could call parliament, chair Privy Councils, take charge of domestic and foreign policy, and make treaties. Although many lords would vote for him, others such as Lord Hume would enter into secret compacts with Beaton.[27] Arran's Protestant sympathies would be reflected in his adoption and imposition of Reformation policies during the first few months of his reign as governor. This tendency would also make him open to friendship and alliance with Henry VIII.[28] Angus and Sir George Douglas had also sent a letter to Arran asking to have their forfeited lands, titles and possessions in Scotland reinstated, and here Arran would have seen an opportunity to strengthen his position against Beaton. Arran seems to have invited the two brothers to Edinburgh.[29]

After the January 3rd 1543 parliament Beaton managed to retain his position as chancellor, ensuring that besides ecclesiastical authority he also possessed significant financial and political position. Whilst defeating Beaton to the governorship was a significant victory, granting the chancellorship position appears dangerously naïve. However Arran could also have been appeasing Beaton with this appointment whilst awaiting for better opportunities to overcome him.

During December and January Henry also receive reports from Scotland about the supposed will of James V. An individual called Archibald Douglas was sent to Sir George Douglas at Berwick by Done Lanerke a Protestant sympathizer from Ayrshire. He reported that the Cardinal on James V's deathbed had asked if either Arran, Moray, Argyll or Huntley should become governor and rule the realm for daughter, and apparently received no reply. There was also talk in Scotland regarding the possibility of marrying the Princess Mary to either a son of the King of

England, or the King of France or Denmark. Arran also had ambitions for Mary to be married to his own son.[30] Such a proposal would need broad-based domestic support, and Arran did not have that.

There was considerable international interest in events in Scotland. The Imperial Ambassador in London, Chapuys, believed that Henry VIII might be delaying renewal of the Anglo-Imperial Treaty with the Emperor. On July 10th 1542, war had broken out between the Holy Roman Empire and France. Prior to that date Chapuys had attempted to negotiate a treaty with Henry VIII for mutual military assistance, and to renew old treaties. Henry did not show any commitment beyond friendly words. Chapuys wrote in January 1543 that French intrigues in Scotland were aimed at diverting England away from Continental operations against the French, and also relates how Scottish prisoners of Solway Moss appeared at Henry's court at Christmas. He reports that Patrick, Earl of Bothwell, banished from Scotland for alleged Lutherism, had entered England two days prior and wanted to join the English in an invasion. The exact reason for Bothwell's banishment is not known, but on 10th December 1540, James had forced him to resign the Lordship of Liddlesdale and the important castle of Hermitage before he went abroad to France.[31]

The French ambassadors were at Hampton Court, and whilst they were treated coldly in public it is believed that there were some private interviews in which exchanges were heated. The new ambassador, Mr de Morvellum, was a former ambassador of Scotland, and had induced James V to invade England on the strength of the French alliance. Chapuys suggests to English deputies that Henry should immediately declare against Francis, King of France, so that the latter would not have the luxury of conspiring in Scotland. The English deputies had fixed a time for any possible invasion of the Continent for July 1st 1543.[32] A war against France, even in alliance with the Empire, would tempt the French to stir up a second front in Scotland. If Henry could conquer Scotland then he would neutralize a potential threat to his continental ambitions. He would then be in a stronger position to face enemies across the water.[33]

Despite any supposed intrigues by France Henry ordered the assured Scots Angus, Cassilis, Glencairn, Fleming, Maxwell, Somerville, Gray, Oliphant and Erskine to go to Scotland in January and deliver letters to the Scottish council. If the council did not agree with Henry's proposals, in respect to marriage contract and other matters, then he expected the above lords to deliver Queen Mary into his hands. They would capture and hand over castles to Henry, and oppose Arran's supporters and any foreigners.[34] There was also the possibility of provocation on the borders between Scotland and England, where it was reported that the powerful Humes of Merse were going to side with the Cardinal.[35]

Having also learned something of the political situation in Scotland, Sir George Douglas would be granted safe conduct by the English authorities. Sir George would prove an assertive and important link between the Scottish and English authorities during the months following James V's death,[36] meeting with Arran and the Cardinal to smooth the way for the return of the Red Douglases to Scotland.[37] The Cardinal and many of the powerful Earls such as Argyll, Huntley and Moray were opposed to the return of the Douglas, but were overruled by the Lord Governor. When Sir George Douglas arrived in Edinburgh in January the Cardinal sought a private interview with him. He asked him his views on religion and Douglas replied he supported the reforming of religious practices. Although the Cardinal was disappointed, he assured him that no bad blood would ensue due to his belief. He then warned Arran against trusting Douglas, and Arran in turn warned Douglas to beware the Cardinal as he was the 'falsest karle in the world', a heavy indictment.[38]

The arrival of Angus and his associates during late January compelled Arran to enter into alliance with them, and he made proclamations on January 16th restoring Angus to his estates.[39] This was not as difficult as it would seem. The vast holdings of the Red Douglas clan had been held by the crown, except for the barony of Abernethy, which had been granted to the Earl of Argyll, so there would be few legal challenges to complicate the restoration. Many of the castles and houses belonging to Angus had fallen into disrepair, and the Earl would have been motivated to ensure some type of durable economic peace between Scotland and England so as to generate wealth and prosperity to his holdings.[40] The marriage proposals were also discussed with Arran, and he appeared open to further discussions. Possibly he was playing for time, as he would have own ambitions to marry his son to Queen Mary. Nevertheless he ordered a council meeting for late January to discuss forming a parliament to discuss the proposals from England.[41]

The Douglas clan, the Earl of Glencairn, the Earl of Cassilis, Lord Maxwell, Lord Somerville and others of note, comprised a political bloc that controlled vast tracts of land, and important castles in the south of Scotland. Whilst the Douglases with their promised restoration would hold land and property north of the Forth-Clyde line, their importance lay in the south, where they became a vital link of communication for English border officials such as Dudley, Lisle, Parr and others. They would also liaise with Ralph Sadler, the ambassador for England, who would arrive in Edinburgh in mid-March, 1543.[42]

Sir George Douglas's four aims in coming to Scotland were to (1) ensure a restoration of the Douglas lands and titles, (2) promote the marriage treaty, (3), ensure the young queen of Scots was taken to England and (4), to ensure Henry was acknowledged as Lord supreme over Scotland, and the important castles were handed over to England. Of the four aims the first was reliant on the Douglases having the backing of Henry, which in turn would convince Arran to acquiesce. The other three would be more difficult, and whilst the Douglas influence and power were significant, to deliver the other three would mean convincing a majority of independent-minded nobles, clergy and burgesses. At first, the threat of English invasion was enough to get the Scots to negotiate, but getting them to agree fully to Henry's demands would be another issue.[43]

Many of the Scottish supporters of the marriage treaty were influenced by the ideas of the reformation, whether from the Continent or from England. One such person was a high-value spy called Alexander Crichton of Brunstane in Lothian, a former servant of Cardinal Beaton. During his period of employment with Beaton he was so well thought of that he was sent to France in 1539 with royal letters.

Returning to Scotland his ship was forced to embark in England, and here he and his correspondence came into the power of the English ambassador Ralph Sadler. The latter would try to use the contents of letters to cause divisions between James and Beaton. At a meeting with James with the Cardinal present, Sadler made the accusation that the letters sent to France had differences compared to the letters authorized by James. The King did not act on this accusation of forgery against Beaton, although he thanked Sadler for bringing the issue to his attention. Despite this Brunstane would go with Beaton to France in 1540, and in November 1542 he sailed to France from Dumbarton to collect rents owed to the Cardinal and Mary of Guise. Upon his return, he was accused of appropriating some monies meant for James from Francis, King of France. Although he was cleared, there are indications that he was in contact with the English and after the death of James these contacts would become more businesslike. The divisions within Scotland would force him to actively take a side, and he left the Cardinal's employ. He would receive an English pension in return for supporting the English marriage and the Protestant reformation in Scotland, as well as producing reports on developments in Scotland.[44]

Robert Maxwell, 5th Lord Maxwell (c.1494-1546), was a powerful land magnate in south-west Scotland, and an important political player during the upheavals of James V's minority, when he would change sides depending on who held the most power, whether it was the Duke of Albany, who would support him as warden of the West March, or Queen Margaret, who supported him as provost of Edinburgh, Steward of Kirkcudbright, and Captain of the

Royal Guard. He would also become an enemy of Angus during the period in which he took control of the young King James. Nevertheless when Angus was ousted from power Maxwell won favour with the King, receiving various rewards and titles and, becoming reconfirmed as warden of West March as well as retaining his position as Provost of Edinburgh.

Maxwell would have his disagreements with James, at one time (1530) being warded in Edinburgh Castle as the King decided to administer royal justice on the borders. At another time he had the honor of acting as proxy bridegroom for Mary of Guise, travelling to France and placing the ring on her finger before escorting her to Scotland. As noted above Maxwell surrendered, or was captured, at Solway Moss, and it was calculated that he was worth 4,000 marks in estates and 3,000 in goods.[45] His faith is unclear up to that time, although a report by the Venetian Secretary, Hironimo Zucculo, of 16th Dec, 1542 claims that Maxwell was a Lutheran.[46] If this was true then Maxwell would have been likely been one of the names on Beaton's list of suspected heretics.[47]

Gilbert Kennedy, 3rd Earl of Cassilis (c.1517–1558) was educated in St Andrews. At eleven years of age he was faced early on with the horror of religious conflict, when he was expected to sign a death sentence for Patrick Hamilton in 1528. In 1530 he travelled the Continent, and was educated by no less than George Buchanan, the influential Latin poet and humanist, who dedicated his translation and Paris publication of Linacre's Latin Grammar to Kennedy in 1533.[48] Buchanan, a former royal favourite, had left Scotland after angering the clergy with a series of satirical

Latin poems which attacked the Franciscans. After being lodged in St Andrew Castle, he managed to escape and make his way to Europe, where he taught Latin in schools and privately offered tuition.[49] In 1536 Kennedy and Buchanan returned to Scotland; shortly afterwards Buchanan wrote his *Somnium* at Cassilis's family seat in Ayrshire.

Young Kennedy built up a power base in the west of Scotland, especially in Ayrshire. He became a member of the Privy Council In November 1538 and was confirmed as Earl of Cassilis with an estimated revenue of £715. After his capture at Solway Moss by Wharton, he was housed in the Tower of London before being put in the care of Archbishop Cranmer and converted to the Protestant faith. Eventually he would become supporter of a marriage between Mary and Edward as a route to a Protestant union between Scotland and England. The hostility of Beaton and the clergy to the reformation would also have directed Cassilis closer to alliance with England, but a pension of 300 marks would also have helped make his decision. Two of his brothers and an uncle were offered up as pledges, allowing Cassilis to travel to Scotland and promote the English agenda.[50]

William Cunningham, 3rd Earl of Glencairn, acted closely with his father Cuthbert, the 2nd Earl, during a distinctly pro-English alliance with Angus and Lennox against Albany during the 1520s. He is identified as acting in English interests as far back as 1516, and was in receipt of an English pension. In 1526 he supported Lennox in an attempt to free James from Angus, in which led to the Battle of Linlithgow and the slaying of Lennox. The Master of Glencairn who had been appointed Treasurer in June 1526 was deprived of his position in in October by Angus. When King James freed himself and assumed government, the Master of Glencairn became an important agent, especially in the area of the Highlands and Isles, where his father owned estates and lands. Overall when William became the 3rd Earl of Glencairn he inherited lands, titles and estates in nine sheriffdoms, including Dunbartonshire and Renfrewshire, which bordered the lands of the mighty Earls of Argyll, and compelled him to enter into alliance with the Earls of Lennox. He also had lordships and baronies in Ayrshire and Dumfriesshire. Prior to his capture at Solway Moss, there are many indications that the Cunningham family was supportive of the reformation, and one of Glencairn's son in 1539 would be accused of heresy, although he would recant. Whilst prisoner in England, Glencairn agreed to promote the marriage treaty between Scotland and England, and was released for the ransom of £1,000[51].

Somerville, Hugh, fourth Lord Somerville (c.1484–1549) was a powerful landowner in Lanarkshire who fought on the side of Angus during the 1526 battle of Linlithgow which ended in Lennox's death. Afterwards he would enjoy good relations with James V, and the King attended the marriage of his daughter Agnes in 1532. He benefited from Hamilton of Finnart's execution and forfeiture, receiving the Baillie of Carnwath in December 1540. During the reign of James, Somerville's religious leanings are unclear. After he was sent to the Tower of London on 19th December, he would be housed with the Lord Chancellor, which would have introduced him to reformation ideals from the highest level of English government. His ransom was calculated at 1,000 merks, however this would be reduced as he would work with Angus to promote the English marriage proposal, and in time he would be offered an English pension.[52]

Another important captive was Gray, Patrick, 4th Lord Gray (1515x20–1584), whose principal seat was Castle Huntley with a number of estates, lands and baronies in Forfarshire and Perthshire. He was also hereditary sheriff of Forfar and received annual rent out of the customs of Dundee, as well as holding the important coastal castle of Broughty. After Solway Moss he was placed under custody of the Archbishop of York. His annual income was estimated at 400 merks sterling. He was ransomed for £500, and Henry VIII gave him a gift of £100. He was put under the charge of Walter Strick at Newcastle, and afterwards went to Carlisle on January 1543 to await pledges before travelling to Scotland. He too was expected to further the cause of the marriage treaty.[53]

The Douglas faction would seek to dominate Scottish policy through the figure of Arran. Whilst the Earl of Angus held the military reputation and muscle, his brother Sir George would be prime negotiator, diplomat and spymaster amongst the assured Scots. Possibly Arran felt he had no choice in his political decisions as Cardinal Beaton had in January 1543 reportedly written to the Queen Mother's brother in France, the Duke of Guise, and also the King of France. He requested that they should send money, arms and men if they wanted Scotland to remain Catholic and retain its ancient friendship with France.[54] He also suggested that Matthew Stewart, 4th Earl of Lennox, should return to Scotland. This lord had a claim as heir presumptive, being descended from a daughter of James II, and was a direct challenger to Arran's designated royal rights.

Lennox had been ten years of age when his father Robert, 3rd Earl of Lennox had been slain at Linlithgow in 4th September, 1526, allegedly murdered after capture by Sir James Hamilton of Finnart.[55] The wardship of the Earldom that Matthew was to inherit as eldest son was administered by the Earls of Angus and Arran. Wardship was passed to Andrew Stewart, Lord of Avondale. Upon marrying Finnart's half-sister they both exploited the Earldom until Matthew came of age on 29th April, 1531 and was able to claim the Earldom himself. He would attend parliament, and become keeper of Dumbarton Castle. He would also agree to forgive Finnart for his father's death. However, before being executed for treason in August 1540, Finnart was a favourite of King James[56] and Lennox possibly decided it would better for his own personal safety, and beneficial to his education to travel to the Continent. In France, under the tutelage of his uncle Robert, a respected soldier, he became a captain of Scots soldiers and would earn French citizenship due to his military exploits in Province and in the wars in Italy.

During the early governorship of Arran, the Queen Mother had written to Lennox in France with hints and suggestions that King James's widow might consider marrying him. Beaton, as noted already, was putting forward an idea to the French court that Lennox could be an effective counter to Arran.[57] There was also the question of the Earl of Arran's legitimate claim as second person of the realm, a claim that the power of the church could investigate.[58] Beaton also sought manpower, weapons and money. If Arran was aware of such plans then he would need powerful allies, and the assured Scots with Henry VIII as ally could be enough to challenge the power of Beaton, the Queen Mother and the French. The potential conflict could also take a religious aspect, with Beaton representing the old religion whilst Arran followed a reforming path. Henry was the enemy of Rome and therefore in the eyes of reformers in Scotland a potential friend and benefactor.[59]

As the widowed Queen of James V, Mary of Guise would have expected to become regent upon his death. What opposed this tradition was that it was also expected that a royal mother should stay a month indoors with a newborn child, whilst partaking in a suitable period of mourning for the King. In mid-January the Queen Mother left her daughter in Linlithgow and travelled to Holyroodhouse. There were indications that she was going to attempt to grasp power. The royal apartments had been taken over by Arran, except for hers at Holyroodhouse. In the King's chambers, which were above her apartment Arran was holding a Privy Council. Beaton was invited to attend at the Governor's chamber, yet this was a trap, as Angus and Sir George Douglas with armed followers entered Edinburgh and made their way to Holyroodhouse. The Queen Mother would learn of the arrest of Beaton when Angus entered her room to explain the shouting and commotion upstairs as Beaton was dragged away by Angus's armed men. Angus would enter her room and assure her the noise was but the capture of a 'false trumping karle', and as the Cardinal was being led away a priest followed with the Cardinal's cross and Angus sarcastically stated that 'he shall pay better than his cross' for what he would be accused of.[60]

At the first opportunity the Queen Mother fled to Linlithgow, and was quickly followed by a party of men sent by Arran, ominously claiming to be her protectors. She believed this was a prelude to her daughter being seized, and this was part of Henry VIII's strategy, to capture the daughter of James V and to capture Cardinal Beaton using the Douglas faction as willing participants. Chapuys mentions the arrest of Beaton by Angus, as prelude to interrogation regarding 'certain affairs'.[61] Angus would accuse Beaton of forging the will of James V and of misappropriating monies left by James V, as well as misappropriating the pensions from France. He would also claim that Beaton and the clergy had compiled a list of individuals to be prosecuted for supposed heresy.[62] In the Palace of Linlithgow the Queen Mother became practically a prisoner, a condition which would last until the summer.[63] Her biggest fear was for her daughter.

Beaton was taken to Dalkeith the home of James Douglas, third Earl of Morton, a different branch from the Angus Douglas. This Douglas was a kinsmen of Arran as the latter had married his eldest daughter, Lady Margaret. Morton had been persecuted by James V, and pressured to resign his lands in inheritance to a kinsman, Robert Douglas of Lochleven. At Brechin on 11th January 1540, after being followed throughout the Highlands by James and armed followers, he resigned his rights, reserving his wife's terce and his life rent. On the following 20th January, Robert Douglas resigned his inheritance rights to the Morton lands to King James. After James died, Morton went to the Court of Session and managed to get the writs by himself and Robert Douglas overturned, citing the pressure by the late King. Morton would enter into agreement with Sir George Douglas, where the former gained annulment of Robert of Lochleven's claims and Sir George paid £2,000 to the Earl. In return his youngest daughter Elizabeth would marry Sir George's second son James, who became Master of Morton and heir apparent to the vast Morton estates and baronies. James and Elizabeth were married between March 18th 1543 and April 2nd 1543. Angus, Sir George Douglas and Arran were now not just linked through common interests but by kinship through marriage and ties of family.[64]

With the imprisonment of their principle enemy Beaton, Arran issued a proclamation calling on all Scots to resist any landing on Scottish soil of the French military. A parliament was also to be called for 12th March, to discuss the prospects of political union with England through marriage, and to publicly condemn Beaton. It was also intended to be a reforming parliament. Knox states that Arran was initially a progressive reformer. As governor he allowed two preachers to travel in Scotland; John Rough, a Dominican Friar, and Thomas Guillaume, a Black Friar, both of whom spoke doctrines that were Protestant and challenged the orthodoxy. Before being imprisoned, Beaton complained bitterly against this preaching, but he could not stop it. Both Rough and Guillaume would act as Arran's family chaplains.[65] In his council he recruited an array of individuals of a reforming tendency, such as Master Henry Balnaves, Secretary of State, Master Thomas Bellenden, Sir David Lindsay, Master Michael Durham, Master David Borthwick, David Forrest, David Bothwell, General of the Mint, and others.[66]

Events in Scotland, such as the arrest of Beaton and Arran's willingness to negotiate a marriage union, may have compelled the English to reach agreement with the Holy Roman Empire. On 11th Feb, 1543, Henry VIII and Charles V signed a treaty, "The enterprise of Paris". Henry would now be expected to declare against France; however he would wait until 21st June 1543, and wait until summer before sending over 5,000 troops to the Continent. It is tempting to suggest that the unresolved matter in Scotland gave Henry reluctance or an excuse not to fully engage elsewhere. Beaton's arrest and Arran's apparent friendship of assured Scots and England, and his reforming tendencies, possibly gave Henry the confidence to sign the treaty. He perhaps held back from declaring against Francis I until the peace and marriage treaties guaranteed a level of security on his northern borders.[67] To add to this sense of insecurity there were reports that Lennox and the Duke of Guise were raising troops in Normandy and Bartaza for an expedition to Scotland.[68] A sighting of a fleet of ships off Holy Isle caused a panic, until it was discovered that they were Scottish ships leading nineteen captured English prizes into harbour.[69]

There were several nobles and prelates supporting the Queen Mother and the Cardinal, who could provide significant forces to challenge the power of Arran and his allies. Archibald Campbell, Fourth Earl of Argyll (1498-1558), known as Roy Oig because of his red hair, owed vast estates and titles in West Scotland and the Highlands, benefiting from the forfeitures of the MacDonald Lords of the Isles in 1493. Argyll was also a hereditary justice-general of Scotland as well as Master of the Royal

Household, which ensured he was active in government and royal councils. Argyll would provide large numbers of Gaelic fighting men during royal campaigns in the West or Highlands, or on the borders. In 1542 he raised 12,000 troops, and had significant contacts with Irish chiefs and lords, which was a concern to the English administrators of Ireland. Argyll would have some sympathy with the ideas of the reformation, and family histories claim he converted to Protestantism in 1536 whilst visiting France. He also in 1541 married Lady Helen Hamilton, daughter of first Earl of Arran and sister to the Governor. Despite these religious and family links he would stay loyal to the cause of the Queen Mother.[70]

George Gordon, fourth Earl of Huntley (1513-1562), was one of the biggest magnates in the north-east, and a representative of royal power in the Highlands as Lieutenant-General of the north and Sheriff of Aberdeen. Local power was ensured through the ability to raise large numbers of troops and consolidated with entering into bonds of manrent with important clan chiefs and families. He married Lady Elizabeth Keith, daughter of the Earl Marshal, potentially a magnate to rival Huntley's power. Huntley was a close associate of James V and frequent member of the Privy Council, and was appointed Regent in 1536 when the King visited France. Like Argyll he could raise large numbers of men, and replacing the Earl of Moray as Lieutenant of the borders he defeated an English invasion at Hadden Rig in 1542. He was a committed Catholic and loyal to the crown of Scotland.[71]

James Stewart, Earl of Moray (1500-1545), was an illegitimate son of James IV and Janet Kennedy, daughter of John, second Lord Kennedy. He was made Earl of Moray, Lord Abernethy and Sheriff of Elgin and Forres. Moray was an ally of Albany during his periods as governor and close to his half-brother James V. He would enter into a marriage alliance with the Earls of Argyll by marrying in 1529 Lady Elizabeth Campbell, daughter of Colin the third Earl. This made him brother-in-law of the fourth Earl of Argyll. He was prominent during the Anglo-Scottish wars and in suppressing rebellions in the north. He visited France several times, which gave him a fuller idea of the importance of the French alliance, and he was assessed by English spies as being anti-reformation, and being a close associate of Cardinal Beaton. It was said that during the campaign that led to the disaster of Solway Moss, the King, Moray and the Cardinal were to raid into England from the East March and deliver a papal interdict on England. Although there is no evidence that this interdict existed, the King's death caused the eastern army to disband.[72]

The power of these three would be difficult for any army to overcome, due to their considerable military power. If there was a means to undermine this power it would need to be from their own territories, either in the Highlands or the Western Isles. A threat to the authority of Argyll and Huntley emerges in the west with the figure of Donald Dubh MacDonald. A claimant to the Lordship of the Isles and the Earldom of Ross, Donald was a tragic figure who had been imprisoned from the age of three. Colin Campbell, the First Earl of Argyll, held him at Innis Chonnel, and then after a brief escape Donald was incarcerated in Edinburgh prison as a state prisoner from 1504/5. His father was Angus Og, and his mother a daughter of the Earl of Argyll.[73] The cost of his long imprisonment, £40 per month, emphasizes the political significance of Donald Dubh. In 1543, Donald who would call himself Earl of Ross, escaped, or was set free. There would be unproven theories that Arran released him so that he could cause trouble in the west.[74]

The Earldom of Ross had been annexed to the crown in 1476, and the Lordship of the Isles had been forfeited in 1493, so Ross was a dangerous figure to the government in the event of a Highland rising in hope of a restoration of the old Gaelic power. James V in June and July 1540 had sought to impose royal power in these districts by leading a fleet to Orkney and the Western Isles. MacKay of Strathnaver, MacLeod of Lewis, and various chiefs of Glengarry, Clanranald, Clan Colla and others were captured and imprisoned in Dumbarton. They would later be dispersed in other prisons across the country. Hostages were also taken to ensure the good behaviour of those left behind, and garrisons installed in important castles in the west.[75]

Ross was a threat to Argyll and Huntley power in the west and north of Scotland respectively. Whether Ross was the inspiration behind the Gaels who would begin mobilizing is not known; however it is very likely. Ross would become more openly active in 1544. Nevertheless he seems to have been enthusiastically greeted when he arrived in the Isles, and Argyll was compelled to sign a truce with Ross to last until May 1st, 1543.[76] This suggests that Ross was free before March, as the signing of the treaty would have allowed Argyll to raise troops in the west. He could then offer military support to the imprisoned Cardinal Beaton. Argyll, Huntley, Moray and the Earl of Bothwell gathered a large force at Perth during March 1543 for the purpose of holding a convention to challenge the Edinburgh parliament.[77] Sir George Douglas relates to Sadler that he had managed to compel the Governor to use the Edinburgh Parliament for the purpose of countering this convention, which was also supported by a large body of the clergy. Douglas admitted to Sadler that lacking force to fulfill the promises made to Henry VIII he would have to try to act through the Governor.[78]

Reid, the Bishop of Orkney, took a petition to parliament, presented by the clergy and commonality with three demands. Cardinal Beaton was to be released unless proved he was guilty of treason. The clergy and the church were not to follow the English example, and the young queen was to be put into wardship with four nobles until of marriageable age.[79] These demands were refused. With penalties of treason being threatened by Arran against the participants of the convention, Argyll, Huntley, Moray and Bothwell dissolved the army on March 12th 1543. They would take the political route, offer submission to Arran and attend the parliament in order to oppose the marriage treaty and challenge the reforming policies of the Protestant party.[80]

The parliamentary session of March 12th was well attended, with bishops and abbots present. To win the favour of the Douglas the acts of forfeiture passed on November 12, 1526 were to be reduced. It was a massive gain for the Douglas as they now had the legal justification to consider themselves once more Scottish lords. The released prisoners were also present and promoting the marriage treaty, and putting their weight behind reforming policies to be introduced. Bothwell was also rewarded by being reinstated in possession of the Lordship of Liddlesdale.[81] Several important English captives from the battle of Hadden Rigg were released, such as Sir Robert and Richard Bowes and others.[82]

At the parliament Arran was reconfirmed as governor and tutor to Queen Mary. The Archbishop of Glasgow introduced the proposals of Henry VIII for a marriage treaty, and the prospect of a peace treaty between Scotland and England. It was agreed that ambassadors should be sent to England for negotiations. There would be one point of disagreement, in regard to the Scottish parliament expecting to keep Queen Mary in Scotland until she was ten years of age.[83] The ambassadors were to be Sir William Hamilton of Sanquhar, Sir James Learmouth of Dairsie and Master Henry Balnaves.[84] There was debate about other details of the peace proposals with a refusal to give up Scottish fortresses, and a determination to retain Scotland's independence, laws, liberties and traditions. And in the event of a child from the marriage, Scotland would still be governed by a native ruler. As keepers of the young Queen, the Earls Marshal and Montrose, and Lords Erskine, Ruthven, Lindsay, Livingston and Seton were chosen. It was also decided that the young Queen would retain a court at Linlithgow under the supervision of the Queen Mother.[85]

On March 14th 1543 the parliament abolished the Act, making it heresy to read the Bible translated into English or any other language besides Latin, Greek and Hebrew. The following day a proposal introduced by Lord Maxwell was debated, then passed into law, which allowed for the scriptures to be spoken in the vulgar tongue, or in any language used by the reader. This allowed English language bibles to be owned and distributed in Scotland.[86] There was a backlash, the clergy in support of Beaton refusing to give mass, carry out baptisms or bury the dead. The Douglas and their supporters were viewed as being prepared to sell their nation's independence for an English pension. Devout Catholics feared that Scotland was a country heading for excommunication.[87] These acts compelled the nobles sympathetic to Beaton to petition once more for his release. Arran refused.

In an interview with Lord Lisle at Berwick, Sir George Douglas would explain in regard to Henry's request that if Beaton was handed over then Arran, he and his brother, as well as the assured Scots, would no longer be trusted by the nobles or people. So it would have been a dangerous measure.[88] Henry VIII would send his ambassador, Sir Ralph Sadler, to Arran in March 1543 to negotiate a treaty between Scotland and England. From reports of the attitude of Arran and the nobles, military action seemed unnecessary. The Laird of Cessford, warden of the Middle March, was especially instructed by the Governor to 'see English complaints redressed to the final penny', indicating that Arran was making a special effort to ensure that hostilities in the borders would not endanger the peace negotiations.[89] Henry however would continue his demand that Beaton be handed over to him, along with Scottish fortresses. It was either a sign of delusion or incredible arrogance.[90]

Sadler would inform his master that resisting the will of the three estates was counter-productive, that they would not go against the general consensus of retaining national independence. They would not give away their sovereign rights and privileges. He suggested that the getting the Scots to reject military alliance with France may be achievable and this would lead to a developing friendship between Scotland and England which would eventually lead to English overlordship. Henry was not satisfied; he wanted all his demands met and threatened invasion, and demanded that all the released prisoners support him in this enterprise or surrender themselves to prison. His attitude would aggravate and turn away former supporters.[91] He made requests that Cardinal Beaton should be delivered to him, and received no satisfactory explanation when his wishes were not granted.[92] Henry would write to Sadler outlining the promises that Sir George Douglas had made regarding helping him gain the crown of Scotland. Henry did acknowledge that these promises, as Sir George stated, were made before Arran was elected governor. This political reality meant that Henry's assured Scots could not vigorously pursue the crown, for in countering the power of Beaton they needed alliance with the Governor.[93]

There is a story quoted by David Hume of Godscroft where in order to convince the Scots over the marriage treaty George Douglas told how a physician at a royal court bragged that he could make a donkey speak within ten years, but would expect to be paid richly for his efforts. When his friends reminded him this was impossible, and he could end up being executed, he replied that he would receive his pay today whilst who knows what would happen within ten years, with either the donkey or the King dead. Sir George was playing for advantages in the present, being well aware how the choppy waters of politics could change.

In several interviews with Sadler at Linlithgow during

March and April, the Queen Mother would offer the opinion that Sir George Douglas was now the main counselor guiding the Governor's actions. But the Queen also feared that if Arran got her daughter in his power, she would not live long. The Lord Governor had also been informing the English authorities that Queen Mary was a sickly child and would not last long. The Queen Mother showed Sadler her child and he admitted that she looked healthy and well.[94] It may be that the Queen Mother was out to slander the character of Arran and also allow Henry to reflect on any dark plans he may have had, since threatening correspondence had been sent to the Queen Mother in regard to the well-being of her daughter.[95] Arran would deny these allegations, and whereas the Queen Mother had told Sadler that she supported the idea of a marriage, Arran replied that she was 'a right Frenchwoman' seeking to cause divisions between Scotland and England.[96] The Laird of Buccleuch and the Earl of Bothwell approached the English crown with an offer to capture the young Queen, but as both were at that time firmly on the side of the Cardinal and Queen Mother, this was possibly a ruse to learn of Henry's plans.[97]

One plan offered by Douglas and the Governor worried Sadler. In order to get power over St Andrew's castle, which was still held by the Cardinal's adherents, and to gain the wealth said to be stored within, they were going to allow the Cardinal to leave Blackness. He was to be accompanied by Lord Seton and travel to St Andrew's, then order its surrender. Once the castle had been possessed the Cardinal would be taken to Tantallon Castle or Dunbar.[98] Sadler was wary of this plan and the Cardinal's cunning, and stated that if the Cardinal escaped then he would not trust Douglas or the Governor again.[99]

Lord Seton was a relative of the Hamilton clan and a Catholic. Despite Sadler's concerns, Beaton was escorted by Seton to St Andrews in late March with only 12 to 16 men. His fears were realised when Sir George Douglas was later sent by the Governor to St Andrews and discovered that the Cardinal was now practically master of his own castle, which was probably inevitable considering Beaton had 300 retainers in the castle.[100] Douglas believed that Seton had been corrupted and rebuked him, although in later intelligence from a spy Douglas was accused of taking a bribe from the Cardinal of 400 crowns.[101]

The Cardinal said he was willing to go to trial and face the accusations that he had entered into treasonable correspondence with France. He also sent his chaplain to Sadler to convey his support for the marriage treaty and the prospects of better relations between Scotland and England. He added that despite his support he would fight any attempt to diminish Scottish independence and sovereignty. This measured message did not reject the marriage treaty, and could have opened the door to more constructive dialogue.[102] On hearing these words of the Cardinal, and upon being visited by the Scottish commissioners, Sanquhar, Dairsie and Balnaves, Henry repeated his demands to be recognised as Lord Paramount of Scotland and for the realm to be handed over to him. The commissioners resisted him, yet the message of his unreasonable and tyrannical attitude served to anger the Scots when learning of it. Even Arran was indignant at being treated so disrespectfully. That faction seeking to promote the marriage through cautious diplomacy found their plans floundering.[103]

Further developments in Stirling were ominous as during late March and early April some nobles and bishops began to gather forces and invited the Cardinal to join them with 'money and friends'.[104] There was a fear that this gathering was for the purpose of surprising and freeing the Queen Mother and her daughter from Linlithgow.[105] Seemingly Arran had granted the Earl of Huntley permission to escort the Queen Mother and daughter to Stirling. Following the advice of the Lords of Council, and Sir George, who were worried about the gathering at Stirling, Arran changed his mind and decided that the Queen Mother and daughter should stay in Linlithgow.[106] An English informer would report on the apparent coldness between the Earl of Huntley and Sir George Douglas when they passed each other in Edinburgh, where the latter sarcastically gave a 'Bonjour, Monsieur Huntley', alluding to the former's allegiance to the pro-French party. Scotland, according to Sir George Douglas, was now dividing into two hostile camps, with Argyll, Moray, Huntley, Bothwell and clergy on one side and the Governor, Angus, Glencairn, Cassilis, Maxwell on the other.[107]

An alliance had also been forged between the House of Maxwell and the Red Douglas, when on April 9th Angus married Margaret, the daughter of Robert, Lord Maxwell. This was a marriage that Arran had initially opposed until under pressure from both Angus and Maxwell he conceded approval. No doubt he was concerned about the implications with regard to the power of these two combined. English reports would indicate that Arran was becoming more reliant on Angus's military advice and power. The Governor had a personal bodyguard of 300 harquebusiers, and Angus had supplied, organized and divided up 1,000 horse to guard the various routes into Edinburgh. These large armed companies and the precautions followed in protecting the Governor's person were a sharp indicator of the sense of danger that was hanging over all parties, but it also indicated the hold that Angus was exerting.[108]

Angus's influence with Arran would face a challenge that April when the Governor's half-brother, John Hamilton, the Abbot of Paisley, arrived from France via England.[109] The Abbot of Paisley was illegitimate, his mother a Boyd from an Ayrshire family. Paisley spent his youth in France and reportedly took an interest in the reformation,[110] and when he visited England en route to Scotland he had been well received and entertained by King Henry.[111] The English had an opinion that Paisley would declare for his brother, and in return Henry would recommend him to replace Beaton as Bishop of St Andrews. The reformers in Scotland had also hoped that Paisley would support their cause.[112] Knox however would claim that he was a French agent when arriving in Scotland, sent by the King of France to oppose the marriage alliance and the Protestant faith.[113] Circumstantial evidence of Hamilton's true allegiance could be found with the Queen Mother's letter of January 24th 1543 to the Pope Paul III, recommending Paisley for the vacant see of Dunkeld, the elderly George Crichton, Bishop of Dunkeld having died, and also asking that he retain the Abbacy of Paisley.[114] It should be noted that at the time of the Queen Mother's letter Arran had been supportive of appointing Robert

Crichton, a kinsmen through marriage of Cardinal Beaton.[115]

When accused of treasonable dealings with France, Paisley offered to have himself subject to trial. Initially he would claim that he supported the government's position on the treaties, and sent his chaplain to visit Sadler to assure him that he could see the benefits of a union between Scotland and England, yet this was subterfuge.[116] In his company were several learned men, including David Paniter, the Scottish ambassador to France and a future player in national and international diplomacy.[117] Paisley was appointed Treasurer of Scotland, depriving Grange of Kirkcaldy, a role which Holinshed stated he had performed with 'great commendation'.

Paisley set about organizing crown resources for the defence of the Kingdom. He also ensured that many of the Hamilton clan, including close relatives, would benefit from gifts, grants and wages, as well as government and military appointments. In 1543/1544 many of the important castles such as Dalkeith, Dunbar, Edinburgh, Linlithgow and others would be be under the captaincy of a Hamilton.[118] One of Paisley's first visits was to Beaton in St Andrews, where he began to work for his release,[119] and for reconciliation between him and the Governor as the best means of resisting aggression from England.[120]

Whilst Paisley sought reconciliation, and we can assume he was working for French and Papal interests, for personal reasons he also needed the Cardinal's support for his bid for the Bishopric of Dunkeld. Herkless and Hannay gathered together some circumstantial evidence that the vacant Bishopric of Dunkeld was offered to Paisley as incentive for support. Cardinal Beaton before his imprisonment was, along with the Lord Governor, promoting his kinsman Robert Crichton to the post,[121], but on May 14th, after Paisley's meeting with the Cardinal, the Lord Governor wrote to Pope Paul III and Cardinal Carpi announcing his withdrawal of support for Crichton and his favour for his brother as Bishop of Dunkeld. On June 17th Arran wrote one of several letters to Pope Paul III asking once more that his brother be appointed as Bishop of Dunkeld and stated that the 'wicked competitor' Robert Crichton, who seemed to be offering a counter-claim to the Bishopric, was causing the issue to be unsettled. For this issue to become settled Cardinal Beaton would need to turn off support for Crichton and switch to Paisley. So the Abbot of Paisley was being offered a substantial incentive to support the Queen-mother and Cardinal. He would next use his influence in turning the Lord Governor away from England and the reformed religion.[122]

Another powerful figure now entered the contest. During the month of March, Matthew Stewart, 4th Earl of Lennox (1516-1571), arrived with a small French fleet at his stronghold of Dumbarton Castle laden with gold, silver, armour, ammunition and powder.[123] Francis I, King of France, was concerned about the growing amity between Scotland and England, which threatened to lead to the end of the Scottish-Franco treaties. He had sent for the Earl of Lennox, who had been serving in Italy, and commissioned him to go to Scotland. He reminded him of his legitimate claims as second person of the realm over Arran. He appointed him French ambassador and promised men, money and munitions.[124]

Lennox met the Queen Mother at Linlithgow on April 5th. Late that month he appeared before the Lords of Articles, a committee set up to consider and access government legislation. He forwarded royal letters from Francis, and also letters of accreditation giving him authority to act on Francis's behalf. He asked the Scots to renew the treaties with France, not to enter into contracts with England, and assured them that if attacked the French king would support Scotland with men, arms and money. Not satisfied with the answers he received from Arran, he conferred with the Earl of Argyll and others who he believed might be sympathetic to French proposals.[125] It appears that Argyll and Lennox spoke to Angus, and Lennox and Angus appeared on good terms.[126] Despite these amicable meetings Angus would continue to support the marriage treaty.

It is stated by Calderwood that prior to sailing from France to Scotland, Lennox had received letters from the Cardinal which stirred up memories of the Lennox blood-feud with the Hamilton family, which had begun with the killing of his father at Linlithgow (1526). Beaton also convinced Lennox that if James V had lived, he would have been confirmed as heir-apparent in the event of King James's death without male heirs. There are also promises of marriage to the Queen Mother, and a twenty-year governorship. During the campaigning of the spring and summer Lennox would still be under the impression that these proposals were genuine.[127]

Rumours began to circulate that Arran was not legitimate and that his father's divorce to Elizabeth Home was flawed and she was still living when he married Janet

Beaton. This marriage would then be considered null and Arran would be illegitimate and deprived of his right to succession. Beaton was accused of being the source of this rumour. He would have the ecclesiastical authority to lobby the Vatican and have Arran declared a bastard. Possibly in reaction to this, Arran at the April convention demanded that Lennox recognise him as second person of the realm, which he refused. Arran then asked him to surrender Dumbarton. Lennox refused this also and fled west.[128]

In one account Arran raised a force of 4,000, and along with Angus marched to Dumbarton. Lennox opened communications with Angus and arranged a meeting in which he agreed to recognise Arran as second person of the realm and to surrender Dumbarton. Seemingly Lennox also proposed that he marry Margaret, Angus's daughter, who was resident at Henry's court. It was reported that he was smitten by her, although it is not recorded whether he had actually met her. It was possibly that he was shown a miniature portrait whilst meeting Angus in Edinburgh, which was common practice in marriage negotiations.

Angus agreed to pass the proposal to Henry and to his daughter. However as Arran arrived at Dumbarton to receive possession of it, he found that Lennox had fled to the Highlands, reneging on any agreement he had with Angus. He also ordered the captain of Dumbarton castle not to surrender.[129] Cardinal Beaton had written to Lennox, no doubt outlining the dangers of handling Dumbarton Castle to Arran or Angus and the possibility of it being handed over to Henry.[130]

As the marriage negotiations carried on during April Henry wanted the young Queen to be educated by English tutors, and he also expected the Scots to support him in his wars with France. If the Scottish council did not agree he wanted Sir George Douglas and the assured Scots to use whatever means, including force against any opposition. The Governor, aware of the unpopularity of these demands, was reluctant to accept.[131] Henry was prepared to offer his own daughter Elizabeth in marriage to Arran's son. Arran however remained committed to the rulings of the parliament.[132]

The Earls of Argyll and Moray stated that they sought a better relationship with England; however they were opposed to the young Queen leaving Scotland. They wanted to preserve the liberty and rights of Scotland, and whilst they would not declare against France on England's behalf they would not wage war against England on France's behalf.[133] Sir George Douglas and Glencairn were then sent south during May to bolster the Scottish ambassadors and to try and get Henry to lessen the harshness of his demands. These efforts were successful, as Henry dropped the article to wage war against France.[134]

The Convention of Clergy at St Andrews in May resolved to resist any English invasion by selling off possessions, melting down church silver to raise funds and taking up arms themselves. Propaganda began to associate Beaton as the leader of resistance against English oppression and the marriage treaty, which they claimed would turn Scotland into a property of English kings.[135] The Cardinal, after returning to St Andrews, set out to win the Queen Mother's support to undermine the marriage treaty. He drew many of the nobles to his camp, either with money and favours raised by the clergy or by arguing that the treaty would lead to servitude to England and the end of the French alliance. There were also threats of French disproval and retaliation. He persuaded some nobles not to send their hostages to England, and those nobles that had been captives he drew so close to him that they were 'careless' to the wellbeing of the hostages left in England.

To test the patience of Sir Ralph Sadler who was waiting the sending of pledges to England, the clergy began to make public speeches against the treaty, and especially against the Ambassador himself. The King of England was a cruel heretic, in their opinion, and the English hated the Scots. They also reminded listeners of the Council of Constance of 1417, which ordained that no contact should be made with 'heretics'. The cardinal was successful in compelling some nobles to breach their agreements with England. However, Gilbert Kennedy, the third Earl of Cassilis, was steadfast in his commitment to the reformed faith and the marriage treaty, and having two brothers as pledges, returned to England. As a reward for his loyalty Henry freed Gilbert and his two brothers.[136]

In late May 1543 Sir George Douglas returned from England with new articles in respect of treaties with England. Arran, who was inclined towards the new proposals, ordered a convention for June. He believed that the article to send Princess Mary to England aged ten might be acceptable to most Scottish lords. He would invite all lords, and no matter the size of attendance he would conclude the business at that convention. He would also prosecute Cardinal Beaton once a peace treaty between Scotland and England had been settled.[137]

On the Continent an agent from Cardinal Beaton, David Vonar, and an agent from the Earl of Lennox, James

Stewart, met with the Patriarch, Marco Grimani, during May 1543 and informed him of events in Scotland. They stated that the Queen Mother and her daughter were housed in the palace of Linlithgow but could not govern whilst Cardinal Beaton was in St Andrews. The lords were close to blows with each other, and Arran sided with the English. He was considered a 'little Catholic' in practices, keeping company with 'bad churchmen'. The Cardinal wanted the Papal legate to come to Scotland and use the power of excommunication to challenge the reformers. After meeting Grimani, James Stewart visited the King of France to plead for ships, artillery, munitions and money, and discussions were held with Montgomery, Sieur de Lorges regarding the possibility of raising a French force.[138]

Sadler in late June expected that peace would soon be concluded between Scotland and England, and advised that Arran should prepare to contend with the Cardinal and Lennox. This after Arran experienced a bout of sickness where he recovered at his home in Hamilton. He would say that Lennox was gaining in strength, and reportedly awaiting shipments of money and arms from France. Sadler advised that he should strike before these shipments arrived. He assured Arran that England would assist.[139] The Lord Governor argued that to open hostilities at this time, whilst he was not strong enough, would threaten the treaties and give the advantage to the Cardinal. Despite his sickness Arran employed the presence of the Rothesay Herald, so that priority correspondence could be sent out, keeping him aware of important developments.[140]

Hostilities with France were intensified with Henry's defiance of Francis issued on June 21[st,] 1543, and with

5,000 English troops planning to arrive on the Continent by late summer.[141] There were reports of 15 to 16 ships landing in Aberdeen, a French fleet claiming to be waiting to stop a fleet of Flemish pirates. According to information they had 2,000 men, 50,000 crowns, 10,000 pikes, 2,000 halbutts and artillery. There was also a rumour that they intended taking the Queen Mother, Queen Mary and the Cardinal to France, with Beaton having supplied two of the ships. Upon hearing these reports Arran went to Linlithgow to make sure the Queen Mother and young Queen were secure, whilst Sadler advised him to take her to Edinburgh Castle.[142] For the English there was the danger of a second front opening in Scotland.

The Scottish ambassadors in England were rejoined by Sir George Douglas along with a party of assured Scots. They met with English commissioners at Greenwich to conclude the Greenwich Treaty on July 1st, 1543. On her tenth year the young Queen Mary was to marry Edward Tudor, and from the date of the treaty there was to be peace between Scotland and England.[143] Sir George Douglas and the other negotiators managed to get the demands watered down so that the ancient league with France was not broken, and Scotland as a national entity would retain its laws, liberties and traditions. Importantly the young Queen was to remain in Scotland.

The role that Sir George Douglas played cannot be underestimated. In his role as an adviser of the Governor of Scotland, whilst offering loyalty to Henry VIII he managed to become the linchpin between the two, helping to produce a peace treaty whilst also helping to conclude an agreement in respect of the Scottish prisoners of Solway Moss. This was signed and sealed by Scottish and English commissioners, allowing the prisoners to be released in return for ransoms and hostages.[144]

Whilst this Greenwich Treaty offered peace, at terms less that the English initially sought, there were English doubts to the sincerity of Arran, and a belief that he was playing King Henry VIII. During early July there were reports that he had openly bragged of his intended betrayal of the promises of the Greenwich Treaty. The English counsellor Parr praised Angus, but considering the role that Sir George Douglas had played in negotiations between Scotland and England the younger brother was considered the intelligence driving the diplomatic games. He also mentioned that he was playing all sides.[145] A servant of Sir George Douglas from Coldingham believed that Arran will turn to the party of the Cardinal, and was waiting for Sir George Douglas to forsake his brother Angus and join in the revolt.

The Earl of Argyll apparently visited Arran whilst he was at Hamilton, and the former tried to persuade him to defect.[146] All the powerful names, except Angus, Cassilis and Maxwell, were joining Lennox and the Cardinal, and there were expectations that Arran would do the same.[147] It should be also understood that Sir George Douglas had to contend with rival counsellors to the governor, such as his brother the Abbot of Paisley and David Paniter. Their influence would be at the most damaging when he was not present at court.

The Treaty of Greenwich was expected to be ratified within two months. However there were secret treaties between assured Scots and Henry, called 'secret devices', in which Scottish nobles in Henry's pay would use all their power and influence within Scottish councils and committees so that Henry would effectively have a secret government in Scotland, and also have a say in domestic and foreign affairs. In respect to divisions in Scotland they would promote the English interest against that of the Cardinal and France, at least in the regions below the Firth of Forth. These agreements were signed on July 1st 1543, the same day as the Greenwich Treaty.[148] The signatories were the prisoners of Solway Moss. In return their ransoms were fixed and they were given leave to pay off what was owed.

Acknowledging that there was a party of Scottish nobles supportive of this treaty, Sadler would relate nearly twenty years later how unpopular it was with the common people. He would quote Adam Otterburn, who stated, 'Our people do not like of it. And though the Governor and some of the nobility have consented to it, yet I know that few or none of them do like of it; and our common people do utterly mislike of it. I pray you give me leave to ask you a question: if your lad was a lass, and our lass were a lad, would you then be so earnest in this matter? ... And lykewise I assure you that our nation will never agree to have an Englishman king of Scotland. And though the whole nobility of the realm would consent, yet our common people, and the stones in the street would rise and rebel against it'.[149]

Whilst a powerful pro-English party began to develop in Scotland, there were reports in late June and early July of a French fleet cruising along the east coasts of Scotland and England. There was a fear that this fleet would be used to take the Queen and her daughter to France.[150] French gold and gifts from the ships were said to be going to the raiding clans and gangs of the borders, who were mobilizing with fresh horses and new harnesses. Borderers of note like Lord Hume and Lord Cessford and others were crossing the Firth of Forth. Hume castle had been fixed by the Cardinal, who had paid for the masons.[151]

As the Scottish commissioners returned northward they had in their company a reforming preacher called George Wishart, possibly the son of James Wishart of Pittirrow, a justice clerk of James V, and patronized in his youth by John Erskine of Dun. He taught as a master at a school in Montrose. He introduced the Greek language, and as this was used in by reformers in their translation of the bible he was accused of heresy, fleeing Scotland in 1538. It was said that he travelled to Germany and Switzerland, finally arriving in England, where he studied at Cambridge's Corpus Christi College.[152] Wishart was supported in his return to Scotland by the Earls of Cassilis and Glencairn, the Earl Marshal, Sir George Douglas and the lairds of Brunstane, Ormiston and Calder. He would travel to and preach in the towns of Montrose, Dundee, Perth and Ayr, speaking against the corruption of the papacy and clergy. He would challenge civil authorities if they attempted to stop him preaching, and could rely on support from his noble sponsors.[153] According to Knox he would be subject to several assassination attempts instigated by the cardinal as he travelled across Scotland.[154] It is clear that those Scots sympathetic to reformation ideas were employing Wishart as part of a wider strategy to challenge church orthodoxy, especially in those districts where the Protestants were growing in strength.

The party of the Cardinal stepped up their own propaganda efforts to undermine the authority of Arran, with the intention of appointing his rival the Earl of Lennox as governor. There was talk that Lennox intended to marry the Queen Mother.[155] To counter this use of Lennox a plan was suggested by John Drummond to approach Lennox and recruit him to the English cause. The Sheriff of Ayr stated that such an approach would make Arran suspicious of the King of England, and he might defect and turn to the Cardinal. It was also accepted that an attempt to turn Lennox would be pointless as long as France continued to provide him with support and finance.[156]

A convention was called for ratification of the Greenwich Treaty for August. Huntly, Argyll, Moray, Bothwell and others would not appear.[157] Countering this convention, the Cardinal and supporters assembled at Stirling for the 20th of July,[158] and the clergy agreed to oppose the marriage treaty and any attempts by England to invade. Arran was stigmatized a heretic, and although there was an obvious religious aspect to this conflict, the strongest cause for recruitment was the threat to Scottish independence. There was an opinion that Arran was prepared to sell Scotland to England in return for Henry making him king above the Firth of Forth, and those that opposed him believed that not only were they fighting for independence of the realm, they were also defending the Catholic church against the reformers.[159] Arran may also have been aware of the 'secret devices' agreed by the Angus faction and Henry VIII, and knowledge of this would have spurred many of the Scots into defence of the realm and religion.[160]

In what Tytler describes as the 'rude politics of Scotland' where crown power is acquired by possessing the 'person of the sovereign', both Arran and the Cardinal made plans to securely hold the young Queen. This would also allow Arran leverage to negotiate profitable terms for a royal marriage. He raised an army at Edinburgh to march to Linlithgow and challenge the army of the Cardinal.[161] He also with his brother captured Edinburgh Castle from Sir Peter Crichton, who had refused to surrender it. The castle was then handed over to the keeping of the Hamilton Laird of Stonehouse.[162] Arran intended taking the Queen out of Linlithgow and housing her in Blackness Castle.[163]

During these military musters during the last two weeks of July, an informant reported that Angus with 1,500 troops was lying in wait for Bothwell and Hume, who with 1,000 men were making passage towards the Cardinal in Stirling. Angus did nothing and let them pass. The same informant believed that Arran would switch to the side of the Cardinal, as he could only raise 10,000 to the Cardinal's 30,000.[164] Another report gave a different, more realistic number, with the cardinal at Linlithgow having 5-6,000 troops whilst the governor 12 miles distant had 7-8,000 troops.[165] However it seemed the figure for Arran's army was an overestimation based on what Arran expected to raise in Edinburgh, and not what he actually raised.[166] Lennox would gather a muster of Gaelic fighters from the west of Scotland and the Cardinal would raise an army from Fife.[167] They would join with Huntley, Argyll and their Gaels, and Bothwell with his followers from the borders. Overall Beaton managed to raise the power of four bishops, six abbots, six earls, eight lords and twenty three lairds.[168] By all accounts Arran was outnumbered and had no choice but to negotiate.[169] Ambassadors were sent by both sides to talk.[170]

Whilst in the company of the Cardinal, Lord Hume instructed his adherents to raid England and undermine any opportunity for peace.[171] The Kerrs and Scotts and other border clans were also to wage war on the borders.[172] The Davidsons, adherents of the Earl of Angus and Sir George Douglas were also raiding England, which sent a contradictory message to their English allies forcing Henry to question the sincerity of the Red Douglas clan.[173] In retaliation English raiders attacked Hume lands on the borders, as an effort to induce Hume to leave the Cardinal. Apparently this tactic worked, as Hume returned to the borders.[174]

During late July there were negotiations between the two armies. The Cardinal's party made four demands. First that the young Queen was to be taken from the custody of the governor, and placed in the custody of four guardians appointed by parliament. Second, that a council was to be formed which was non-prejudicial and representative of all parties. Third, the Governor should resign, and fourth that Angus and Sir George Douglas should leave court whilst governor negotiated with the Cardinal's people. Glencairn announced that the first two conditions were acceptable but the last two were not. The Cardinal's party dropped these last two demands, knowing that any further delay could threaten the break-up of the army due to supplies running out. Angus and Brunstane believed that the rebellion was an attempt to threaten peace, and to sabotage the Treaty of Greenwich.[175]

The Cardinal's party however outwardly appeared supportive of the marriage treaty and did not disagree that Queen Mary should leave for England when she was 10 years old.[176] However the Cardinal also made secret approaches to the Governor offering the hand of Queen Mary to his son the Master of Arran, which would secure the succession to the House of Hamilton instead of that of Henry Tudor. The Cardinal understood that this was a dynastic ambition of Arran's, but he was playing for time and seeking to disrupt the ratification of the marriage. Arran, who had also received an offer for his son to marry Henry's daughter Elizabeth, which he declined, also refused the Cardinal's offer, knowing full well that it was not sincere.[177]

In respect of the fourth demand to rid the Governor of the influence of Sir George Douglas, we have here another indication of the power of this individual, and the fear he inspired on the other side. It should also be noted that the Abbot of Paisley, allied with David Paniter, was also present at council, and whilst he had some influence with his brother, getting rid of the Red Douglas faction would make it easier for him to persuade the Governor to change sides. Whilst Arran was the formal head of the Hamilton clan, his brother would become a powerful influence, helped no doubt by his association with France or as Knox described it, "enchanting boxes" filled with "promises and terrors". These related to letters from the French king, and offers of pensions and monetary rewards to those remaining loyal to the Catholic faith and the French alliance.

Understanding that Arran was surrounded by a council of men of a reforming tendency, the Hamilton family began a campaign of intimidation against them, and this opposition was openly expressed in council when the Abbot suggested that it would be in his brother's best interests if a number of protestants were hanged.

With the hostile Hamiltons gaining ascendancy in court, many of Arran's protestant advisers began to leave, such as Balnaves, Bellenden, Sir David Lindsay, Durham, Borthwick, Forrest, David Bothwell and others. At some point Friar Guillaume and Friar Rough were dismissed as Arran's chaplains and both fled respectively to England and to Kyle. The Abbot Hamilton also threatened Arran, saying his acts would anger the King of France. The papacy could investigate and make a judgment, whereupon his father's first divorce of Elizabeth would be judged invalid. Therefore the second marriage to Janet Beaton, his mother, would also be made invalid and Arran would be declared a bastard and exempt from the royal succession.[178] Here a powerful pressure was placed on Arran. As head of the Hamilton clan he was expected to ensure prosperity for the family and there was no higher honour than royal succession, yet he continued to follow the road of treaty ratification.[179]

Whilst both sides agreed that the young Queen was to be taken out of Arran's custody and appointed four guardians, the Cardinal whilst in Linlithgow took charge of Queen Mary and the Queen Mother.[180] Lennox, with 2,500 mounted men and 1,000 foot, escorted the two to Stirling, arriving there on the 26th of July, 1543.[181] Four guardians for the Queen were appointed: Graham, Erskine, Lindsay and Livingston. During their stay in Linlithgow Queen Mary and the Queen Mother's expenses were covered by Lord Alexander Livingston, who would be reimbursed at the end of August to the huge sum of £143. Angus and the Cardinal then apparently had a friendly reconciliation, meeting between Edinburgh and Linlithgow, where the two embraced. The Cardinal used his meeting with Angus to convey that he wished to speak to Sadler in a bid to earn favour with Henry VIII.[182]

This message proved to be insincere, for as soon as the Cardinal travelled to Stirling he sent Huntley to Edinburgh. He announced that there was to be a convention in Stirling to rival the Parliament in Edinburgh which was to ratify the Greenwich treaty. Arran stated that if the Cardinal's party did not comply with the promises made, he would seek financial assistance from England. He added that if the Cardinal and his party came to Edinburgh he would forgive them. Huntley added that if Arran left his allegiance with England then all barons would support the marriage between Arran's son and Queen Mary. Angus, Glencairn, Maxwell and Somerville believed that the Cardinal was genuine about peace and better relations with England, and Glencairn and Maxwell expressed the opinion that Arran was playing a game to attempt further support and money from Henry VIII. Angus stated that the truth would be known if the Cardinal came to Edinburgh. There were also reports that the French king was outfitting ships with munitions and money to be sent to Scotland. A French ambassador and papal representative would accompany the ships, which were meant for the Cardinal and Lennox.[183]

In late July Robert Reid, the Earl of Orkney was sent by the Cardinal to pass on a message expecting certain conditions to be followed if the Cardinal's party attended the Edinburgh Parliament. Arran offered his own son as pledge, and 'if any of them afraid of Sir George Douglas', he would offer Douglas's son, the Master of Morton, as a hostage.[184] This assertion emphasized the dark reputation that Sir George Douglas possessed, and whilst Sadler stated that the

Cardinal's party feared and hated him, Arran decided to employ Sir George's diplomatic talents to persuade the Cardinal to be at Edinburgh and ratify the Greenwich Treaty.[185]

Whilst negotiating with the Cardinal's party, Arran also sought money from England to sustain him.[186] In return Henry kept insisting that the Governor should fully ratify the treaty and surrender castles below the Firth of Forth. He also asked that Arran should delay French ships in Leith so that his own naval forces could capture them. Henry was surprised that Angus, Cassilis, Maxwell and Somerville had been taken in by the words of the Cardinal. Henry also stated that English ships sent into Leith would ensure Arran kept his promises to Henry.[187] Henry also offered to send two divisions of 5,000 men into Scotland through East and West Marches if the Governor asked. Arran wanted money and arms, but he wanted no Englishmen as this would turn friends and servants against him.[188]

The Cardinal was at Stirling and Henry suggested that Arran should raise forces and drive him across the water or capture him.[189] However Sir George Douglas had arranged to meet the Cardinal at St Andrews and Seton was offered as a hostage.[190] Whilst he was kept well informed by Sadler, Henry's bullish behaviour was at odds with the complex negotiations needed to get both sides together. Diplomatic efforts were being made to try and persuade the Cardinal to ratify the treaty, yet Henry made little attempt to help this happen and seemed incapable of offering anything beyond war and treachery. This attitude added to the distrust of the Cardinal's party and compelled them to drag out negotiations so as to gather strength. Added to this was a belief that French money and arms were going to be sent to the Cardinal.[191]

Maxwell thought the Cardinal was genuinely seeking favour with the English King, whilst Sir George Douglas agreed with Sadler's assessment that the Cardinal was playing for time.[192] Sadler met with the Queen Mother during the first week of August, reporting that she claimed to support the marriage treaty. The rebellion was principally against Arran, who regarded her daughter and herself as prisoners, even though tutors had been appointed by parliament. She blamed secret councils for leading the Governor astray. Sadler disputed this, saying all diplomacy regarding the peace and marriage treaties was done openly.

Upon returning to Edinburgh Sadler learned that Lennox and Huntley were building up an army, and were expecting arms and money from France through the efforts on the Continent of James Stewart, a Captain of the Scots Guards. The Governor prepared his own forces for a march towards Linlithgow, in a bid to pressure the Queen Mother and Cardinal, whilst the French ships were still in the Firth of Forth awaiting a favourable wind.[193]

With the threatened approach of Arran and further prospects of war, Huntley wrote to the Queen Mother in mid-August that he, Argyll, Lennox and Bothwell would devastate with 'fire and sword' the lands and possessions of Arran and his allies on both sides of the Forth-Clyde divide. His wife also wrote that the Governor had been trying to get her husband to switch sides. This was possibly an attempt by Arran to create dissent within the opposition ranks by approaching Huntley and then reporting it widely. It seemingly worked, as Huntley's wife had to report his innocence, and he had to impress on the Queen Mother his intention to wage total war against the Governor, as if to absolve himself from accusations of treachery.[194]

Threatened by these powerful nobles, Arran requested 5,000 crowns from Henry but received an offer to put military forces at the ready 'at no small charge'. Henry did not believe that the French were capable of supplying the Cardinal, and believed that any word otherwise from the Cardinal's party should be considered bluff.[195]

Knox mentions that during August 12th ships from Edinburgh and several from other cities landed in English ports such as Yarmouth, and felt secure and relaxed in their visit because of the 'late contracted amity'. Henry however would disrupt this sense of 'security' and 'merriness'[196] by ordering that any Scottish ships sailing to France without safe conduct through English waters should be detained and their wares considered to be victuals for France. Henry admitted to detaining five to six ships which were taking victuals to France, which was against the treaty as read by Henry. Writing on August 16th he claimed that five to six ships were of the Cardinal's faction, and the occupants had insulted the Governor and his associates, calling them traitors to the Queen.[197] The Governor reported that the ship *Boneaventure,* belonged to Edinburgh merchants, had been taken at the Port of Rye. The Ross Herald sent this message to Henry VIII.[198] Calderwood claimed that Henry had grabbed the ships and imprisoned the sailors in retaliation for Beaton's activities, as many of the nobles were turning against prior agreements.[199] Sadler himself was targeted by angry Edinburgh citizens and his house briefly surrounded.[200] Arran raised concerns about safe conducts needed to be issued for Scottish merchants sailing to France, and any ships failing to fulfill these conditions were to be detained by English. The Scots began to interpret the peace offered by the Greenwich Treaty as false, and this was proved by the detainment of the ships and sailors.[201]

Sir George Douglas met the Cardinal at St Andrews in mid-August. The Cardinal said that he wanted Douglas to help him win favour with the English king. The Cardinal also said that he did not fully trust the nobles that followed him as he believed they were using him to get what they wanted. Douglas accused him of supporting the late rebellion for the sake of the church, an accusation that the Cardinal agreed with, saying that he feared the Governor would follow the English King in changing the structure of the church. When Douglas asked him to come to Edinburgh and ratify the Greenwich Treaty, the Cardinal claimed he could not do so without getting permission from the nobles he was associated with. He also feared the 'malice' of Arran's wife the Countess Margaret Douglas, who appeared to hold a particular grudge against the Cardinal. This dislike would have been due to the support of King James during the persecution of the Douglas, not only against her father, but also the burning of Lady Glamis.

Sir George Douglas was a much more pragmatic individual, recognising that the Cardinal was needed alive and healthy so as to contribute to a political settlement. He assured him that with regard to the governor's wife he could be 'sure of her good mind' if the cardinal had a similar attitude to her husband.[201] The Cardinal suggested that the Governor should ratify the treaty even if the Cardinal was not present, and he would do his utmost to unite both sides so that his side could go to Edinburgh, or the Governor to St Andrews.[203] Despite this interview the Cardinal wrote to the Earl of Bothwell informing him of the summoning to Edinburgh of August 20th and requested that he and other allies assemble at Stirling to make ready to go to war within twenty-four hours, each man to have victuals for 15 days.[204]

Upon learning that the cardinal was seeking favours with England, Henry wrote on August 24th that if he moved away from Rome and France he would remain Archbishop and Primate, and any lost profit from France would be recompensed through friendship with England.[205] During this period the Queen Mother complained that at Stirling she was being pressured by Argyll to marry his son to the young Queen. Lennox and Bothwell competed for the Queen Mother's hand by courtly activities at night and games and sports through the day. Lennox proved to be the better at these pastimes, but it was also becoming clear that the Queen Mother had no intention of marriage despite what Lennox had been led to believe.[206]

The tough marriage negotiations of Argyll were postponed, as he had to leave the court of the Queen Mother and travel with an armed force to his lands and dominions in the west of Scotland. Arran, at the instigation of Argyll's hated rival Glencairn, had released the Gaelic leaders imprisoned in Tantallon, Dunbar and Bass, such as MacKay of Strathnaver, MacLeod of Lewis, and various chiefs of Glengarry, Clanranald, Clan Colla and others. Arran entered into a bond with the chiefs that they 'should not make any stir or breach in their country, but at such time as he should appoint them'. They were appointed to harass the lands of Argyll and Huntley.[207]

A force of 1,800 was raised, and they killed Argyll's servants and lifted goods and cattle.[208] According to Gregory these freed chiefs had joined with Ross, the truce with Argyll having expired in June.[209] Argyll must have been aware of Glencairn's part in the release of the chiefs as he wasted Glencairn's lands in the Highlands and threatened the lands of the Sheriff of Ayr, and those of Cassilis.[210] This also suggests that Glencairn, Cassilis and the Sheriff of Ayr were offering some kind of support to the Gaels. This diversion allowed the Governor and others to travel to the other side of Firth of Forth to meet the Cardinal.[211] Reportedly there was an exchange of hostages, with Sir George Douglas going to St Andrews as Arran's pledge and Sir John Campbell acting as the Cardinal's pledge.[212] The Cardinal was reluctant to speak to the Governor, despite the latter travelling across the Firth of Forth. Within St Andrews Castle Sir George Douglas attempted and failed to persuade the Cardinal to meet Arran.

Arran arrived in the town of St Andrews and proclaimed treason against the Cardinal. The Cardinal's party began to mobilize forces at Stirling, whilst the Governor's party also raised forces.[213] The Governor returned to Edinburgh and on August 25th, at the Abbey Church of Holyrood, he ratified the Greenwich treaties with a small number of pro-treaty supporters present.[214] The Cardinal's party refused to recognise the treaty, claiming it invalid as it was the work of a small clique of individuals and was not supported by the people of Scotland or the will of the vast number of members of parliament.[215] The Governor informed Sadler that he could not fulfill the full terms of the treaty in the time expected by Henry VIII, and he could not hand over the strongholds to England as such an act would lose him support.[216] Money was being sent to the Governor to aid his struggle, and the Governor was asked if he wanted the English to harry the Cardinal's allies on the borders. They also want Dunbar castle handed to the English.[217] About this time there were plans to send Lord Wharton with 2,000 men along the west march, whilst Lord Eure with 2,000 would invade the east march.[218]

During late August and September, Lennox, Huntley and Bothwell were gathering forces around Stirling. They intended to crown the young Queen, appoint four regents and deprive the Governor. The date for the coronation was set for September 9th at the Chapel Royal in Stirling Castle. Argyll would have difficulty being present as he was busy fighting the Gaels in the west of Scotland. However Sir George Douglas believed Arran would change sides once war broke out, and it is likely that with Douglas's absence from Arran, the Abbot of Paisley and David Paniter were pushing the Governor to defect. Douglas left St Andrews, not wanting to be in the Cardinal's power if Arran did defect. There was also anger in Edinburgh at the detaining of merchant ships in English ports, with Sadler a continuous target of this anger. Arran sends the English pensioner Brunstane to negotiate the release of ships if possible.[219]

It was then reported that the Governor was supposedly going to Black Ness to meet with his wife, who was in labour. There was also a rumour that the Governor was actually going to meet the Cardinal at Culross Abbey, and this meeting was induced by the Abbot of Paisley and David Paniter.[220] It was soon learned that Arran, along with the Abbot of Paisley and David Paniter, would defect to the

Cardinal. They met between Linlithgow and Stirling at Lord Livingston's house on September 3rd. Once reconciled, they both left for Stirling. At Greyfriars Church in Stirling, before the Queen Mother and councilors, Arran sought absolution from the Cardinal and recanted his adherence to the reformed faith. He also broke the solemn pledge to support the marriage treaty with England.[221]

The Abbot of Paisley and David Paniter went to Linlithgow to dispatch letters to be sent to noblemen, requesting they cease from raising troops.[222] The reasons for Arran's defection were given to be fear that his allies were 'drawing from him by bribes and rewards' and that in the English opinion 'he was now become vile'. He also had pressure from his brother and Hamilton kinsmen to switch sides, with pleas not 'to destroy yourself and house'.[223]

Paisley was astute enough to know he would need to buy time with the English. He travelled to Edinburgh and met with Sadler to attempt to explain that whilst the Lord Governor and the Cardinal were reconciled, the terms of the marriage treaty would still be fulfilled. He also stated that the sudden violence in Edinburgh against the ambassador was due to the taking of the merchant ships and Sadler was a convenient target. He assured him that this was the actions of the 'common people', which was meant to assure Sadler it was not sanctioned by the nobility, or people of means.[224]

On September 4th in Dundee the houses of Grey and Black friars were sacked,[225] an act that was possibly influenced by the preaching of George Wishart, who was resident in Dundee at that time and enjoying the support of the Earl Marshall[226] and a 'bodyguard of mail-clad barons and retainers'.[227] In the Highlands there was still much violence and warfare which kept Argyll in the west, whilst the Cardinal's forces at Stirling were estimated at 5,000.[228]

With the defection of Arran, Henry had to postpone the twin invasion of Wharton and Eure on the borders until he could raise an even larger force. In early September he offered money and men for Angus to go against the Cardinal and Governor. He asked him to raise as many people as he could and go to Stirling and attempt to take the Cardinal, Governor and young Queen. Henry promised to send 8-10,000 men by land and 2-3,000 by sea.[229] He also sent a Herald to Edinburgh, where a proclamation was made threatening war if the treaties were not fulfilled, and also threatening the Edinburgh magistrates if any harm should come to the English ambassador, Sadler.[230]

There was a marked increase in organized violence on the borders, with the Humes, Kerrs and Scotts given license to raid England in support of the Cardinal. The English retaliated against the above families and supporters of the Cardinal[231] and Wharton released those Scottish reivers in English captivity, such as the Armstrongs,[232] the Storeys and Crosers, who themselves were given license to attack borderers loyal to the Cardinal.[233] Sir George Douglas travelled to the borders to meet with English officials, and supplied a list of names of those to be spared,[234] these being his kin, servants and friends who were now subject to attacks from English raiders and their Scottish helpers. In return for having their lives, lands and possessions saved they were expected to wage war against Henry's Scottish enemies. These assured Scots now became an important military and psychological weapon on the borders, where former friends and even close kin were fighting against each other in return for assurance.

Arran and the Cardinal asked Angus and his followers to come to the Queen's coronation, with the aim also of attending parliament so as to unite against a threat from England.[235] Angus declined, refusing to go to the coronation unless the Cardinal and Governor fulfilled the terms of the Greenwich Treaty. At Angus's Castle of Douglas on 8th September, a bond was subscribed by the assured Scots, where Somerville and Maxwell were tasked with representing their views to Henry VIII.[236]

The Cardinal and Arran met at Falkirk, and then to Stirling where they met Huntley and Argyll who had returned from the warfare in the west and north. Moray and Bothwell joined them. The Cardinal revealed to Sandy Pringle, an English spy, that whilst warded at either Blackness or Dalkeith, he had given Sir George Douglas 500 crowns to help him get released into the care of Seton, with Douglas and Seton being cousins. He was to be warded at St Andrews under the bond of four lords, and was not to depart St Andrews without the Governor's agreement. Sir George and the Laird of Grange would release him of this bond, because Douglas believed Beaton would have got himself released by other means, and Douglas wanted the Cardinal to remember it was he that had released him.[237] Sir George was once more playing all sides against each other. Getting rid of Beaton would have been favourable to Henry and his Scottish supporters, but it could have led to English military and political domination with no significant figurehead to counter opposition. Sir George was aiming for the Marriage Treaty to be ratified, and Beaton's approval was needed to give the treaty some measure of legitimacy and to avoid a dangerous civil war.

Whilst Sir George had worked hard to get rid of the harsher articles that Henry sought, this was subterfuge, as the 'secret devices' would have put Scotland in the power of those Scots seeking an English and Protestant alliance. This might have been what Sir George was seeking, with the Douglas to be major players in this alliance. These grand plans were bound to fail with the release of Beaton. Possibly Sir George thought he could manipulate Beaton to ratify the treaty, but he miscalculated badly and Beaton would use all means to undermine Angus and his allies.

Arran was the first significant ally to turn, and at Stirling on September 8th before the Cardinal, Queen Mother and Council, he renounced the Protestant faith, returned to the Catholic faith and renounced the marriage alliance with England. He handed over his eldest son James, housed by the Cardinal in St Andrews, as a pledge. Beaton had proposed that young James, the Master of Arran, mere five or six years of age, would be a suitable candidate to marry Mary, Queen of Scots. However this was not a genuine ambition of the Queen Mother and the son became a hostage, retained to ensure the good behaviour of the Governor.[238]

Sadler also reported a conversation that Argyll had had with Arran where he stated that if Arran had not turned against England his lands would have been devastated. To make his point he mentioned how he had devastated the land of Hector Mor Maclean of Duart, killing nearly 2,000 livestock and burning numerous homes and strongholds. MacLean would prove an interesting character and possibly one of the most effective double agents during the wars. In early 1543 Hector Mor had entered into a bond of manrent with Argyll, in which he agreed to become Argyll's man. In return he was to be gifted 40 marks of land in Mull and Morvern, although these were crown lands that Argyll could not fully guarantee beyond a promise. Despite this it would never be totally clear whose side he was on.[239] The MacLeans may have been supporting Lennox, or even in communication with Ross, and Argyll's raid was a reminder of who held the real power in the west.

References: (1) (HP, vol.1, (260), pp.338-340. Lisle, Cumberland, and Tunstall to Henry VIII, Dec 18th, 1542). (2) (HP, vol.1, (240), pp.339-340. Sir George Douglas to Lord Lisle, Dec 18th, 1542). (3) (HP, vol.1, (261), pp.341-343. Lisle to Henry VIII, Dec 19th, 1542). (4) (Calderwood, pp.150-154. Knox, pp.32-35). (5) (Melville.pp.1-5). (6) (Marshall, pp.45-47). (7) (Hume-Brown, Vol 2, pp.3-4, Thomson, Vol 3, pp.51-53). (8) (Tytler, pp.254-256. (9) (Holinshed, pp.529-530. Lesley, pp.170-171. Tytler, pp.254-257). (10) (Hume-Brown, Vol 2, pp.3-4, Thomson, Vol 3, pp.51-53). (11) (Tytler, pp.256-257. (12) (CSPS, Chapuys to Queen of Hungary, Jan 1st, 1543). (13) (CSPS, Eustace to Queen of Hungary, Dec 23rd 1542. Chapuys to Queen of Hungary, Jan 1st, 1543). (14) (Calderwood, pp.154-155.Tytler, pp.257-258). (15) (Thomson, Vol 3, pp.52-53). (16) (Hume-Brown, Vol 2, p.3). (17) (Calderwood). (18) (Holinshed, p.530). (19) (Calderwood). (20) (ODNB, vol.24, pp.827-833). (21) (SP, vol.4, pp.366-367), (22) (MacCulloch, pp. 203-204, 246). (23) (Calderwood, 154-156). (24) (Knox, pp.35-36. Thomson, Vol 3, pp.52-53. CSPS, Chapuys to Queen of Hungary, Jan 15th 1543. CSPS, Chapuys to Emperor, Jan 15th 1543). (25) (Knox, pp.27-28, 35-36). (26) (Tytler,pp.259-261). (27) (ODNB, vol.24, pp.827-833. SP, vol.4, p.459). (28) (ODNB, vol.24, pp.827-833). (29) (Lesley, pp.171-172). (30) (HP, vol.1 (272), pp.357-359. Lisle and Tunstall to Henry VIII, Jan 5th 1543). (31) (CSPS, Chapuys to Emperor, Jan 15th 1543). (33) (Merriman, pp.128-133). (34)

(HP, vol.1, (276), pp.367-376. Henry's second instruction to Southwell. January, 1543). (35) (HP, vol.1 (268), pp.351-353. Lisle to the Privy Council, Jan 1st 1543). (36) (HP, vol.1 (268), pp.351-353. Lisle to Council, Jan 1st 1542). (37) (Fraser, p259). (38) (Herkless, Cardinal Beaton, pp.208-210). (39) (Merriman, pp.113-115). (40) (Fraser, p.260). (41) (Lesley, pp.171-172). (42) (Merriman, pp.113-115). (43) (Thomson,pp.52-53. Tytler. 262-264). (44) (ALHTS, p.275. SSP, vol.1, pp.25-28, 42-44). (45) (ODNB, vol.37, pp.526-528. (46) (CSPV, Hironimo Zucculo, Venetian secretary in England to the Church of the Ten, 16th Dec, 1542). (47) (ODNB, vol.4, pp.551-556). (48) (ODNB, vol.31, pp.241-242). (49) (Roper, pp.36-37). (50) (ODNB, vol.31, pp.241-242. SP, vol.2, pp.469-470). (51) (ODNB, vol.14, pp.701-702. SP, vol.4, pp.236-238). (52) (ODNB, vol.51, pp.612-613). (53) (ODNB, vol.23, pp.447-448. SP, vol.4, pp.280-289). (54) (Thomson, p.53). (55) (ODNB, vol.52, pp.729-733). (56) (Hume-Brown, vol.1, p.312), (57) (ODNB, vol.52, pp.729-733.Tytler, p.276-277). (58) (Hume-Brown, vol 2, p.5). (59) (Thomson, pp.53-54. CSPS, Chapuys to Queen of Hungary, Jan 17th, 1543). (60) (Herkless, Cardinal Beaton, pp.209-211). (61) (CSPS, Chapuys to Queen of Hungary, Jan 28th, 1543. Marshall, pp.48-51). (62) (CSPS, Chapuys to Queen of Hungary, March 17th, 1543). (63) (LP, The Patriarch, Marco Grimani to Cardinal Farnese, 5th June, 1543). (64) (Knox, pp.35-37). (65) (Thompson, p.56). (66) (Knox, pp.42-43). (67) (Merriman, pp. 128-133). (68) (HP, vol.1, (325), pp.458-459. Suffolk, Lisle, &c, to the Privy Council. March 8th, 1543). (69) (Tytler, pp.263-264). (70) (ODNB, vol.9, pp.698-699). (71) (ODNB, vol.22, pp.878-882). (72) (ODNB, vol.52, pp.684-685). (73) (Williams, p.234, p.243). (74) (Merriman, pp. 71-72. pp.150-151). (75) (Williams, pp.244-245). (76) (Gregory, p.155). (77) (Thomson, Vol 3, pp. 54). (78) (HP, vol.1 (337), pp.474-488. Sadler to Henry VIII, March 20th, 1543). (79) (HP, vol.1 (332), pp.468-469. Lisle to Suffolk. March 16th, 1543). (80) (Thomson, Vol 3, pp. 54). (81) (Letters and papers, Henry VIII, Parliament of Scotland, March 15th, 1543). (82) (Lesley, p.172-173). (83) (Tytler, pp.269). (84) (Knox, pp.41). (85) (Tytler, pp.270-271). (86) (Thomson, pp.54-55. Knox, pp.37-40). (87) (Tytler, pp.264-265). (88) (Tytler, pp.265-267). (89) (LP, Lisle to Suffolk, 17th March, 1543. Merriman, pp.115-

116). (90) (Thomson, pp.53-54). (91) (Thomson, pp.54-55). (92) (HP, vol.1 (334), pp.470-472. Lisle to Suffolk, March 16th, 1543). (93) (HP, vol.1 (354), pp.514. Henry VIII to Sadler, 14th April, 1543). (94) (Marshal, pp.49-50.Reid, David, David Hume of Godscroft's History of the House of Angus, vol. 1 (2005), 107–108). (95) (Marshall, pp.47-48). (96) (Marshall, pp.49-50). (97) (Herkless, Cardinal Beaton, pp.219). (98) (Herkless, Cardinal Beaton, pp.219-220). (99) (HP, vol.1 (338), pp.488-489. Sadler to Henry VIII, March 23rd, 1543). (100) (Herkless, Cardinal Beaton, pp.219-220. Tytler, pp.272-274). (101) (HP, vol.1, (30), pp.38-42. Parr to Suffolk, Sept 13th 1543). (102) (Tytler, pp.274-275). (103) (Tytler, pp.275-276). (104) (HP, vol.1 (351), p.512.Sadler to Henry VIII, 9th April, 1543). (105) (HP, vol.1 (353), pp.512-513.Privy Council to Sadler, 13th April, 1543). (106) (SCML, Huntley to Queen Dowager, Edinburgh, 28th March, 1543). (107) (HP, vol.1 (354), pp.514. Henry VIII to Sadler, 14th April, 1543. LP, Lisle to Suffolk, 17th March, 1543). (108) (Fraser, p.262. LP, Lisle to Suffolk, 17th March, 1543). (109) (HP, vol.1 (358), pp.520-521. Sadler to Henry VIII, April 19th, 1543). (110) (ODNB, vol.24, pp.862-864), (111) (Holinshed, pp.531-532. (112) (Herkless & Hannay, pp.20-22). (113) (Knox, pp.42-43). (114) (Dowden, pp.88-91). (115) (Herkless & Hannay, pp.23-24). (116) (Tytler, pp.273-275). (117) (Merriman, p.106). (118) (ALHTC, vol.8, pp.lxxxii-lxxxviii. Holinshed, p.531). (119) (ODNB, vol.4, pp.551-556). (120) (Thomson, pp.55-56). (121) (Herkless & Hannay, pp.8-11). (122) (Dowden, pp.88-91). (123) (ODNB, vol.52, pp.729-733). (124) (Holinshed, p.532). (125) (Lesley, pp.173-174.Merriman, p.123). (126) (LP, Sadler to Henry VIII, 26th April, 1543). (127) (Calderwood, pp.163-164). (128) (Hume-Brown, pp,4-5.Knox, pp.43-44.Thomson, pp.55-56). (129) (Fraser, pp.262-264). (130) (Herkless, Cardinal Beaton, pp.227-228). (131) (HP, vol.1 (371), p.533. Sadler to the Privy Council, May 1st, 1543). (132) (Tytler, pp.272-273). (133) (HP, vol.1 (367), pp.530-531. Sadler to Henry VIII, 1st May, 1543). (134) (Merriman, pp.119-121). (135) (Thomson p.56. Tytler. pp.279-280). (136) (Calderwood, pp.162-164). (137) (HP, vol.1 (375), pp.534-535. Sadler to Suffolk, Parr and Tunstall, 3rd June, 1543). (138) (Herkless, Cardinal Beaton, pp.229-229. LP, The Patriarch, Marco Grimani to Cardinal Farnese. 5th June, 1543).

(139) (HP, vol.1 (354), pp. 548-549. Sadler to the Privy Council, 29th June, 1543). (140) (ALHTS, vol.8, pp. xl-xli. Herkless, Cardinal Beaton, p.232). (141) (Merriman, pp.128-129). (142) (Herkless, Cardinal Beaton, pp.232-233. HP, vol.1 (390), p.550, Sadler to Council, 30th June, 1543). (143) (Thomson, pp-55-56. LP, Greenwich Treaty, 1st July, 1543). (144) (LP, The Scottish Prisoners, July 1st, 1543). (145) (HP, vol.1 (397), pp.554-557, Parr to Suffolk, 6th July, 1543). (146) (HP, vol.1 (400), pp.562-563, Parr to Suffolk, 7th July, 1543). (147) (HP, vol.1 (402), pp.565-566, Parr to Suffolk, 8th July, 1543). (148) (Thompson, vol III, pp.56-57). (149) (David, SHR, p.23. Tytler, pp.282-283). (150) (HP, vol.1 (401), pp.563-565, Sadler to Council, 8th July, 1543). (151) (HP, vol.1 (404), pp.567-568. Suffolk, Parr and Tunstall to the Privy Council, 11th July, 1543). (152) (Thomson, pp.66-67). (153) (Tytler.340-342). (154) (Knox, pp.52-56). (155) (HP, vol.1 (404), pp.567-568. Suffolk, Parr, and Tunstall to the Privy Council. 11th July, 1543). (156) (HP, vol.1 (406), pp.569-570, Sadler to Henry VIII, 13th July, 1543). (157) (HP, vol.1 (406), pp.569-570, Sadler to Henry VIII, 13th July, 1543). (158) (HP, vol.1 (408), pp.572-573, Sadler to Henry VIII, July 16th, 1543). (159) (Tytler, pp.283-285). (160) (Thomson, p.57). (161) (Calderwood, pp.164-166). (162) (Lesley, pp.174-175). (163) (HP, vol.1 (408), pp.572-573, Sadler to Henry VIII, July 16th, 1543). (164) (HP, vol.1 (418), pp.582-584, Parr to Suffolk, 22nd July, 1543). (165) (LP, Sadler to Parr, 23rd July, 1543). (166) (LP, Sadler to Parr, 22nd July, 1543). (167) (Marshal, pp.52-53). (168) (Paterson. p.174). (169) (Calderwood, pp.165-166). (170) (LP, Sadler to Parr, 23rd July, 1543). (171) (HP, vol.1 (408), pp.572-573. Sadler to Henry VIII, July 16th, 1543). (172) (HP, vol.1 (418), pp.582-584, Parr to Suffolk, 22nd July, 1543). (173) (HP, vol.1 (421), p.587, Henry VIII to Sadler, 22nd July, 1543). (174) (LP, Sadler to Parr, 23rd July, 1543). (175) (HP, vol.1 (424), pp.589-591, Sadler to Suffolk and Tunstall, 24th July, 1543). (176) (HP, vol.1 (424), pp.589-591, Sadler to Suffolk and Tunstall, 24th July, 1543). (177) (Thomson, vol.3, p.57). (178) (Knox, pp.42-44, Thompson, p.56). (179) (Hume-Brown, vol.2, p.5). (180) (HP,vol.1 (427,429,430,437), pp.597-616, Parr to Suffolk, 26th-31st July, 1543). (181) (Marshal, pp.52-53). (182) (ALHTS, pp. xli-xliii. HP, vol.1 (425), pp.591-

594, Sadler to Henry VIII, July 26th, 1543). (183) (HP, vol.1 (433), pp.602-609, Sadler to Henry VIII, July 28th, 1543). (184) (HP, vol.1 (436), pp.602-609, Sadler to Henry VIII, July 31st, 1543). (185) (HP, vol.1 (443), pp.622-626, Sadler to Henry VIII, 5th August, 1543). (186) (HP, vol.1 (436), pp.612-613, Sadler to Henry VIII, July 31st, 1543). (187) (HP, vol.1 (438), pp.616-618. Privy Council to Sadler, August 2nd, 1543). (188) (LP, Sadler to Suffolk, Parr and Tunstall, August 3rd, 1543). (189) (HP, vol.1 (440), p.620, Henry VIII to Sadler, 4th August, 1543). (LP, Sadler to Suffolk, Parr and Tunstall, August 3rd, 1543). (191) (HP, vol.1 (443), pp.622-626. Sadler to Henry VIII, 5th August, 1543). (192) (HP, vol.1 (443), pp.622-626, Sadler to Henry VIII, 5th August, 1543). (193) (HP, vol.1 (446), pp.629-632. Sadler to Henry VIII, 9th August, 1543). (194) (SCML, Huntley to Queen Dowager, 16th August, 1543, Huntley, Countess of Huntley to Queen Dowager, 16th August, 1543, Huntley). (195) (HP, vol.1 (451), pp.636-639. Henry VIII to Sadler, 16th August, 1543). (196) (Knox, pp. 42-43), (197) (HP, vol.1 (451), pp.636-639, Henry VIII to Sadler, 16th August, 1543). (198) (LP, Arran (Governor) to Henry VIII, 16th August, 1543). (199) (Calderwood, pp. 164-166). (200) (Tytler, pp.286-287). (201) (HP, vol.1 (460), pp.655-656. Sadler to Henry VIII, 25th August, 1543). (201) (HP, vol.1 (452), pp.639-644. Sadler to Henry VIII, 17th August, 1543). (202) (LP, Sir George Douglas to Cardinal Beaton, 16th August 1543, Edinburgh). (203) (HP, vol.1 (452), pp.639-644. Sadler to Henry VIII, 17th August, 1543). (204) (SCML, Cardinal Beaton to the Earl of Bothwell, 17th August, 1543). (205) (HP, vol.1 (457), pp.650-654. Henry VIII to Sadler, 24th August, 1543). (206) (Calderwood, pp.167-169). (208) (LP, vol.1 (456), pp.622-626. Suffolk, Parr, and Tunstall to the Privy Council, 19th August, 1543. Calderwood. Williams, pp.245. Ronald, p,245). (209) (Gregory, pp.156-157). (210) (HP, vol.1 (460), pp.655-656. Sadler to Henry VIII, 25th August, 1543). (211) (HP, vol.1 (456), pp.646-650. Suffolk, Parr and Tunstall to the Council, 21st August, 1543. HP, vol.1 (466), pp.662-663. Sadler to Suffolk, Parr and Tunstall, 27th August, 1543). (212) (SCML, Communication (by Methven?) Cupar?, 27th August, 1543). (213) (HP, vol.1 (469), pp.664-665. Sadler to Henry VIII, 29th August, 1543). (214) (Hume-Brown, vol.2, pp.6-7). (215)

(Thomson, p.57). (216) (HP, vol.1 (469), pp.664-665. Sadler to Henry VIII, 29th August, 1543). (217) (HP, vol.2 (2), p.5, Privy Council to Sadler, Sept 1st, 1543). (218) (Holinshed, pp.533-534). (219) (HP, vol.2, (2), pp.2-5. Sadler to Henry VIII, Sept 1st, 1543.Marshal, pp. 53-54). (220) (HP, vol.2 (11), pp.15-16. Sadler to Suffolk, and Tunstall, Sept 4th, 1543). (221) (Calderwood, pp.165-167). (222) (HP, vol.2 (13), pp.18-20. Sadler to Henry VIII, 5th Sept, 1543). (223) (Calderwood, pp.166-167). (224) (Herkless & Hannay, pp.12-13). (225) (HP, vol.2 (11), pp.15-16. Sadler to Suffolk, and Tunstall, Sept 4th, 1543). (226) (Tytler, pp.342-343). (227) (Luckoch, pp.121-123). (228) (HP, vol.2 (11), pp.15-16. Sadler to Suffolk, and Tunstall, Sept 4th, 1543). (229) (HP, vol.2 (28), pp.34-36. Henry to Angus, 11th Sept, 1543). (230) (Tytler, pp.289-290). (231) (HP, vol.1 (458), pp.622-626, Privy Council to Suffolk, Parr and Tunstall, 24th August, 1543). (232) (Tytler, pp. 289-290). (233) (MacDonald Fraser, pp.256-257). (234) (HP, vol.2 (16-18), pp.16-18. Parr to Suffolk, Sept 5th, 1543). (235) (Tytler, pp.288-289). (236) (HP, vol.2 (26), pp.31-33. Sadler to Henry VIII, 11th Sept, 1543). (237) (HP, vol.2 (30), pp.38-42. Parr to Suffolk, 13th Sept, 1543). (238) (Calderwood, pp. 166-167). (239) (MacLean-Bristol, pp.116-122).

Chapter Three

Effusion of blood

On September 9th 1543 at Stirling, the infant Mary was crowned Queen of Scotland with Arran carrying the crown, Lennox the scepter and Argyll the sword of state. The Cardinal conducted the coronation. Arran remained Lord Governor, and he and the Estates agreed that the young Queen was to reside in Stirling with her mother, and funds were allocated to provide maintenance. The Lords Livingston, Erskine and Graham and John Lindsay were to stay by her side as tutors and protectors. A bodyguard of 400 'men of weir' was also employed, led by Captain James Dog and Patrick Kincaid, at the price of £1,200, whilst a smaller company was led by Hew Hommyll and paid £46.[1] As Arran was now siding with the Cardinal and the Queen Mother,[2] Lennox found it difficult to remain allied with them. Not only was Arran a rival for the succession and governorship, there was his family feud with the Hamiltons. In September Lennox began to conclude that he had been played by the Cardinal and Queen Mother, and despite suggestions otherwise there was little possibility of his winning the hand of Mary of Guise.[3]

There were attempts to reconcile both Arran and Lennox, but this was a near-impossible prospect. The Cardinal suggested that the Queen Mother should write to the French king, asking him to recall Lennox to France. Better he were out the country, instead of causing divisions or joining the party of Angus. Lennox however was disillusioned with his current allies, and left for Dumbarton. Holinshed considered that Lennox had a 'greater stomach' than Arran, yet the Cardinal and the Queen Mother were prepared to betray him and favour his hated rival despite Lennox having contributed to freeing the Queen Mother from Arran and undermining the pro-marriage agenda. The decision was tactical. They could wreck the project of Henry VIII and the Angus faction by causing the defection of their only claimant to the succession, whilst also reversing the treaty ratifications and the reformation legislation introduced in March.

The handing over of the Lord Governor's son as hostage was an unusual situation, where the head of government was now bound to the councils of the Cardinal. The Cardinal would use his influence to introduce anti-heretic legislation and involve the Governor in campaigns against suspected heretics that were aimed at showing the power of the Cardinal but also at humiliating Arran, the former champion of reform, whereas if Lennox had been Governor,

Scotland would have been ruled by a fairly independent-minded individual.[4]

To the Queen Mother Lennox, was an ambitious suitor seeking a dynastic marriage to bolster his claims to the crown of Scotland, whether through marrying Mary's mother or being promised an adult Mary as his wife and Queen. The Queen Mother would be happy to see him return to France after being used ruthlessly by the Cardinal and herself.

Lennox would obviously be angry; he had been commissioned by the French King to promote the French alliance and defeat the pro-English Protestants. This he had done valiantly, yet now, despite the promises of the Queen Mother and Cardinal, he was to be discarded in favour of the Hamiltons, those who had slain his family. Lennox would join the party of Angus, although the circumstances of his joining are not known for certain.

As reported by Sadler to his English associates in late September, Lennox began to look towards Lady Margaret Douglas, the daughter of the Earl of Angus, as a possible wife. As a granddaughter of Henry VIII she might be sufficient compensation for Lennox's failed efforts with Mary of Guise.[5]

There were also attempts to reach out to the Earl of Angus and bring him away from allegiance to King Henry. A few days after the crowning of Queen Mary there was a meeting of councillors, and on the advice of the Abbot of Paisley it was suggested that Angus be invited to join the Privy Council. Paisley and Lord Fleming were appointed to make this announcement to Angus.[6] During these political changes Sadler arranged to meet the Cardinal, the Queen

Mother, Moray and Arran at Black Friars in Edinburgh during late September. The latest upheavals were discussed, and the Cardinal explained that the majority of nobles disagreed with the Greenwich Treaty and resented the private meetings and councils of certain individuals. The Cardinal stated that the taking of ships was not justified, and reminded Sadler that Henry had not ratified the Greenwich Treaty. Sadler replied that Henry was waiting the handing over of hostages, and then would have ratified the treaty. Afterwards Sadler had a meeting with Angus and his party and they continued to stand by their promises with regard to the treaties and agreements, even if the Cardinal would not.[7]

Counselled by his brother the Abbot of Paisley and David Paniter, Arran agreed to meet Sir George Douglas between Edinburgh and Dalkeith in late September. Both travelled to Dalkieth for talks, this being the stronghold of James Douglas, Earl of Morton, the father of the Governor's wife Margaret. As already noted Morton's youngest daughter Elizabeth would marry Sir George Douglas's second son James between March 18th 1543-April 2nd 1543, with the husband becoming Master of Morton and heir apparent to the vast Morton estates and baronies.[8]

Arran promised to bring the Cardinal from St Andrews, to provide hostages and negotiate the treaties. Sir George doubted his sincerity.[9] Nevertheless, during the meeting there was an attempt to lure the Douglas clan away from the pro-English agenda, whilst Douglas no doubt tried to tempt Arran away from the Cardinal.[10] Sir George Douglas left Dalkeith and had talks with Sadler during the first week of October. He reported that the Queen Mother was safe in Stirling Castle, and that the Angus faction did not have the artillery or ordinance to besiege or capture it. There was also the danger that an assault could prompt the Queen Mother and Queen Mary to be taken into the Highlands. Sir George required English money and aid to besiege the Cardinal at St Andrews. Edinburgh Castle would also be difficult to take by force, yet there was a Hamilton who was captain of Edinburgh Castle, a family according to Douglas, 'all false and inconstant of nature'. He suggested that bribery might win the castle.[11]

Upon hearing of Sir George's meeting with Arran, Henry apparently 'marveled' that Douglas had not captured him at Dalkeith. The King also said to Sir George that if he and Angus got licence to visit the Queen Mother at Stirling, they should ensure that they had the means to capture the young Queen.[12] In reply to Henry, Sir George explained that Arran had visited Dalkeith under trust, and in regard to Henry's suggestion that he should have captured him, he considered this dishonorable.[13] Douglas was advised not to show too much favour to Arran in case Lennox switched back to the Cardinal's party.[14]

In early October a small French fleet of five ships arrived in Dumbarton, with ambassadors Jacques de la Brosse and Jules de Menage and the Papal Legate Grimani, Patriarch of Aquileia, along with James Stewart, a captain of the Scots Guards and relative of Lennox. The ships were believed to be transporting 500 men, 50,000 crowns, 10,000 spears, 4,000 halbutts and hackbutters and powder and ammunition.[15] The Legate was also authorized to investigate the extent to which the reformed religion had grown in Scotland.[16] Lennox, Cassilli and Glencairn offered to capture these French ships at Dumbarton. There were also concerns within the camp, as discussed by Sadler and Sir George Douglas that James Stewart, returning from the Continent, would try to persuade Lennox back to the French favour.[17]

Sir George Douglas found it difficult to trust anyone, especially with both Arran and Lennox switching sides. He suggested ensuring Lennox's loyalty by allowing him to marry Lady Margaret Douglas, daughter of Angus, and supporting his claim as heir presumptive of Scotland and as governor of Scotland. In early October Arran went to Edinburgh to meet Angus and to offer to mediate between the two sides. He also stated that he would not side with Lennox unless he relinquished his claim as second person of the realm.[18] Sadler also reported that the Angus faction were uncertain how to serve Henry as they did not know if he would bring an army to Scotland, or as Maxwell put it, declare himself King of Scotland.[19]

Lennox and Glencairn took command of the French convoy at Dumbarton, whilst the Cardinal's party were at Stirling trying to learn what was happening to the cargo.[20] Lennox did not need to use force, for the French king was not aware of the state of the country or the present loyalty of Lennox. He had even issued orders that Lennox was to be given the honour of distributing the gold and coin to supporters.[21] A surgeon called John Moore spoke with Lennox and Glencairn at Dumbarton during October.[22] He reported that Lennox wanted to marry Lady Margaret and become heir to the Angus Earldom, but that the Earl of Angus refused. Moore advised Sadler to leave Edinburgh because of the growing violence.[23] There was a belief that the Legate, who had arrived on ships from France to Dumbarton, would be killed if he went to Edinburgh. A large number of Edinburgh residents had embraced the reformed religion and were hostile to the Catholic religion. Friars were reportedly attacked in their homes. The Papal legate and French Ambassador were taken to Glasgow, and the Cardinal's party sent orders for Lennox to allow both to come to Stirling with the French cargo.[24]

The French ambassador arrived first in Stirling, but for some reason the Legate was held back and there was a failed attempt to capture him by Glencairn, which had been ordered by Henry.[25] The legate would later recount how Lennox brought him to Glasgow, and whilst groups of men began to show up and Angus himself was due to arrive, it was only delegations from the Queen Mother and Cardinal which alerted him that Lennox was of the party of Henry VIII. He escaped the trap by putting on a disguise and travelling to Stirling. The Legate was surprised that Lennox had switched sides as he had a long and profitable history with France. Arran, who was still governor, was considered by the legate to be a good prospect for the fight against the assured Scots and Henry VIII.[26] There were requests for Lennox to come to Stirling, yet he refused and kept the French cargo, money, artillery and arms.[27]

La Brosse reached Stirling by late October. He had an audience with Mary of Guise and suggested she offer the hand of her daughter to Lennox once she was of age. The French ambassador had authority to revise the Scot-Franco Treaty and to grant pensions to nobility, whilst the Legate, apparently desperate to leave Scotland, had 'bulls, facilities, and pardons' to bestow.[28] It was reported on October 30th that Lennox would change sides again and go to Stirling to join the French commission and parcel out and distribute pensions.[29] According to reports from the Spanish ambassador he shifted his allegiance from England back to France because he received favourable terms.[30] Taking la Brosse's advice, the Queen Mother was prepared to offer Lennox marriage to Queen Mary. Lennox did not reject the offer, but he refused to hand over the French cargo.

Whilst Lennox was in Stirling, La Brosse used the opportunity to get the gold out of Dumbarton, although the means are unknown. Lennox learned of this action and left Stirling. He managed to recover the gold, and seeing that he had been tricked by the French ambassador he returned to the Angus party.[31] Despite this serious altercation between the two there would still be efforts by the Queen's side to keep him on their side.

Having failed to recapture the gold, la Brosse devoted his efforts to breaking the treaties between Scotland and England. He examined the parliamentary register and found that the seizure of the ships was a clear breach of the Greenwich Treaty. The treaty was supposed to guarantee peace, and the seizures made the treaty invalid. Also of importance was the fact that Henry did not ratify the treaty signed by Arran and sent to him.[32]

Sadler, under instruction from Henry VIII, attempted to win the merchant classes to the English side, promising that their ships and property would be released if they agreed to support the marriage treaty. The merchants refused any approaches, stating that they would prefer to lose their lives and all their goods rather than agree to Henry's plans to usurp Scottish independence.[33] The merchants would be preparing for a new type of livelihood. With the threat of war with England and her imperial allies, this would open up possibilities for privateering under Letters of Marque. The Queen Mother would grant such a letter in November, to a merchant called John Barton, who had had his goods taken by Portuguese ships whilst travelling from Flanders. The letter gave him authority to seize goods from Portuguese shipping as restitution.[34]

Unlike the merchants, the nobles of Angus's faction were prepared to give full allegiance to Henry. Lord Somerville and Lord Maxwell intended travelling to England in early November and presenting Henry with the Douglas Bond and various letters.[35] Whilst they both stopped at Maxwell's house in Edinburgh with 30 men, the Abbot of Paisley led 60 horsemen to the house. He requested that Maxwell and Somerville confer with him on the High Street. This they did, possibly under promise of safe conduct, but they were immediately faced with another 80 men, led by a sergeant-in-arms who arrested them in the name of the Queen. Whilst Somerville, realising that Paisley had 'betrayed' them, was prepared to resist, Maxwell stated that he would not disobey the Queen's command. Both were taken to Edinburgh castle. Somerville reportedly had in his possession, whether on person or in the house, the bond written up at Douglas Castle on September 8th, agreeing to support Henry VIII against the Cardinal, and also other letters that Arran called proof of high treason.[36] Sadler was uncertain how Angus would react to the captures of Maxwell and Somerville. After a brief stay in Edinburgh Castle, Somerville was taken to Black Ness castle.

There is an allegation that Maxwell went to a meeting

with the Abbot of Paisley in order to have himself captured. This suggests he set up Somerville to be caught with letters which the Angus party had asked him to take to the King of England.[37]

How Maxwell persuaded Somerville to meet Paisley is unknown. One possibility may be that Paisley let it be known that he wanted to send a message to Henry, and this was passed to Somerville with Maxwell's connivance, thereby luring him into a trap. These letters would be evidence of high treason, by which the assured Scots intended to cause 'confusion' to the realm.[38] Whether Maxwell did defect is unclear; he would spend the next few months in prison, which may have been the safest place for him if he had betrayed the Angus faction and the King of England.

Arran considered putting Somerville to the torture, to learn the 'credence' sent to Henry from Angus.[39] Since Maxwell had been captured by Paisley, Wharton on November 5th asked his son Master Robert Maxwell to prepare himself against assault by Arran and his allies, and promised English aid if Robert could guarantee Lochmaben Castle, the Eskdale, Annandale and Ewesdale. He commissioned Maxwell to gather 100-200 light horsemen and hurt enemies within a 40-mile radius.[40]

Sir George Douglas advised Sadler to go to Tantallon Castle for refuge, as the towns were unsafe, especially in the west.[41] Sadler would go to Tantallon either on or after November 6th, and stay there for some time before being escorted by Sir George Douglas to England.[42] Brunstane was still using ciphered correspondence with Sadler even after he arrived at Tantallon. Whilst the marriage treaty was losing support in Scotland, Brunstane was still recruiting supporters for the English cause, such as John Charter, a former favourite of Beaton, and John Sandilands of Calder. He persuaded Calder's neighbors not to accept French money. He stated that the Scottish government was determined to wage war.[43] A prior request by Henry for the Angus faction to apprehend the Cardinal, Queen and Arran was unfeasible as they were now too busy trying to survive attacks by their growing number of enemies.[44] Sadler reported that on November 7th Arran had laid siege to Dalkeith Castle, part of a concerted attack against the Douglas faction, whilst the passages around Tantallon were blocked off. Fourteen horses were used to pull cannon to Dalkeith, and twenty-three horses were needed to bring carts laden with smaller cannon, powder and bullets.[45]

At Dalkeith the Master of Morton held the jails, along with James Douglas of Parkhead and Alex Drummond, but they lacked artillery and were running out of victuals.[46] During this period Sir George Douglas was in Berwick requesting money and aid, which the Earl of Suffolk granted. There was a suggestion that if the assured Scots could unite, England would help them take Scotland below the Forth-Clyde line, although the strongholds would have to wait until the countryside was pacified.[47]

The Master of Morton surrendered Dalkieth on condition that his people and baggage were free to go. The Governor said to Morton that if his father Sir George and his uncle Angus would leave their allegiance to Henry then he would 'esteem them above all in Scotland'. The Master replied that the King of England had shown them so much favour that they could not betray him. Sir George Douglas's castle of Pinkie was taken, and the Abbot of Dunfermline captured.[48] Arran next focused his attack on Sadler, accusing him of coordinating actions and rebellions against the Scottish crown. Writing to Arran in November 11th, from the protection of Tantallon, Sadler refuted this. Arran would request that he answered charges against him, or left the realm.[49]

Brunstane reported that the French were offering the services of 6,000 knights from Denmark and money to pay 10,000 Scots soldiers. The Cardinal also crossed the Firth of Forth to campaign against suspected Protestants. He took with him Arran, who having campaigned against the assured Scots was now forced to face the dangers caused by the spread of the reformed religions. Beaton was also possibly concerned that if Arran was outside his watch he might become swayed to rejoin the pro-English party of Angus.[50] The Cardinal would continue to hold Arran's son as hostage, as a guarantee against betrayal and possibly an indication of how little Beaton trusted the Governor.

The issue of religion was also becoming political. The Lord Ruthven was one who openly practised the reformed faith and he was also Provost of Perth, or St Johnston. Arran had used his authority as governor to impose John Charters as Provost, but the people of Perth refused to accept this change, which they claimed was 'hurtful to their freedom of election'. John Charters with Lord Gray, and Norman Leslie, Laird of Rothes, advanced towards St Johnston but were beaten off by Ruthven. However, it was suspected that the defeated party was not fully loyal to the cardinal, since they had expected favours and received none. John Charter was also the name accredited by the English spy Brunstane as being a potential recruit.[51] The Governor and Cardinal went to Dundee along with the Abbot of Paisley, David Paniter, and the Laird of Buccleuch.

The suspicions about Leslie may be valid as there was contention between the Leslies and the Cardinal. Before the King's death the lands of Wemyss in Fife had been granted to the Leslies, however the Cardinal reversed this and restored the lands to the prior owners. Norman Leslie was also one of the Scots captured at Solway, and released in return for favouring the marriage treaty. The Leslies were also with the Fife party which favoured church reform, such as the Melvilles of Raith, Kirkcaldy of Grange, Lindsays of the Byres, and the lawyer Henry Balnaves. Gray, Rothes and Balnaves at Huntly Castle are ordered by Arran to come to a meeting at Dundee.

The Cardinal however attempted a stratagem in which before time of meeting, an armed force would ride to Perth and surprise them. Forewarned, the men of Perth assembled 300 men in readiness. Faced with this defence the Laird of Kirkcaldy and the provost of St Andrews were sent forward to negotiate, and ask why they prepared for battle. They replied that they were only defending themselves, and that they distrusted the cardinal. They were offered a protection under trust if they disband their forces and come into Dundee. This they did, however as they approached Dundee they became wary and distrusted, but they were not allowed to return to Perth. Once they entered Dundee they were apprehended.[52] By late November it is reported that Bannaves has been put under custody of the Cardinal, the Governor has Rothes, and Gray is in Dalkieth.[53] Sadler related the capture of Gray, Rothes and

Balnaves. He also believed that the Cardinal did not fully trust the Governor as he still has his son as hostage in St Andrews.[54]

Sir George Douglas continued to correspond with Henry and his chief men, seeking favourable conditions for himself, friends and adherents. The English king replied to an assertion of Sir George that he and his family and friend had suffered through service to him. Henry believed that he himself had gained little, despite agreeing to all Sir George's requests for money, aid and arms. He also knew that offers had been made to Angus and Sir George. Henry also said that whilst Sir George asked for assurances for certain friends and adherents on the borders, many of them had by hostile actions proven themselves enemies.[55] He offered further details, in that people in Tynedale for whom Sir George wanted assurances had injured the King of England's subjects.[56] Sir George however continued to work to the English interest, escorting Sadler to Berwick later in December when the warfare intensified.[57]

At the parliament at Edinburgh during the month of December Arran was to remain governor and Lennox was offered a post on the Council of 16. Possibly this offer left Lennox feeling isolated and betrayed, having arrived in Scotland hoping to undermine his hated rival Arran, and now his chances of becoming governor, or heir presumptive were minimized.[58] The invitation had conditions, in that Lennox should hand over the French cargo; this he had no intention of doing. Despite being a Catholic, Lennox decided to fully join with the pro-English party. Invitations were also extended to Angus and Glencairn to serve in the council, either a prelude to reconciliation or possibly a trap.

It was now becoming common for the Cardinal and Governor to use invitations under trust to capture enemies. The two did not take up the invitation, stating their reluctance to serve with Arran.[59]

Beaton was also confirmed by the Three Estates as chancellor, no doubt a severe blow to the pro-English party.[60] The office of Lord Privy Seal was granted to the Abbot of Paisley.[61] Arran's change of politics and religion, evident during his journey with Beaton north of the Firth of Forth, was now confirmed by the introduction of legislation to investigate all accusations of heresy, with a claim that 'heretics increase more and more' across Scotland. During this time, Arran, who had once been an advocate of reformation, became a fierce opponent, adding further to the accusations that he was a tool of the cardinal and the clergy.[62]

There was an ambition to form a unified parliament, and a declaration was made whereby no one who supported the Queen Mother or Arran during the recent troubles that had brought the young Queen out of Linlithgow was to be accused of any crime, and were free of any punishment in respect of the above.[63] However, there were exceptions, and having rejected an invitation to attend parliament as a counselor, no doubt not wanting to share the fate of Maxwell and Somerville, Angus, along with his brother Sir George Douglas, was charged with treason. A supplication was raised in connection with an event in 1526. During that year, whilst James V was in their power, they had destroyed and burned the lands and properties of Patrick Hepburn of Bolton and taken him captive. However during a session of parliament, King James V deemed that Angus and Sir

George were innocent of any crime, and the parliament passed this. Hepburn used the December parliament to ask the lords of articles that the decision of James V and his parliament be reversed.[64]

The mention of the Douglas and their status as rebels and traitors prior to James V's death was highlighted in a summons by James, son of James Hamilton of Finnart,[65] and in a summons raised by Margaret Forrester.[66] The event of several summonses coming into the parliament would remind the three estates of previous traitorous activities by the Douglas faction. This would have real significance in respect of the Summons of Treason that was to be made against all those lords that added their names to the Douglas bond and other correspondence in the possession of Lord Somerville.[67]

The December parliament also renounced the Greenwich Treaty, where the seizure of the merchant ships in England were seen as an act violating the peace, the English authorities acting as 'enemies' to the Scots. Arran and the Queen Mother had approved and ratified the two contracts for marriage and for peace before expiry date of September 1st, but having received those contracts Henry failed to approve or ratify them, causing them to expire after that date.[68] The three estates also, with the two ambassadors La Brosse and Jacques Mesnage, reviewed all the old contracts of alliance between Scotland and France, and then renewed and ratified the former treaties between them whereby each would support the other against the King of England, or any other enemies.[69]

It was reported on December 12th that Moray and Argyll were considering joining Angus as they were unhappy with the Cardinal and Governor seizing people under trust and without trial. If they could usurp the Cardinal and Governor, Angus, Lennox, Huntley and Argyll would be chosen as regents. If Moray and Argyll did not join they would nevertheless attack the Abbot of Paisley's lands and burn the town of Hamilton.[70] Argyll's consideration of switching may also have something to do with the devastating attacks by the Scottish Gaels and Irish levies, which Henry may be funding. The King of England around this time would seek to negotiate with Argyll, to get him to change sides using the threat of Gaels and Irish against his lands as a lever.[71]

At Douglas during the first two weeks of December the Master of Maxwell and the Laird of Donlanark assembled armed forces, intending to do harm to their enemies.[72] Open war was now a viable alternative for Lennox. Seeking to marry Lady Margaret Douglas, daughter of Angus and Margaret Tudor, sister of Henry, he now had the prospect of forming marital links with the English king and the powerful Douglas faction. He would side openly with the Douglas, Glencairn, and Cassilis in December 1543, and would muster forces in Glasgow before marching against Beaton and Arran. Lennox and his allies intended to make proclamation against the Cardinal and Governor, and cite their falsehoods and treasons as having provoked war.[73]

There is some question that Lennox may have initially marched towards Stirling. Arran appears to have been present with the Queen and Queen Mother at Stirling, as it is recorded that he was granted £160 from the treasurer to play cards with the Queen Mother over Christmas. The playing of games during an approaching civil war may seem like a cool-headed response; nevertheless Arran was prepared for any imminent actions by his enemies. On January 2nd three hundred 'men of weir' were raised to await 'the cuming of the Erll of Lennox, Casillis, Glencarn, and otherris to the toun of Striviling'. Arran also sent letters to Lennox, Cassilis and Glencairn from Stirling to Glasgow, though the contents are unknown. However during the first weeks of January Arran seems to have been continually on the move, sending letters from Stirling, Linlithgow, Hamilton and Edinburgh. Arran also dispatched artillery and specialized gunners by a convoy of carts, and employed ships to transport other artillery from Leith. There was a storm which caused several of the ships to scatter, and after dogged efforts to reorganize the small fleet and get to Stirling it appears they only stayed a few days before the artillery was transported back to Leith. It appears that Lennox, after an initial march to Stirling, instead decided to lead the army towards Leith, reaching it on January 10th, 1544. Arran apparently reached Edinburgh around the same time.

Lennox's army then gathered outside Edinburgh and called on the Governor and Cardinal to meet them in battle. They decided to do nothing and wait as Lennox and his army began to use up vital provisions, Both Arran and the Cardinal had been prepared for conflict, for summons had been sent out to Haddington, Lauder, Jedburgh, Selkirk and Peebles for men to arrive at Edinburgh by December 28th, whilst those from Fife, Forfar and Kincardine were to appear by January 7th. Right up to Lennox's appearance before Leith the Governor sent out messengers to collect horses and men, whilst ferrymen in Kinghorn and

Queensferry were under instruction to cooperate fully and fairly with men travelling to assist Arran. Lennox had no cannon, and the defender was not going to lose his advantage by fighting out in the open, especially when he had enough cannon with adequate range to stave off an assault on Leith or Edinburgh. Arran also had a spy in Lennox's camp supplying information on the movements of his armed companies. During this period many of Lennox's allies entered into secret negotiations with Arran and the Cardinal. This compelled Lennox to do likewise and agree to meet with Arran.[74]

Sir George Douglas may have inadvertently opened the door to peace talks. With the Lennox army at Leith, Sir George was leading five hundred horsemen from the Merse when at Musselburgh he was set upon by the Earl of Bothwell, and instead of fleeing to Leith went to Stirling. It is said he had an audience with the Governor. If this is correct then Arran appears to have returned to Stirling whilst the Cardinal held Edinburgh.[75]

Sir George Douglas added further details of the campaign in correspondence to England. From 10th to 14th January the army of assured Scots had been outside Edinburgh offering battle on the field. They could not assault Edinburgh due to better artillery and the larger number of troops serving the Governor. Sir George Douglas reported that many of his allies began to make secret arrangements with the Governor. The Master of Maxwell went to Stirling to visit his father, and then changed sides. Sir George said that alongside the other great men he made arrangements with the Governor to save himself.[76] At Rood Chapel of Greneside, Commissioners from both sides met to agree to set aside divisions in the realm. Through the 'Greneside Agreement', Angus, Lennox, Cassilis, Glencairn and allies promised to be true to the Queen, and to support Arran in defending Scotland. Securities were provided by the lords.[77]

Lennox was invited to further talks in Linlithgow, and although outwardly friendly with Arran he learned of a secret plot against him. Without a word he departed Arran's company and went to Glasgow.[78] Those that remained were to promise to defend the realm and turn away from the opinion of England. Rather than offer his two sons as pledges, as he believed they would be put to death, George Douglas offered himself. Glencairn offered his son and Cassilis a brother, while Lennox before fleeing west had offered a brother and 10,000 crowns. Despite this development Sir George still claimed to be the King of England's servant.[79] The Spanish ambassador Chapuys believed that the assured Scots had submitted out of 'compulsion' and they had indicated to the English that they would switch sides once England invaded Scotland. He offered the opinion that Scotland and England were not in a formal state of war, but that there were numerous raids from both sides, conducted with 'much animosity and cruelty'.[80]

Henry was also applying diplomatic pressure through his ambassadors to get the Emperor to declare the Scots enemies of the Empire. Henry asked in January 1544 for the Emperor to transfer 500 Spanish troops, harquebusiers, to England for use against the Scots, even though these troops were vital to the cohesion of Imperial military tactics and would be missed. The Emperor also wanted to know for certain whether Scotland and England were actually at war, since the military alliance only counted if there was a genuine state of war. The Emperor was also reluctant to break commercial treaties with Scotland.[81] The English ambassadors also asked the Emperor to seize all Scottish ships that had been preying on English shipping. The Emperor ordered arrests of privateers or pirates, but still refused to end trading relations with Scotland. The Scots claimed there was no war, whilst the English asserted that there was.[82] To counter English demands for the Emperor to declare war against Scots, he asked the English ambassador to ask Henry to declare war against Holstein, King of Denmark. The Emperor passed on information that French agents were stirring up trouble in Scotland and Ireland.[83]

During January Beaton and Arran crossed the Firth of Forth once again and arrived in Perth, where the Cardinal opened his spiritual court and instigated judicial measures against many accused heretics. The court put to death by hanging several heretics, and one woman was drowned. This was a campaign to drive the reformed worship out of Perth, which Calderwood described in some detail. They were accompanied by the Earl of Argyll, Justice Sir John Campbell, Lord Borthwick, the Bishops of Dunblane and Orkney and other nobles. These forces were needed, as when sentences were proclaimed there was pleading by the townspeople to Arran for mercy, and there were fears of armed rebellion. Although Calderwood stated that Arran was sympathetic to the pleading of the townspeople, he could do nothing to save them because of the dominance of the clergy. It was such persecutions that formed an opinion from the protestant party that alliance with England was the best protection from inquisition and French vassalage.[84]

On January 28th 1544 Henry declared war against the Scots and asked the Emperor to do the same,[85] receiving the now standard Imperial reply that if Henry wanted the Emperor to declare against the Scots then the English must declare against Holstein. Henry did not want to take this action because of mercantile links, and noted the danger to English interests if Holstein were to send an army of Germans to Scotland.[86] His fears seem to have been justified, as there were reports of 10,000 troops in the Duchy of Holstein, which could be gathering for the Low Countries or Scotland.[87]

After the religious campaign during January, Arran retired to his residence in Hamilton. The Queen Mother was at Stirling and the Cardinal at St Andrews. According to reports they did not take care to defend the realm. Lennox believed that the Cardinal and royal household might flee to France.[88] Scots ambassadors arrived in England in February to talk peace; they insisted that marriage between Mary and Edward should occur when both were of marriageable age, but the English Privy Council had no faith in this proposal.[89] They believed they now desired peace so as to earn time to grow and sow crops, and to receive aid from France and Denmark. King Henry decided on full-scale raids into Scotland.[90]

The English decided that the lands of the Douglas were to be wasted and if Sir George Douglas complained then it was to be explained that wasting Douglas land would appear as if they were out of credit with England. If he continued to serve in secret he would be compensated.[91] In

March, as the raids were set to intensify, the King suggested putting a notice on the church door of every plundered village, 'Yon may thank your cardinal, for if he had not been (cardinal), you might have been quiet and rest, for the contrary whereof he has travelled, much as he can by to bring you sorrow and trouble'.[92]

At Normandy the French were building up a fleet, and Italians and other foreign troops were mustering to prepare for crossing to Scotland. Henry was said to be outfitting a fleet with 20,000 men to obstruct this crossing.[93] A later report would count a fleet of 150 sails outfitted on the Thames on March 20th, capable of transporting 15,000 infantry and cavalry. Winds stopped the fleet from sailing. There were also considerable forces on the borders of Scotland.[94]

Lennox seems to have reneged on his arrangement with Arran, and fortified Glasgow Castle in March 1544.[95] The Governor sent out letters to the regions of Fife, Forfar, Kinross, Perth, Strathearn and Kincardine for men to muster at Stirling with eight days' supplies. Robert, the Master of Maxwell, travelled from Dumfries to act as mediator between Angus and Arran. Angus at this time was in Tantallon castle.[96] Angus asked Henry to send an army to Scotland. Henry however wrote to scold Angus, as not being decisive enough when he had his enemies in his power, such as when Beaton was imprisoned. Lennox's secretary, Thomas Bishop, had also explained the situation in Scotland, as had the King's chaplain Mr Penwen. As for the 'assurance' that Angus asked for, the King stated that Angus needed to ensure certain conditions and requirements.[97] There was definite distrust of Angus by the

English, yet he was considered too useful and dangerous to be discarded. Sir William Paget suggested negotiating a 'long treaty' between England and Earl of Angus, which should have ensured that Angus did not help the Scottish governor or hinder the English invasion.[98]

Sir George Douglas said all freeholders and others had been ordered to host at Stirling on last day of the month of March, with 12 days' supplies for each man. The purpose was to oppose Lennox, Angus and the other assured Scots .[99] Possibly in response to Henry refusing to send an army at that time, Maxwell or Angus managed to get writs of protection authorized by Governor, Queen and Cardinal so as to allow for negotiation.

Maxwell brought Angus to Glasgow to meet with Arran on April 3rd 1544.[100] Angus and Maxwell would also attempt to negotiate on behalf of Lennox, and travelled to one of Arran's lodgings. Whilst their forces were arrayed outside, Angus and Maxwell entered to meet with Arran. Despite the writ of protection, the Governor ordered them captured and taken through the postern gate and to his castle in Hamilton. James Douglas of Parkhead and George Douglas of Waterside were also taken, and it was alleged that Maxwell's capture was with his own connivance.[101] Angus stayed at Hamilton Castle for five weeks, and was then taken to Blackness Castle on the southern shore of the Firth of Forth, where he and his kin and followers were expecting to be executed.[102]

At the siege of Glasgow Castle, the Governor used professional soldiers and brought up cannon to bombard the walls and steeple. The military train that Arran brought from Edinburgh consisted of artillery, cannon and culverins from the castle and likely from Stirling where the muster had been called. 153 horses gathered from the districts surrounding Edinburgh were gathered and used in the train, many to pull the carts, such as four wagons of ammunition. 60 laborers were also employed with shovels and picks to level out any uneven pathways.[103] The garrison surrendered at the beginning of April and despite promises of freedom, 18 of Lennox's supporters were hanged on gallows erected on the Tollbooth of Glasgow.[104] Lennox was not in the castle when it was surrendered and fled, possibly to Dumbarton. During that period, apart from asking Angus and Maxwell to negotiate on his behalf, he had written to the Queen Mother in early March to defend himself against accusations by Arran that he was the main cause of division within the realm. He stated that he was willing to answer that charge in front of the three estates.[105]

Lennox would also write to the French King explaining how he had been wrongly treated by the Cardinal's party in favour of Arran, who he describes as his enemy. He reminded the King of the services he had performed for him, and how he had promised to support him in his rights as second person of the realm. Disappointed that Francis had not supported him by using his influence with the Cardinal and Queen Mother, he had renounced his allegiance.[106] He now wished to be reconciled with France. He described Arran as a 'faithless man' who 'changed friends with foe upon every light occasion'. He took credit for saving the Queen Mother and young Queen when he took them from Linlithgow to Stirling. Lennox would receive no positive word from France, and when the French King learned that Lennox had sided with England he had his brother, John

Stewart, Lord of Aubigni and a captain of Scots Guards, put in jail, and his lands and possessions forfeited.[107]

Sir George Douglas, despite being incarcerated, was able to collect information and compose letters. He managed to get correspondence smuggled out of Blackness prison, and informed the English that six ships were sailing from Scotland to Flanders, with three ambassadors, one each for the Imperial, French and Danish courts.[108] Sir George and his brother Angus were either to be executed or sent to France in these ships. One ship, the *Lyon*, was to transport the Papal Legate, the French Ambassador and David Paniter. The small convoy was expected to sail with 16 merchant ships, and the Master of Morton invited Henry to capture them.[109] The Imperial ambassador would later confirm that Grimani, the Patriarch of Aquileia and Papal Legate had set sail to France in April to avoid the English fleet.[110]

Suspicions about Angus and his followers were spreading among the English, and there were accusations that Angus and Maxwell had both consented to capture and that Angus had defected to Arran.[111] However the Master of Morton revealed that his Uncle Angus was a captive, and he related how there was a plan to rescue him if he was to be taken to France. Angus's jailers feared to take him to the ships, possibly because there was a force of 100 horses lying between Edinburgh and Leith with the purpose of falling on them.

On April 7th, the ship meant to take Angus and the other Douglas sailed without them. Morton agreed to hold Dalkieth and Tantallon until an English army arrived. He desired assurances for certain friends and allies.[112] In relation to a suggestion that Maxwell had led Angus into a trap, it was considered common practice by Governor and Cardinal to offer protections, and then breach those trusts.[113]

An agent of the Douglas, Sandy Jardine, was negotiating over the handing over of Tantallon to England. He insisted on assurances for Morton's friends and adherents, repeating the story that Angus had been taken whilst under safe conducts issued by the Cardinal, Queen and Governor. The Master of Glencairn and Thomas Bishop, Lennox's secretary, had conference with Hereford. They stated their belief that Maxwell had betrayed Angus, and Hereford was warned to beware the Sheriff of Ayr as he had been picking faults with Angus and his capture in order to distract from his own falsehoods. Lennox and Glencairn were asked to visit Carlisle for talks, and then visit Henry at his court.[114]

A person called 'Wysshert', which may have been George Wishart, arrived in Newcastle on April 17th bearing a message from Brunstane, who can be identified as Alexander Crichton of Brunstane. On March 1544 Wysshert had passed a letter to Henry Ray at Berwick, to be sent to Henry VIII. He was also given a cipher for further correspondence to the English. A meeting with Henry VIII occurred on April 21st. Henry VIII alluded to a scheme whereby some Scottish lords were prepared to enact a 'feat against the cardinal', and once completed they expected Henry to provide them with refuge. The principal actors were the Laird of Grange, Norman Leslie, the Master of Rothes, and John Charters, the former adherent of Beaton. Leslie had apparently been reconciled with the Cardinal after his imprisonment in 1543. His name was on a list of those pardoned for questioning the scriptures, and on April 24th he entered into bond of manrent with the Cardinal.[115]

There were no details of what type of 'feat' was offered, yet with the apparent better relations between Leslie and the Cardinal this would give the former better opportunities to harm the latter. There was also an offer by the Earl Marishal, Lord Gray and associates to burn church lands, the abbey and the town of Arbroath once the Cardinal went south to resist the English invasion. Henry suggested that if the lords wished to burn and waste church lands he would pay 1,000 pounds sterling. If this was George Wishart, we know from Knox that after leaving Dundee in September 1543 he was then supposed to travel to Ayrshire to preach. During a hostile visit by the Archbishop of Glasgow he was given protection by the Earl of Glencairn and gentlemen of Kyle. Knox's chronology may be wrong, as from late 1543 Glencairn was busy conspiring against the Scottish government. The report by the Privy Council suggests that at time of writing he was in company of assured Scots from Lothian, such as Brunstane, and may have travelled to England to meet the King. If true this suggests that Wishart, a devout preacher, was being used to support protestant opposition in Scotland.[116]

Although Henry was interested in these plans, his first priority was the planned attack on Scotland. Negotiations were underway with the Master of Morton and David Douglas to hand over Tantallon once the English army arrived.[117] To do it before would lead to the execution of Morton's father and uncle and other family and friends. The Cardinal and Governor compelled Angus and Sir George to sign a bill to hand the Castle of Tantallon over to the Abbot of Paisley, who was preparing for a long siege. Hereford wrote to the Douglas asking them to hold out for eight days, and he would send forces to lift the siege, bragging that he would do this despite the power of the Lord Governor and the Cardinal.[118] Lennox and Glencairn were summoned to appear before parliament under charge of treason on May 7th, whilst Sir George Douglas and Angus would face the same charges.[119]

The Scottish government was aware of the plans for a naval invasion and sent word on April 23rd for all east coast towns to fortify and prepare themselves, although the Governor and the Cardinal were possibly not prepared for the scale of what was to come. On May 3rd 1544 Hereford sent a fleet into the Firth of Forth with 114 ships. The fleet cast anchor at Leith Roads. The next morning 11,000 troops disembarked at Granton, west of Edinburgh. Arran and Beaton called for a host to gather at Boroughmuir, and Argyll, Huntley and Bothwell were in their company. Hereford marched towards Leith on May 4th. Six thousand Scottish horse and a number of footmen gathered at a nearby valley, and artillery was placed before two straits that needed to be crossed. Hereford sent in his vanguard, led by the Lord Admiral. There was an exchange of artillery fire before the Scots withdrew and allowed the English to pass, losing eight pieces of artillery. A contingent of harquebusiers was given credit during this action, a disciplined body of soldiery that the Scots could not match as they had few themselves. They would prove decisive in much of the fighting that would occur.[120] After a few more skirmishes Hereford occupied Leith, bringing in supplies and artillery from the nearby ships. By the next morning Leith had been plundered, ships had been captured and 1,500 men were left to occupy as Hereford advanced towards Edinburgh.

Learning that Bothwell and Lord Hume had entered Edinburgh, the English vanguard forced through the Cannongate with artillery, firearms and archers covering the advance and driving defenders away from the walls. Resistance from the townspeople was hard, with street-to-street fighting offered, whilst defenders fired guns from windows and alleyways. Three to four hundred Scots were said to have been slain. Bothwell and Hume retreated to the castle. An attempt to position artillery from the High Street of Edinburgh was beaten off by guns from the castle. The efforts and actions of the men within Edinburgh Castle during this attack would be especially mentioned in the treasury accounts, not just the soldiers, gunners and men who brought in supplies but also surgeons who supplied drugs to the wounded and even barbers who acted as auxiliary surgeons with their sharpened instruments. There was payment to a trumpeter and a minstrel for playing morale-lifting tunes during the conflict.

The remedy to this resistance from the castle was to put Edinburgh to the flames, which they did thoroughly over two days of burning houses, including Holyrood Palace.[121] Lord Eure and 4,000 horse from Berwick and the borders joined Hereford, laying waste and pillaging the surrounding countryside.[122] Craigmillar castle was captured and there were sea raids across the Firth, with Kinghorn plundered. Numerous small towns and villages along the coasts would suffer devastation from the fleet.

It appears that the Governor and the Cardinal ordered the release of Angus, Sir George Douglas, Somerville, Lord Maxwell and the other assured Scots from Blackness Prison prior to Hereford's raid. Maxwell however was taken by English forces outside Edinburgh, and due to a belief that he deliberately allowed himself to be captured and was an agent for Arran; he was taken to London and housed in the Tower.[123] Arran and the Cardinal had freed them because they did not want their followers to join the English, and they also wanted to win some favour with the populace. Sir George would sarcastically praise the invasion for forcing his captors to make this decision to release him, thanking 'King Harry and my gentle masters of England'.[124]

After his release Sir George made approaches to Hereford in respect of saving his lands and adherents from the warfare. The advice from the Privy Council to any offers of friendship, or 'pretext of friendship', was for Hereford to continue to execute a policy of burning and wasting lands in Scotland, including those of Sir George Douglas.[125] The wasting would be precise and thorough, Eure being joined with numerous border Scots such as the Armstrongs, the Nixons, the Crosers, the Rutherfords, all putting on the Red Cross of St George and employing reiving tactics across a wide area around Edinburgh.[126]

On May 15th the fleet set off for home filled with plunder, including 80,000 iron shot. The town of Leith was burned as a leaving gesture. Hereford began a slow march to Berwick, reaching it on May 18th after destroying towns and villages on the way. Seton Castle and the surrounding area were given especially destructive attention, due to Lord Seton having released the cardinal. Musselburgh, Preston,

Haddington and Dunbar were all set on fire. At Dunbar Hereford employed 500 harquebusiers and 500 horsemen to capture the town, this being a new developing military formation that the English would employ during the Scottish wars, where the fire of harquebusiers broke up a Scottish formation and the horse and foot finished it off. At a strait called the Pease, Lord Seton, Lord Hume and Buccleuch were waiting with a reported 10,000 men, but a thick mist hampered any engagement. When the mist rose the Scots withdrew as the English vanguard advanced.[127]

The Emperor would declare war against the Scots, calling them enemies of the Emperor's allies the English, who were allied with the Emperor's enemies the French, who in turn were allied with the Turks.[128] This declaration, which was opposed by mercantile interests in the Low Countries, and initially by Scottish merchants and government, would in turn have severe economic implications for the fishing industries of Holland, Zealand, Flanders and Friesland, depriving them of access to the herring fisheries of the North Sea. Denied access to trade with the Low Countries, many of the Scottish merchants turned to piracy as justifiable warfare against the Empire.[129] These merchants-turned-pirates would attack not just English ships but vessels from the Low Counties, Spain and Portugal.[130]

The issue of whether Sir George Douglas and his family, friends and servants should be granted assurances was much discussed. Eure makes the point that when Sir George's lands were raided by the English he would seek redress for family, adherents and servants, but if his own raided English lands and their victims sought redress, he would claim he was not connected to them and it was not his concern. Eure suggested that Sir George should produce a list of family, adherents and servants he sought assurance for, and then compare them with people Douglas had previously disowned.[131] Hereford however advised that this should be granted for a short time for tactical reasons, so that the horses and men were refreshed before launching an attack on Jedburgh. Once the attack had been carried out, sufficient pledges and hostages should be expected from Douglas to assure his loyalty and good behaviour.[132] The Privy Council however disagreed and refused assurance to Douglas, as his 'saying doth far differ and disagree with his doings'.[133] Eure stormed Jedburgh and put the town to the torch. Kelso suffered the same fate. During these raids the assured Scots wore identifying labels, such as the Red Cross of St George.[134]

The Earl of Lennox had sent John Campbell to France, to speak to the King and ask his leave to return to that country. He sought to remind the King that it was through his actions at Linlithgow that the Queen Mother and the young queen had been set free. His present misfortune and that of his friends he blamed on Arran, a person keeping faith 'neither with God nor man'. Campbell was not allowed an audience, due to the King's closeness to the Guise family, so Lennox decided to accept an offer to go to England and offer his services to Henry VIII.[135] Lennox placed a garrison in Dumbarton castle and called his vassals to arms before leaving for England.

At Carlisle on the 17th of May 1544, Lennox met with Glencairn and his son Alexander. They entered into a treaty with Henry VIII by which the English king was recognised as Lord Protector of Scotland. Henry also sympathized with the way Lennox had been treated by the King of France and Cardinal Beaton, who had denied his claim to being second person of the realm. Henry promised to support Lennox's claim and other causes, and 'thankfully received his gentle offer of service'.[136] Lennox would allow the English to use Dumbarton and the Isle of Bute as bases to attack Arran. He agreed to do everything in his power to deliver Queen Mary into the power of Henry VIII. Henry in turn recognised Lennox as rightful governor of Scotland. Lennox also relinquished his right to the crown of Scotland. The Bishop of Caithness, a hostage for Lennox, was sent to Court at Westminster. Glencairn and son would receive a pension from the English crown.[137]

Lennox next left for Dumbarton, where he planned to muster forces, and then meet up with Glencairn at Glasgow. They were planning to waste the lands of the Hamiltons along Clydesdale. At Glasgow Glencairn had 500 men, mostly spearmen, made up of the levies of the barons, lords and gentlemen of Lennox and Renfrew, as well as the burgesses and clergy. Arran, possibly learning of the intent of his enemies, managed to raise 1,000 men and artillery, including 26 gunners. He advanced towards Glasgow and sought to engage Glencairn before he linked with Lennox. Once reaching the town he positioned his forces at the Muir of Glasgow, a mile from the city. Glencairn, with 500 spearmen, decided to attempt victory himself and attacked Arran. Initially it appeared Glencairn would win the battle, as Arran's front ranks were driven back and the artillery taken. At a critical moment Lord Boyd and his forces appeared, and whilst there was uncertainty about which side he would favour he joined with Arran and Glencairn was routed. Glencairn lost two sons and three hundred men, although he managed to escape. Arran also lost 300 men, and there were many wounded. Like the recent defence of Edinburgh Castle, barbers were employed to tend to wounds and dig out bullets.

The victorious side plundered the town of everything movable, even doors and windows. Several captured lords were hanged at Glasgow Cross. Glencairn escaped to Dumbarton with a small force. There were reports that despite Arran's victory, the Queen Mother was planning to oust him from the position of Governor. He was blamed for the failure to defend Edinburgh against Hereford's raid. Despite Lennox's followers advising him to stay in Scotland to observe the power struggles between Arran and the Queen Mother, he decided to sail to England, leaving George Stirling to captain Dumbarton.[138]

The Battle of the Muir of Glasgow was small, yet important. A defeat for Arran would not have won Scotland for Henry, but it would have weakened the opposition and allowed a pro-English party led by Lennox to operate in the west of central Scotland, especially Glasgow. Whilst Arran was in the west the Queen Mother took advantage of the general unpopularity of the governor among all classes, and demanded that a convention be called at Stirling on June 3rd so that power would be transferred to her.[139]

Up to this period the Queen Mother had been a practical spectator with no real power except in possessing the person of the future Queen of Scotland. Whilst the Lord Governor's defence against Hereford's invasion had proved inadequate, no major strongholds had been captured. However the devastation that the English armies and their Scottish helpers had brought to Scotland must have filled the Queen Mother with a fear that she, and no doubt her daughter, would not have a country to govern if matters were to continue unchecked. She may have also realised that despite her devout Catholic upbringing and the Guise family tradition of opposing the reformation, Cardinal Beaton's inquisitions and anti-Protestant acts were dividing the country and putting one section into alliance with England. A new political agenda would develop in which the Queen Mother would attempt to build up a Catholic-Protestant coalition, and with this she would be helped by a surprising source.

On May 26th Sir George Douglas had written to the Queen Mother offering his services to 'protect the realm' to the utmost of his abilities.[140] It was a pragmatic proposal, since the English were wasting his lands and attacking family, friends and servants, and isolated as he was, he needed powerful alliances. The Queen Mother would accept his offer, also a pragmatic move since the power of the Red Douglas clan would help her undermine Arran. It would also bring a possibility of a general reconciliation amongst the nobility. Tytler suggests that Angus and Sir George Douglas were the instigators of a new coalition between Catholic and Protestant parties, a fact which is reflected in the make-up of the gathering at Stirling on June 3rd when Arran was asked to resign.[141]

The Earls of Huntley, Argyll and Moray, joined with the Protestant sympathizers such as Lord Somerville, the Earl of Cassilis, Robert, Master of Maxwell and others to add their signatures to the motion.[142] Here we have an instance where former rivals and enemies unite against a common enemy despite their history and their religious differences. Henry VIII and Cardinal Beaton probably deserve some credit because of the former's savagery and diplomatic ineptitude and the latter's religious intolerance and cruelty. It could also be argued that Arran was being used as a scapegoat, since the machinations of the pro-English party had contributed to the weakening and dividing of Scotland.[142] This faction was now to feature in the new government, a reflection of political realities rather than sentiment. Arran however was not going to accept the blame or surrender easily and fled to Edinburgh. The Queen Mother was declared governor and was to be guided by three earls, three lords, three bishops and three abbots. Angus now joined the Scottish government, and was appointed Lieutenant-General.[143]

On June 11th Sir George Douglas once more wrote to the Queen Mother, also sending a herald who would take letters from her to Henry VIII, requesting safe conduct for Scottish ambassadors visiting England.[144] Here we have a pragmatic arrangement between the Queen Mother and Sir George, where he could use his diplomatic influence to earn some time for the new government, badly threatened not just by the English and the Habsburg Empire but by the Gaels to the west and Ireland. Douglas was also trying to move himself into a position of influence between Scotland and England, in order to play both sides to his advantage.

In the following months the English would learn more about the nature of Douglas's diplomacy and that of his associates, when a Scottish ship was taken off Scarborough. Discovered on board were letters from Mary of Guise to the

French King. The letters revealed that Angus, George Douglas, Cassilis and Robert, Master of Maxwell had pledged loyalty to the Queen of Scotland.[145] In the autumn Sir George would write to the Queen Mother thanking her for 1,000 crowns, and asserting that he would serve her 'in all matters'.[146] Obviously the Queen Mother was buying Sir George with French gold in an attempt to keep him away from England.

During these upheavals the Highlands and Isles had also risen up against crown authority. Soon after the May invasion of Hereford and prior to the June 3rd meeting at Stirling, Huntley as Lieutenant-General of the Highlands, Orkney and Shetlands, and Argyll as Lieutenant-General of the West of Scotland and the Isles, advanced north and west respectively to quell the violence. Huntley had raced to Knoydart and Moidart, where John Moidart of Benbecula, chosen as leader of the Clanranald MacDonalds, was burning and harrying in the Highlands. Initially it was a clan leadership dispute with a rival named Ranald Galda, whom the Frasers were supporting. John Moidart was joined by Ewan Allanson, leader of the Camerons of Lochiel, Ronald MacDonald of Keppoch, assorted MacKenzies and other clans. The dispute developed into a serious rising. They occupied Abertarf and Stratherrick, vast tracts of land pertaining to Lord Lovat of Clan Fraser, as well as Castle Urquhart on Loch Ness, and Glenmoriston, belonging to the Grants. This direct challenge to Huntley's authority compelled him to levy a large army, consisting of Grants, Rosses, MacKintoshes, Chisholms and Frasers. With the approach of Huntley's army the Highlanders retreated into the hills and valleys. Huntley reached Inverlochy and established Ranald Galda as ruler of Modart. The Highlanders were driven out of the lands of the Frasers and Grants and their possessions restored.

Satisfied with this campaign, Huntley returned south, marching towards Strathspey by Lochaber and Badenoch. At Glen Spean Lord Lovat decided to separate from the army, and despite warnings from allies not to go alone, decided to return to his lands in Abertarf and Stratherrick. As they marched along the Great Glen with 400 men and Ranald Galda and his few followers, they were shadowed by the Clanranald, who quickly gathered a force of 500 and advanced towards the Frasers. Lovat and the Clanranald engaged in battle at the head of Loch Lochy. According to tradition both sides fired off arrows at each other, and then closed in for close combat with swords, axes, spears and daggers. The fight was bloody, with only a few on both sides surviving. The encounter was called Blar-na-leine, or 'Field of shirts', on account of the July heat which caused many of the combatants to fight in their shirts.[147]

Lord Lovat, an important government agent, died in this encounter, along with his son the Master of Lovat and Ranald Galda. Huntley returned to the north, entered Lochaber and harried the country, executing many captives. It would be several years before principal captains such as Ewan Allanson and Ronald MacDonald of Keppoch were given up. Other captains, such as John of Moidart, escaped to where Huntley could not find them, the hills or the isles.[148] Donald Dubh, the Earl of Ross is not mentioned in these accounts, although he would become a significant threat to the Scottish government the following year. After this campaign Huntley and Argyll returned to the south to side with the Queen Mother against the Governor and the Cardinal.

During July and August, Arran, supported by the Cardinal, the clergy and a small group of nobles, fortified Edinburgh Castle, Holyroodhouse and even the Church of St Giles, ensuring that the garrisons were amply supplied with enough ammunition and beer.[149] He appointed a new Edinburgh provost, another act in clear defiance of the Queen Mother and her parliament in Stirling.[150] Arran, who had had recent counsel with Beaton at Dunfermline, could still rely on the power of the regions of the Mearns, Angus and Fife. He also employed 62 harquebusiers as his bodyguard at Holyroodhouse. Arran was determined to stop the Queen Mother holding a parliament in Edinburgh.[151] Civil war was threatening to break out, all due to the stubbornness of Arran in refusing to concede his position as Governor even though he was widely blamed by the people for the failures to oppose the raids of Hereford.

To add to the confusion, the Earl of Lennox was appointed Lord-Lieutenant of the South of Scotland and North of England by Henry.[152]

A form of compensation for his losses in Scotland was gained by Lennox when he was allowed to marry Margaret Douglas, daughter of Angus and niece of Henry VIII, on June 26th. This while his new father-in-law was now an enemy. On the 10th of July Lennox would become an English subject and be granted lands in Temple Newsam, Yorkshire, worth 1,700 marks yearly. A parliament at Linlithgow made Lennox forfeit and this punishment extended to his brother in France, Lord D'Aubigny, who at the insistence of the Scots lost his position as captain of the Scots Guards and was thrown in prison.[153]

Lennox in August would sail from Bristol, in command of 18 ships and 600 men, a mix of harquebusiers, archers and pikemen. He returned to the Firth of Clyde, where he was joined by 140 MacFarlanes of Ardleish, wearing shirts of chain mail and carrying two-handed swords,[154] and a contingent from Hector mor MacLean, who although having entered into a bond of manrent with Argyll was seemingly offering manpower to Lennox.[155] They would support Lennox in wasting the Isle of Arran and destroying Brodick Castle, and then wasting the Isle of Bute and capturing Rothesay Castle. These were possessions of the Earl of Arran which Lennox would hand over to English captains accompanying him. Lennox attempted to take possession of Dumbarton Castle, but this held against him. His captain, Stirling of Glorat, whilst acknowledging Lennox as his liege lord, would not turn against his sovereign, or hand the castle to the English.[156]

Lennox would attempt bribery, and Stirling this time seemed open to a monetary transaction in return for handing over Dumbarton and allowing an English garrison. Glencairn was also within the castle, having stayed there since the battle in Glasgow. Accordingly the Queen Mother had communicated with Glencairn and persuaded him to take part in a plot to capture Lennox. As Lennox approached the castle with 300 men, he then took a smaller retinue with the bribe into the castle. But just as the money changed hands it appears that Lennox suspected a trap and left quickly, leaving behind the money.[157] Learning that Sir George Douglas was leading an army of 4,000 and had entered the town of Dumbarton, Lennox hurried back to his ships and sailed off. His fleet then passed Dunoon Castle, the town occupied by a force of 700 men commanded by the Earl of Argyll, arrayed with banners displayed. As they passed through the narrow straits of this part of the Clyde River, the ships were fired on by artillery from the castle. Lennox ordered his own guns to fire back. Using the cover of the guns he landed his men and engaged Argyll, who, losing 80 men withdrew and dispersed. Dunoon was burned, and the church in which locals had stored their goods was plundered. Argyll lost more men as he tried to hamper the retreat of Lennox's men with their spoils, which they loaded onto the ships.

Lennox's fleet next landed on a part of Argyll and wasted the surrounding countryside. The Earl of Argyll, having recruited up to 2,000 men, did not engage the smaller force as their defensive array was too strong. Two thirds of Lennox's forces were harquebusiers and bowmen. Lennox's fleet then wasted Kintyre, belonging to James MacDonald of Duvivaig, then burned and harried the highland lands and estates of his former ally Glencairn before raiding Kyle, Carrick, Cunningham and Galloway on the route back to Bristol. Beacons were lit along the coasts as communities feared being victims of Lennox's forces. Many gentlemen or clan chiefs would approach Lennox and enter into assurances to protect the lands and properties of themselves and adherents.[158]

Once back in England, Lennox sent his secretary, Thomas Bishop, to Henry VIII at the siege of Boulogne in France and explained the activity of Glencairn and his son. Henry, although angry at Glencairn's treachery, was pleased to learn that Lennox had entered into bonds with clan chiefs from the Isles which could bode well for any future intrigues involving the west coast of Scotland.[159]

On the borders the English lords Eure, Laylan and Bowes kept up a relentless wasting and destroying of the border lands. Between July and November 1544, 192 towns, villages, farms, castles, fortified dwellings and hamlets were burned, whilst 10,886 cattle were lifted along with 12,492 sheep and 1,496 varied forms of livestock. This was brutal economic warfare, and the fact that so few people were killed suggests that the population were not resisting and were instead withdrawing to the woods, hills and marshes to survive the onslaught.[160] The fortified Abbey of Coldingham became an important base camp for the English, and allowed them to plan and co-ordinate their raids and counter-raids against the Scots.

Arran decided to hold his alternative parliament for Edinburgh on November 6th. Sir George Douglas, writing from Dalkeith on October 13th, advised the Queen Mother to hold a parliament at Stirling and to contact all the lords, ordering that they attend.[161] Sir George next travelled to Angus's castle at Tantallon and wrote again, discussing joining the forces of Angus, the Earl of Bothwell and himself to those of the Queen Mother at Stirling, and then marching to Edinburgh to confront Arran. If Arran did not take the field, then they would 'hunger them to death'.[162] The Queen Mother called a parliament at Stirling for November 13th and called on Arran to attend under charges of treason. The Queen Mother was calling all classes to turn away from Arran and give their allegiance to her.[163]

At the Edinburgh parliament Arran declared by the authority of the three states that the parliament that the

Queen Mother had called was 'pretended' and 'unlawful', and that a summons for him to appear was without force or legality.[164] Although taking a forceful stand, Arran, under advice of the Three Estates, agreed to send a delegation to Stirling with the purpose of opening an amicable dialogue under the pretense of uniting against the English enemy, but more likely to avoid civil war. He sent William Keith, the Earl Marischal and the Earl of Montrose, in the company of Lord Seton, the Master of Sempil, and Sir James Learmouth of Balcomie.[165]

The Edinburgh parliament also agreed to continue to side with Arran, even if the Queen Mother's parliament at Stirling could not agree to join forces.[166] He also ordered a muster for November 10th at Edinburgh, requiring all able-bodied men, on horse or foot, to prepare for war and bring victuals for four days. It was not stated to what purpose this muster was raised, but four days' supplies suggests a march against Stirling. Whilst sending a delegation for peace he was also preparing armed force if peace was rejected.[167] Arran also raised three summonses for treason against Angus, Sir George Douglas, and Patrick Hepburn, Earl of Bothwell. The latter was in heavy debt to creditors, making him open to bribery whether from English or French sources.[168]

Arran gave the Douglas brothers until November 17th to appear at Parliament. Here also we have Arran prepared to use legal means to attack one of the most dangerous factions in Scotland, but if Arran were to win the power struggle with the Queen Mother, the Douglas would have to make some kind of decision: whether to make peace with Arran, or once more face the threat of forfeiture.[169] As if to show that he could be open to negotiation, Arran, with advice from the three estates, remitted all accusations of treason against Glencairn, Cassilis, Hugh Campbell, Sheriff of Ayr, and all their kin and adherents.

This was a significant act in that these three were major supporters of the English agenda, and it was also an attempt to bring them to his side. The three above had suffered due to Lennox's recent wasting of the west coasts of Scotland, and Arran would find them useful allies against his hated rival. During the judicial proceedings the treasonable crimes of Angus, Sir George Douglas and the Earl of Bothwell were listed, and this revealed that the Scots had themselves a good intelligence network, especially as there was knowledge of the secret agreements made with King Henry and Hereford, as well as of correspondence with other English agents. The accusations included assisting the English during several invasions before and after James V's death, and of giving council, advice and promises to the invaders.[170]

With a civil war becoming a strong possibility at some point, a compromise was reached between Arran and the Queen Mother. Lord Methven took credit for stopping the 'effusion of blood' between the two parties, which suggests he took a major part in negotiations.[171] On November 24th at the court of the Edinburgh parliament, present amongst the commissioners was a 'special commission' sent by the Queen Mother.[172] Angus, Bothwell and Sir George Douglas were pardoned in late November, by the authority of the Queen and the Governor, and on the advice of the three estates.[173] This was a decision where the three estates in Edinburgh realised that the power of the Red Douglas faction on the borders is vital for the defence of the realm.

A new political structure was agreed whereby the Queen Mother became principle member of the council of 16 lords. Arran remained Governor, and Angus remained Lieutenant-General.[174] Lord Methven also assured the Queen Mother that the balance of power was with her, since she was the principle of the council and Arran would need its permission to act.[175] Reports also reach England that after the apparent reconciliation the Scots had begun to muster forces. At Lauder the Cardinal, Governor and allies met, whilst Angus raised levies at Peebles. The wealth of vacant abbeys and bishoprics were to be used for funding warfare, and 12 days of victuals were to be acquired.[176]

A proclamation in the name of Queen Mary was to be made at Jedburgh by the Sheriff of Roxburgh, ordering all loyal Scots to gather weapons and 12 days' victuals and assemble on the 26th of November at Edinburgh. The proclamation acknowledged that the merciless warfare of Henry VIII with 'burnings and killing of women and children' had compelled riders from Teviotdale, Liddlesdale, Hawis, Hewisdale and parts of the Mersh to side with England.[177] Further information cited Coldingham as the target of the Scots and they had great ordinance and artillery, although travelling in such weather and ground conditions was considered 'cumbersome'.[178]

Coldingham Abbey was garrisoned by 100 men and some gunners from Berwick.[179] During November Sir Ralph Eure suggested that 1,000 horse from Northumberland, Tynedale and Reddisdale, and additional gunners from Berwick would be enough to challenge the Scots. Although the assured Scots were good fighters there was still some distrust.[180] Advice to the English council was for the wardens of the East, Middle and West marches not to take undue risks against the Scottish army and just work within their means.[181] With Angus, Glencairn and Cassilis at Peebles, the English could not determine their intentions, in consideration of their prior loyalty to Henry.[182] Once the Governor's army had advanced to Dunbar, the Earl of Glencairn and Sir George Douglas joined him, along with the Earl of Bothwell, the Earl of Crawford, Lord Seton and Lord Ruthven. The Cardinal stayed in Edinburgh,[183] possibly experiencing a reluctance to join the expedition, having little faith in the effectiveness of an army so riddled with suspicion.

Tytler writes that Sir George may have been responsible for spreading dissent and rumours within the camp in order to undermine the campaign. It is not difficult to imagine the level of distrust that must have been felt within the Scottish army considering Douglas and Glencairn's past dealing with England, and that recently Arran had accused Sir George, Angus and Bothwell of treason.[184] The English also tested the unity of the Scottish army by ordering on December 2nd that important hostages of any individual having given an oath to Henry would be executed, in a way that would spread terror to the other lords. The hostages for the Master of Erskine and Lord Fleming would be the first.[185]

Arran and Angus finally joined and led an army of 7,000 men to besiege Coldingham. Angus, Glencairn, Cassilis, Somerville and the Sheriff of Ayr were in the vanguard,[186] which commenced the siege with artillery. The men stood before the walls for a day and a night in a bitter cold winter,[187] and when news reached Arran that an army was coming from Berwick, he withdrew to Dunbar with a small party of supporters. He would claim that he feared he was to be betrayed to the English by men within the army, because of 'hatred they had conceived against him for many of his offences'. Once the bulk of the army learned of the Lord Governor's escape there began a disorganized retreat. The artillery was about to be abandoned, and some experienced soldiers suggested filling the cannons with powder and blowing them apart so they could not be used by the English.[188] It was Angus who was credited for saving the artillery,[189] organizing a group to pull them back to Dunbar. He personally led a small troop to cover them whilst being constantly assaulted by English horsemen.[190]

Another opinion is that Sir George Douglas spread the rumour that 10,000 English were advancing from Berwick, and that it was Bothwell at the rear and not Angus who tried to rally those forces retreating.[191] Giving the reputation of Angus and Sir George, there would have been a very understandable fear that the vanguard, made up of assured Scots, would join the advancing English and turn on the contingent of Arran. A report to Henry VIII said that the Scots withdrew from Coldingham at the approach of the wardens of East and Middle Marches, and praises the Teviotdale Scots for their contribution. Interestingly, Angus and Sir George Douglas are cited as having 'showed their untrue hearts to their perpetual shame'. This suggests that in the opinion of the writer, the Earl of Shrewsbury, Angus and Sir George had once more betrayed Henry,[192] and there possibly was an expectation that the Douglas brothers were going to set up the Scottish army for destruction and they failed to fulfill this. And saving the ordinance would have denied important prizes to the English.

Even before the Coldingham siege there is evidence that Angus was in communication with the Earl of Lennox. There is a suggestion of a plan to capture Queen Mary and take her to England. Whether this came from King Henry or Douglas is not clear. Henry instructed Wharton to welcome Lennox at Carlisle and supported him in setting up a meeting with Angus at Solwaysands. Lennox was to bring letters from his wife to Angus, which scolded him for his treatment of the King, his brother-in-law and her uncle. Henry stated that if capturing Queen Mary was not feasible, Lennox should sow seeds of dissention amongst the Scots.[193] What Angus was really intending is unclear, although it could have been a ploy to capture Lennox.

There is no evidence as to whether this meeting occurred, and it seems unlikely as events changed significantly for Angus and his brother when at a parliament on December 12th 1544 at Edinburgh, Angus was to remain as Lieutenant-General with 1,000 horsemen. The clergy agreed to pay 12,000 crowns towards maintaining this force.[194] The failure of the Coldingham expedition brought home to the Scots the need for a unified front and for past actions to be forgiven. They would also have to pay to keep Angus on side and away from the English. The French ambassador present at Edinburgh would not give money due to the divisions amongst the Scots, although he promised money and men during the spring. It has to be assumed that this was on condition of some kind of military and political cohesion.[195] There was also an agreement by the Cardinal and Governor to strengthen ties with France, and there was even talk, instigated by the French

Ambassador, of marrying Queen Mary to the Dauphin and sending the young Queen and Queen Mother to France.[196]

There were still tensions within the Scottish camp, as well as shifts in the dynamics of power. Sir George Douglas would begin to enjoy better relations with the Cardinal despite religious differences. The relationship between Arran and the Cardinal was more strained, due to the fact that Arran's son was still a hostage in St Andrews. Failure to release him emphasized distrust by the Cardinal and a lever to control the governor. At a meeting at Edinburgh in late December, the Cardinal and Arran had a falling out; the latter drawing a sword in anger over a matter whose details are not reported. Although they settled their dispute these tensions would be reported to the English.[197]

The Lord Governor was not a popular figure; his failure and flight at Coldingham 'which break the hearts of the Scots, and advanced the minds of the English' was added to his failure to counter the Hereford invasion. Despite this he still held power, not through popular mandate but through the complex political machinations that dominated state and government.

The Queen Mother was also busy, writing to both the Pope and Cardinal Carpi, reporting how Robert Stewart, Bishop of Caithness and brother of Lennox, was a willing participant in the treasons and crimes against Scotland. She recounted the latest escapades of Lennox and how he had led a fleet of English soldiers into Scotland and attacked and wasted lands and dwellings. She asked the pope to recall Robert Stewart to Rome and assign the bishopric of Caithness to Alexander Gordon, brother of the Earl of Huntley. Here she sought to bind the house of Huntley closer to government by patronage. She also reminded the Pope and Cardinal that Lennox had now married the niece of the English king, the enemy of the Catholic faith.[198]

References :(1) (ALHTS, vol.8, pp. xliii-xliv, p.228. Holinshed, p.534). (2) (CSPS, Chapuys to Emperor, Dec?, 1543), (3) (HP, vol.2 (50), pp.81-82, Sadler to Suffolk and Tunstall, 30th Sept, 1543). (4) (Calderwood, pp.169-171.Holinshed, pp.534). (5) (HP, vol.2 (50), pp.81-82. Sadler to Suffolk and Tunstall, 30th Sept, 1543). (6) (Accounts of the Lord High Treasurer of Scotland, vol.8, 1541-1546, vol.9, 1546-1551. Paul, J.B. (ed.), (1911), H.M. General Register House, Edinburgh) (ALHTS, vol.8, pp. xxv-xxix. Herkless & Hannay, pp. 13-14). (7) (HP, vol.2 (38,43), pp.56-73. Sadler to Henry VIII, 20th & 24th Sept, 1543). (8) (SCML, Moray to Queen Dowager, 30th Sept, 1543). (9) (HP, vol.2 (50), pp.81-82. Sadler to Suffolk and Tunstall, 30th Sept, 1543). (10) (Herkless & Hannay, pp.13-14). (11) (HP, vol.2 (55), pp.90-92. Sadler to Suffolk and others, 5th Oct, 1543). (12) (HP, vol.2 (60), pp.97-100. Privy Council to Sadler, 11th Oct, 1543). (13) (HP, vol.2 (62), pp.105-106. Sadler to Council, 13th Oct, 1543). (14) (HP, vol.2 (60), pp.97-100. Privy Council to Sadler, 11th Oct, 1543). (15) (CSPS, Chapuys to Emperor, Oct 18th, 1543). (16) (Tytler, pp.290-291). (17) (HP, vol.2 (60), pp.97-100. Privy Council to Sadler, 11th Oct, 1543). (18) (HP, vol.2 (61), pp.100-105. Sadler to Henry VIII, 13th Oct, 1543). (19) (HP, vol.2 (62), pp.105-106. Sadler to Council, 13th Oct, 1543). (20) (HP, vol.2 (61), pp.100-105. Sadler to Henry VIII, 13th Oct, 1543). (21) (Calderwood, pp.167-168). (22) (HP, vol.2 (65), pp.110-111. Suffolk and Tunstall to Council, 16th Oct, 1543). (23) (HP, vol.2 (63), pp.106-109. Sadler to Council, 16th Oct, 1543). (24) (HP, vol.2 (63), pp.106-109. Sadler to Council, 16th Oct, 1543). (25) (HP, vol.2 (67), pp.112-113. Sadler to Council, 18th Oct, 1543). (26) (LP, The Patriarch, Marco Grimini, to Dandino, 24th Oct, 1543). (27) (SCML, Communication (by Methven?) c. Oct, 1543, XXX & XXXII. HP, vol.2 (63), pp.106-109, Sadler to Council, 16th Oct, 1543). (28) (HP, vol.2 (73), pp.120-123. Sadler to council, 25th Oct, 1543). (29) (HP, vol.2 (79), pp.131-134. Sadler to Council, 30th Oct, 1543). (30) (CSPS, Chapuys to Emperor, Dec?,

1543). (31) (SCML, William Cunningham of Glengarnock to the Queen Dowager, after 25th Oct 1543). (32) (Marshal, pp.53-56). (33) (Tytler, pp.292-293). (34) (LP, Scotland and Portugal, Nov 1st, 1543). (35) (HP, vol.2 (81), pp.136-137. Sadler to Suffolk, Nov 1st, 1543). (36) (Tytler, pp.292-293). (37) (HP, vol.2 (85), pp.141-143. Sadler to Council, 6th Nov, 1543). (38) (HP, vol.2 (92), pp.150-152. Sadler to Suffolk and Tunstall, 10th Nov, 1543). (39) (HP, vol.2 (99), pp.161-163. Sadler to Council, 13th Nov, 1543). (40) (HP, vol.2 (83), pp.138-140. Wharton to Suffolk, 5th Nov, 1543). (41) (HP, vol.2 (79), pp.131-134. Sadler to Council, 30th Oct, 1543). (42) (Merriman, note (9), pp.138-139). (43) (HP, vol.2 (88), p.146. Laird of Brunston to Sadler, 7th Nov, 1543). (44) (HP, vol.2 (85), pp.141-142. Sadler to Council, 6th Nov, 1543). (45) (ALHTS, pp.235-236. HP, vol.2 (87), pp.145-146. Sadler to Suffolk, 7th Nov, 1543). (46) (HP, vol.2 (89), pp.146-147. Sadler to Suffolk and Tunstall, 8th Nov, 1543). (47) (HP, vol.2 (91), pp148-150.Suffolk to Sir George Douglas, 9th Nov). (48) (HP, vol.2 (92), pp.150-152. Sadler to Suffolk and Tunstall, 10th Nov, 1543). (49) (LP, Sadler to Arran, 11th Nov, 1543). (50) (HP, vol.2 (99), pp.161-163, Sadler to Council, 13th Nov, 1543). (51) (Calderwood, pp.168-171. HP, vol.2 (88), pp.146 Laird of Brunston to Sadler, 7th Nov, 1543). (52) (Calderwood, pp.168-171). (53) (HP, vol.2 (116), pp.186-188. 26th. Sadler to Henry VIII, Nov, 1543). (54) (HP, vol.2 (117), pp.pp.188-189. Sadler to Suffolk and Tunstall, 26th Nov, 1543). (55) (HP, vol.2 (128), pp.207-210. Suffolk to Sir George Douglas, 2nd Dec, 1543). (56) (HP, vol.2 (128), pp.207-210. Suffolk to Sir George Douglas, 2nd Dec, 1543). (57) (HP, vol.2 (135), pp.221-223. Sadler to Suffolk, 12th Dec, 1543). (58) (RPS, 1543/12/53). (59) (Merriman, p.137-139). (60) (RPS, 1543/12/57). (61) (Herkless, Cardinal Beaton, p.247-248). (62) (RPS, 1543/12/63). (63) (RPS, 1543/ 12/ 14). (64) (RPS, 1543/12/35). (65) (RPS, 1543/12/47), (66) (RPS, 1543/12/48). (67) (RPS, 1543/12/12). (68) (RPS, 1543/12/31). (69) (RPS, 1543/12/32). (70) (HP, vol.2 (135), pp.221-223. Sadler to Suffolk, 12th Dec, 1543). (71) (Williams, pp.244-247). (72) (HP, vol.2 (135), pp.221-223. Sadler to Suffolk, 12th Dec, 1543). (73) (HP, vol.2 (146), pp.245-247. Suffolk to Sir George Douglas, 30th Dec, 1543). (74) (ALHTS, vol.8, pp. xlvi-li, pp.249-250. Calderwood, pp. 167-168). (75) (Fraser, p.264-265). (76) (HP, vol.2

(149), pp.250-252. Sir George Douglas to Suffolk, 15th Jan, 1544). (77) (LP, Parties in Scotland, 13th Jan, 1544). (78) (Calderwood, pp. 167-168). (79) (HP, vol.1 (149), pp.250-252. Sir George Douglas to Suffolk, 15th Jan, 1544). (80) (CSPS, Chapuys to Queen of Hungary, Jan 23rd, 1544). (81) (CSPS, Emperor to Chapuys, Jan 3rd, 1544). (82) (CSPS, Queen of Hungary to Chapuys, Jan 10th, 1544). (83) (CSPS, Emperor to Chapuys, Jan 19th, 1544). (84) (Calderwood, pp.171-175. ONDB, vol.4, pp.551-556. Thomson, vol.3, pp.59-60). (85) (CSPS, Henry to Emperor, Feb 1st, 1544). (86) (CSPS, Chapuys to Emperor, Feb 2, 1544). (87) (CSPS, Queen of Hungary to Chapuys, Feb 14th, 1544). (88) (HP, vol.2 (162), pp.270-272. Privy Council to Suffolk, 5th Feb, 1544). (89) (CSPS, Chapuys to Emperor, Feb 2, 1544). (90) (HP, vol.2 (182), pp.294-295. Hereford and Others to Henry VIII, 8th March 1544). (91) (HP, vol.2 (183), pp.294-295. Hereford and Others to Henry VIII, 8th March 1544). (92) (CP, March 11th, 1544. Sir Wm Paget). (93) (CSPS, Chapuys to Emperor, March 2nd, 1544). (CSPS, Chapuys to Prince Philip, April 13th-22nd, 1544). (95) (Hume-Brown, vol 2, pp.9-10). (96) (ALHTS, vol.8, pp.274-277.LP, Wharton to Hereford, 8th March, 1544). (97) (HP, vol.2 (191), p.310. King Henry VIII to Earl of Angus, 21st March,1544). (98) (CP, Sir Wm Paget to Earl of Hereford, March 21st, 1544). (99) (CP, Edward Shelley to Earl of Hereford, March 22nd, 1544). (100) (HP, vol.2 (206), p.324. Hereford and Others to Henry VIII. 8th April, 1544). (101) (HP, vol.2 (206), p.324. Hereford and others to Henry VIII, 8th April). (102) (Fraser, pp.265-266). (103) (ALHTS, vol.8, pp.li-liv, pp.274-277. Holinshed, p.543-544). (104) (ALHTS, vol.8, pp.li-liv, pp.274-277. Hume-Brown, Vol II, pp.9-10). (105) (SCML, Lennox to Queen Dowager, 7th March, 1544). (106) (Holinshed, p.534). (107) (Calderwood, pp.178-180). (108) (CP, Edward Shelley to Earl of Hereford, March 22nd, 1544). (109) (HP, vol.2 (206), p.324. Hereford and Others to Henry VIII, 8th April, 1544). (110) (CSPS, Chapuys to Prince Philip, April 13th-22nd, 1544) (111) (HP, vol.2 (205), p.324. Hereford and Others to Henry VIII, 7th April, 1544. HP, vol.2 (207), pp.325-327. Privy Council to Hereford, 10th April, 1544). (112) (HP, vol.2 (206), p.324, Hereford and Others to Henry VIII, 8th April 1544). (113) (HP, vol.2 (210), pp.329-330. Hereford to Henry VIII, 13th April, 1544).

(114) (HP, vol.2 (220), pp.345-347. Hereford, Lisle, &c., to Henry VIII, 21st April, 1544). (115) (ODNB, vol.33, pp.448-449). (116) (CP, Privy council to Earl of Hereford, 26th April, 1544. SP, vol.6, pp.46-47. Knox, pp.47-50). (117) (LP, Lisle and Sadler to Henry VIII, 26th April, 1544). (118) (Herkless & Hannay, p.18). (119) (HP, vol.2 (226), pp.353-354. Hereford to Master of Morton and David Douglas, 27th April, 1544). (120) (ALHTS, vol.8, pp.lvi-lvii. .Lesley, pp.180-182. Thomson, vol.3, p.260). (121) (ALHTS, vol.8, pp288-293. Thomson, vol.3, pp. 60-61, Merriman, pp.1145-150). (122) (Calderwood, pp.177-179). (123) (Calderwood, pp.177. ODNB, vol.37, pp.526-528). (124) (Calderwood. p.177). (125) (CP, Privy council to Earl of Hereford, 16th May, 1544). (126) (MacDonald Fraser, pp.255-257). (127) (Pollard (ed.), pp.39-51). (128) (CSPS, Declaration of the Emperor, 8th May, 1544). (129) (Merriman, pp.184-186). (130) (Merriman, pp.194-195). (131) (CP, Sir Wm Eure to Earl of Hereford, May 25th, 1544). (132) (CP, Earl of Hereford to the King, May 27th, 1544). (133) (CP, Privy Council to Earl of Hereford, 28th May, 1544). (134) (Fraser, pp.258). (135) (Calderwood, pp.178-180. CSPS, News From Scotland: (89)). (136) (Holinshed, p.543). (137) (SP, vol.4, pp.239-240). (138) (ALHTS, vol.8, pp.lix-lxi. Calderwood, pp.179-180. Lesley, pp.177-178. Thomson, vol.3, pp 61-62. Tytler, pp.305-306). (139) (Tytler, 306-307). (140) (SCML, Sir George Douglas to Queen Dowager, Calder, 26th May, 1544). (141) (Tytler. pp.306-308) (142) (Tytler, pp.306-308). (142) (Tytler, pp.306-307). (143) (Tytler, pp.307-308). (144) (SCML, Sir George Douglas to Queen Dowager, 11th June, 1544). (145) (LP, Henry VIII to the Council, 1st Aug, 1544). (146) (SCML, Sir George Douglas to Queen-Dowager, 28th Sept, 1544). (147) (Gregory, pp.162-164). (148) (Lesley, pp.183-185. Strathspey, pp.110-112). (149) (ALHTS, vol.8, pp.lxi-lxiii. Marshal, p.59. RPS,1544/11/1). (150) (HP, vol.2 (298), p.437 Sir Ralph Evers to Shrewsbury, 1st Aug, 1544). (151) (ALHTS, vol.8, pp.lxi-lxiii. LP, Alex Brand, vicar of Evan to Hugh Crage, 8th August, 1544). (152) (LP, Alex Brand, vicar of Evan to Hugh Crage, 8th August, 1544). (153) (Merriman, p.141-142. ODNB, vol.52, pp.729-733. Thomson, vol.3, p.62). (154) (MacFarlane, pp.42-44). (155) (Maclean-Bristol, pp. 116-122). (156) (Tytler, pp.309-310). (157) (Gregory, pp. 164-165. Holinshed, p.539),(158)

(Holinshed, pp. 539-540). (159) (Gregory, pp. 165-167, Tytler, pp.309-310). (160) (Tytler, pp.310-311). (161) (SCML, LXXXVI, 13th Oct, 1544). (162) (SCML, LXXXVII, 18th October, 1544). (163) (Tytler, pp.311). (164) (RSP, 1544/11/8). (165) (RPS, 1544/11/14). (166) (RPS, 1544/11/15). (167) (RPS, 1544/11/16). (168) (SP, vol.2, pp.157-161). (169) (RPS, 1544/11/9). (170) (RPS, 1544/11/20. RPS, 1544/11/30). (171) (SCML, 28th Nov, 1544, XCIII). (172) (RPS, 1544/11/20). (173) (Tytler, pp.310-311, RPS, 1544/11/31, 1544/11/32, 1544/11/33). (174) (Marshal, pp. 58-59. HP, vol.2 (370), pp.517-520.,Shrewsbury, &c. to the Privy Council, 26th Nov, 1544). (175) (SCML, XCIII, 28th Nov, 1544). (176) (HP, vol.2 (370), pp.517-520.,Shrewsbury, &c. to the Privy Council, 26th Nov, 1544). (177) (SCML, Mary Queen of Scots to sheriff of Roxburgh, 19th Nov, 1544). (178) (HP, vol.2 (373), pp.520-521. Shrewsbury, &c, to the Privy Council. 30th Nov, 1544). (179) (LP, Sir Wm Eure to Shrewsbury, 1st Dec, 1544). (180) (LP, Shrewsbury to Sir Ralph Eures, 28th Nov, 1544). (181) (HP, vol.2 (374), pp.521-523. Shrewsbury, &c to the Privy Council, 1st Dec, 1544). (182) (HP, vol.2 (375), p.522. Shrewsbury, &c, to the Privy Council, 2nd Dec, 1544). (183) (HP, vol.2 (524), p.524, Shrewsbury, &c., to the Privy Council, 3rd Dec, 1544), (184) (RPS, 1544/11/20, Tytler, pp.310-311). (185) (HP, vol.2 (377), p.524. Privy council to Shrewsbury, 2nd Dec, 1544). (186) (Tytler, pp.311-314), (187) (Holinshed, pp.540-541). (188) (Holinshed, pp.540-541). (189) (Thomson, vol.3, pp.63-63). (190) (Fraser, p.268). (191) (Tytler, pp.311-313). (192) (HP, vol.2 (381), pp.525-526. Shrewsbury, &c., to Henry VIII, 5th Dec, 1544). (193) (LP, Henry VIII to Wharton, 9th Dec, 1544). (194) (HP, vol.2 (391), pp.535-536. Shrewsbury, &c., to the Privy Council, 29th Dec). (195) (HP, vol.2 (391), pp.535-536. Shrewsbury and others to the council, 29th Dec, 1544). (196) (HP, vol.2 (394), pp.537-538. Lord Evers to Shrewsbury, 1st Jan, 1545). (197) (HP, vol.2 (394), pp.537-538. Lord Evers to Shrewsbury, 1st Jan, 1545). (198) (SCML, Mary Queen of Scots to Paul IV, 12th Dec, 1544. SCML, Mary Queen of Scots to Cardinal Carpi, 12th Dec, 1544).

Chapter Four

Not with painted words

———◆———

The King of England, disappointed and angry with the double-dealing of the Red Douglas brothers, decided to offer a bounty for their capture, 2,000 crowns for Angus and 1,000 crowns for Sir George.[1] He would also grant to the warden of the East March, Sir Ralph Eure and Sir Bryan Layton all the land they could conquer in the Merse, Teviotdale and Lauderdale.[2] The reports of the reconciliation at the Scottish parliament between the Cardinal, Governor and assured Scots must have been a massive insult to Henry after he had invested so much energy and money into acquiring Scotland, and then lost the opportunity when it looked a formality. What Henry achieved was to turn southern Scotland into a desert short of victuals. His attempts to place garrisons in the lands of assured Scots would be hampered by the inability of these men to live off the land, and they in turn would have to rely on supplies brought in.[3]

The Scots however seemed to be more successful in the field of piracy. Sir George Douglas in November had reported that merchants from Leith and Edinburgh seeking to redress their losses during the Hereford invasion were now capturing English ships off the English coasts.[4] They were led by John Barton, who took his plundering to the coasts of Netherlands, where 24 'Hollander' ships were taken and led to Leith.[5] Whilst the Treaty of Crepi, signed 18th September 1544, created a peace between France and the Habsburg Empire that would last for seven years, the Scots were not included. This exclusion was due to pressure from England. Technically Scotland was still at war with the Emperor Charles V. Many of the merchants who had been averse to warfare with the Empire were now finding it profitable to raid the Low Countries and venture against Spanish shipping and commerce.[6]

Whilst the Queen Mother wrote to Charles V asking him to stop oppressing the Scots and to include them in the treaty,[7] she may have also been benefiting from a royal share of the lucrative privateer trade, having backed John Barton with letters of marque. There were profits to be made attacking both English and imperial shipping during a time of war, and little chance of victims getting redress in the legal courts. She would also grant letters of marque to Nicholas Hay, who would prove to be another successful privateer, to use against the English.[8] The Imperial ambassadors at the English court were prepared to counter English opposition to Scottish-Imperial peace, and would offer advice to the Emperor that hostilities with Scotland should cease since this was depriving trade between Scotland and the Low Countries, especially the access to herring fishing off the North Sea coasts.[9] The Emperor however needed the English alliance, uncertain though it was, to counter threats from France.[10]

The Emperor heard of a defeat of the English in Scotland, with 1,400 lost. The reason given was that the Spanish and German mercenaries that were transferred to Henry were billeted in York and Newcastle and too far away to assist the English. In following letters it was related that defeat was not so drastic and only 200-300 were lost.[11] There is no other account of this encounter, although on January 2nd, the Abbot of Paisley, John of Clydesdale and Patrick Hume led 500 to 600 horsemen on the East March, and met up with a Lord Warden and a foraging party from Berwick which because of its smaller numbers was forced to withdraw.[12] An estimated 3,000 mercenaries were active on the borders, ranging from Spanish, Italians, French, Germans and Greeks to Irish,[13] which emphasizes the growing importance of the foreign professionals in the wars against the Scots.

The strategy of the English in devastating their enemy's lands also meant that the assured Scots would have to rely on aid and supplies from outside their areas, as there was little of worth to plunder. The assured Scots were also open to attack from those border riders still loyal to Edinburgh, such as Sir Walter Scott, the Laird of Buccleuch, who was relentless in leading raids against Teviotdale to the extent that they were threatening to switch sides if the English did not supply aid.[14] Ominously, the warders of the East and Middle Marches were receiving reports that the Scots were assembling an army, which was surprising, due to the dearth of victuals. It was advised that the English on the borders should get ready for campaigning and each man was to be provided with ten-day victuals. Recognising the importance of the Teviotdale riders, it was recommended that money and men should be provided.[15]

If the Scots were now raising a second army within three months of the Coldingham failure, it was quite an achievement considering the economic destruction of towns, villages and the land, and the fact that the French were withholding funds and men until April/May. Also, Angus was said not to be receiving the promised funding from the clergy for 1,000 horsemen and had offered his resignation in February, which was not accepted. Angus and Arran had a heated discussion in which Arran complained that the nobles and lords would not follow him, whilst Angus claimed that Arran was seen as a tool of the clergy. Angus pleaded with him to join him in raising a force and fighting the English, saying 'I am accused of treachery, you of cowardice; let us, by doing at once what it will be impossible eventually to avoid, wipe out those accusations, not by words, but deeds of battle', or as Holinshed wrote, 'not with painted words but with bloodied weapons'. It was Buchanan's and Holinshed's writing later that put these words into Angus's mouth, with some artistic licence, nevertheless Arran called a council and authorized a muster. Without waiting for the full call-up, Angus and Arran took 300 men to the borders.[16] It was a small force, but they were determined to do what they could to hinder the invaders.

Acknowledging previous recent correspondence with Sir Ralph Eure, Sir George Douglas penned a letter to the

English king in which he explained why he had turned from allegiance to him. During the 1544 invasion by Hereford his goods, possessions and lands and those of his friends and family had been wasted, at great cost to himself. He was critical of the brutality of the war, in which 'women and young children' had been killed. And it had been reported to the Scots that the English plan was to turn the nobles into no better than shepherds. Sir George claimed he still supported a union between the two realms, but suggested a more diplomatic approach. He related how recently the Queen Mother, Governor and nobles had been prepared to talk with Henry's ambassadors with regard to marriage, but had been told that before any discussions the Scottish prisoners had to be returned to England. This they refused and no meeting of any note took place. It is clear that Henry's thuggish approach to negotiation was counter-productive.

Still playing several sides at once, Sir George offered to keep Henry informed of matters within government.[17] This letter was sent from Dalkeith or Lauder on February 25th. Two days later Sir George was present at Ancrum when the Scots engaged an English force led by Sir Ralph Eures and Sir Brian Layton, the Captain of Norham Castle.

Eure and Layton led a number of devastating raids into Scotland, with little military opposition due to many of the inhabitants and districts entering into assurances. Those that did not have assurances fled into woods or marshes, or sought protection living behind strongholds. An assured Scot would be expected to show his worth to the English by effecting an action against fellow Scots. In that way bitterness and vengeance would keep the borderers divided.

Those assured Scots would continue to identify themselves by wearing red crosses.

In mid-February Eure entered Scotland with 4,000 men, made up of English, and assured Scots, foreign mercenaries and Irish levies. Arriving first at Jedburgh, he attempted an early-morning foray to Melrose, where Arran and Angus were reported to be. With 300 men they quickly withdrew at Eure's approach to the hills. The English forces ransacked the town and abbey, desecrating and defacing the tombs and monuments of Angus's Douglas ancestors. They then returned to Jedburgh, this time shadowed by Arran and Angus, who would be joined by the Master of Rothes with 1,200 horsemen, and Scott of Buccleuch with 500, which increased the forces to 2,000. Eure then attacked the tower of Broomhouse, where an old lady and family were said to have been burned alive. Eure then made camp in the valley of the River Teviot.

Arran and Angus managed to position themselves on low ground out of sight of the English camp. They dismounted and arrayed before an old Roman road that crossed Ancrum Moor. The horse were led along the road onto higher ground in such a manner as to make it look as if a company was retreating in disarray. The English camp spotting them quickly mobilised and chased after them.[18] Once coming onto the lower ground they were faced with the spears and firearms of Scots, and with the added disadvantage of having the sun in their faces. As the English forward ranks fired their guns, the wind blew the smoke of their powder towards the middle and rear columns, causing confusion and disorder in the ranks.[19] Many of the assured Scots ripped off their crosses and turned their weapons against the English.[20] Arran and Angus pressed forward their advantage and 200 English were slain, including Eure and Layton, whilst 2,000 were captured. In the poet Leyden's words, 'Dark Ancrum's heath was dyed with deeper red'.[21]

After this defeat the English border was now considered vulnerable. With a lack of victuals the garrisons were ordered to withdraw into their fortifications and prepare to defend the country.[22] Lennox would complain that his absence from the battle at Ancrum was due to him being summoned by King Henry to go to Carlisle and prepare to 'practice' with his father-in-law, Angus.[23] The story of Ancrum spread to the Continent, and Angus gained some fame as the leader in a battle in which the English lost 2,000 horsemen.[24] As far as Turkey the battle was reported, although with differing details and some exaggeration. The English were numbered at 7,000 infantry and 500 horsemen, with the Scots killing or capturing all of them.[25] In May the story of a Scottish victory still carried, with 4,000 English reported dead.[26]

David Paniter would arrive at Brussels with letters to remind the Queen-Dowager of Hungary of ancient friendships between Scotland and Low Countries. She would also have to hear the arguments of the English ambassador, who insisted that only when the Scots made peace with England could they legally reconcile themselves with the Emperor, in accordance with the terms of the Anglo-Imperial Treaty.[27] The English also reported that Henry VIII was angry that the Scottish ambassador had stayed such a long time in Brussels, and the English ambassador was concerned that Princess Mary of Scots will marry the son of the Emperor.[28] A compromise was agreed, and the merchants of Scotland and the Low Countries were allowed to trade with each other under safe conducts.[29]

Despite these trade and peace negotiations the attacks were increasing against Spanish and Portuguese shipping as Scottish privateers or pirates became more organized. They were now operating out of Normandy and from there sailing into areas around Brittany.[30] It was reported that the French King had also sent the Scots to Brittany to chase away English, and that he had forbidden them to touch Spanish shipping. In what sounds like a subtle threat, the King also stated that the Scots could do more damage by commanding a strait between Flanders and Spain. Goods captured were sold in the Normandy ports.[31] In the summer it would be found that the French king was actually supporting Scottish piracy, when a Scot called Gilbert Scot of Dieppe was granted letters of marque by the French king to prey against Portuguese shipping as restitution for the loss of a ship. When Gilbert brought a Portuguese prize to Scotland the Governor and council decided that the ships goods could be sold there, as a letter of marque absolved privateers from criminal prosecution.[32]

By early 1545 another powerful figure would become involved in the political intrigues surrounding Scotland. Donald Dubh MacDonald, or the Earl of Ross, as he was titled in correspondence, sought to become head of the Gaels in a bid to restore the Lordship of the Isles and challenge the Scottish government. He is not reported to have been involved in the wars in the Highlands and Western Scotland that had plagued Huntley and Argyll in 1544, yet according to reports he had been expected to spend Christmas in

Inverness. There were also reports from as far away as Antwerp that a new king had been chosen amongst the 'Scottish Irish.'[33] Early in 1545 he would approach Lennox to form an alliance.[34]

Hector mor Maclean's brother Patrick, who was Baillie of Iona and Justice Clerk of the South Isles, was chosen to negotiate between Ross, Lennox and King Henry. It was agreed that the English would pay Ross 800 crowns, but payment was at Lennox's discretion. The Privy Council would advise that this offer should be withdrawn when it was discovered that Ross had entered into truce with Huntley and Argyll to last to May 1st 1545, and that he had tried to gain safe conduct to visit the Queen Mother at Stirling.[25] Ross however was not invited to meet the Queen Mother, and whether insulted or not he would later throw in his lot with Henry VIII.

Ross would have a rival in the figure of James of Dunivay, a MacDonald of Islay and the Glens who controlled the wild wooded glens of Antrim where many MacDonald kinsmen had settled. As Dunivay sought to expand in Ireland he would pursue an agenda of neutrality for which Arran would later express gratitude. On April 21st, 1545, Dunivay would be given a grant of Kintyre, Islay, Jura, Sunart and Morvern,[36] and it is possible these lands were targeted by Ross and his cohorts during raids reported in June.

With the English losing the military initiative in southern Scotland, Henry attempted to buy time with some diplomacy. At a convention in Edinburgh on April 17th 1545, Cassilis once more presented the case for Scotland forging a union with England through marriage between Mary and

Edward. With more than a hint of irony Henry stated that he would forgive the Scots the past hurts against him. As a threat, 30,000 English were made ready on the border. The Scots however were in a stronger position, and Cassilis's argument was rejected. To further frustrate Henry, Cardinal Beaton was confirmed by the Pope as legate in Scotland.[37] Arran would later quip that Beaton could replace the Cardinal's hat with the Royal Crown, an indication of how much power Beaton possessed.[38]

Tytler also wrote that during April Cassilis, with encouragement from Henry, was organizing yet another plot to kill Beaton. A ciphered letter from Cassilis, the same cipher used by Crichton of Brunstane, was sent to Henry, dated April 20th. This was three days after Cassilis's appearance in parliament and possibly a response to the rejection of Cassillis's proposals. Henry sent John Foster as envoy to meet with Cassilis, Angus and Sir George Douglas. After stopping off at Dalkeith, then travelling to Douglas, then Dumfries, he joined Angus, Cassilis and Sir George at a hunting party, a cover for their traitorous meeting. At this time the Douglas were developing a keen hatred for the Cardinal.[39] In April the death of the Bishop of Aberdeen had created a vacancy whereby Angus was hopeful of placing his illegitimate son George. The Cardinal though would recommend the Earl of Huntley's uncle, William, the Chancellor of Moray, to that position. This support for a rival candidate would damage Angus's plans and possibly give him the incentive to contemplate assassination plots against the Cardinal.[40] Cassilis however at that time was cautious about giving support.

Sir George Douglas decided to send a more enthusiastic

response to Henry via the Earl of Hereford, which Foster was to deliver. The message said: '...to tell my lord lieutenant, if the King would have the cardinal dead, if his grace would promise a good reward for the doing thereof, so that the reward were known what it should be... he thinketh that that adventure would be proven'.[41] The letter from Douglas appears to have been an attempt to call Henry's bluff and get him to openly announce his intention to kill Beaton. Internationally such an announcement would have made him a pariah, but if he had put words into writing then this would have given the Douglas a powerful weapon to recruit willing assassins. The King of England was not prepared to move outside the sphere of innuendo and dark hints, or make a concrete contractual agreement. He apparently backed down from the plan, as there was no evidence of a reply to Douglas's message.

Rumours and hints of these dark negotiations may have reached the ears of the Queen Mother. On April 24th it was decided by an Act of Parliament that Lords Erskine and Livingston were to be appointed Guardians of Queen Mary. As a source of funds Lord Livingston was granted on June 10th a Charter of dominical lands of Manuel.[42] By July the Governor and counsel at Linlithgow had instructed Livingston and Erskine to recruit a body of Stirlingshire lairds and gentlemen to act as the Queen and Queen Mother's personal bodyguard. They were given permission not to attend any wars or invasions against England or to obey away summons or proclamations that would divert them away from their main duty to the Queen and Queen Mother. They would also be exempt from any legal action if they refused, and the names of the bodyguard were to be registered in the book of counsel in respect to their terms of duty to Queen and Queen Mother.[43]

There were obviously fears of a plot of some kind, but no indication of its nature. At the Council meeting the Queen Mother was not present and the participants, apart from the Lord Governor, Secretary and Clerk of Register, were prelates, Beaton, the Bishop of Orkney, the Abbots of Paisley and Culross. The fact there were no nobles or lords suggests that this council was more secret than most, wanting to keep the recruiting as secret as possible out of fear that it could be sabotaged or disrupted by hostile forces.[44] The bodyguard was also made up of gentlemen and gentry; many of them trusted friends and associates of Erskine and Livingston. The idea of refusing proclamations and summons to war is suggestive, since only the parliament could legitimately raise such commands. There may have been word of a plan to snatch Queen Mary during a mustering for war when the Queen Mother would have been had fewer people to protect her, hence the Act to raise a stronger bodyguard with a clear legal obligation not to leave her side. This personal bodyguard would also develop into a network of informants that would stretch across Scotland, gathering information about enemies and potential enemies. It would not only report on the usual suspects like the Red Douglas, but keep an eye on the Lord Governor and the Cardinal.

In the build-up to the renewal of warfare, the Seigneur de Lorges was assigned by the King of France to raise troops, 2,500 foot, 600 horsemen (100 Scots) and with 60,000 crowns.[45] At the end of May a French fleet landed near Greenock with troops and horse, and enough money to pay the wages of the French soldiery for six months. There was also a bodyguard of 100 archers gifted to Arran.[46] The commander of the small army, otherwise known as Jacques de Montgomery, Seigneur de Lorges, was a Frenchman of Scottish descent.[47] He led the French out of Greenock on 4th June and marched to Glasgow with a train that included 108 carts, each drawn by two horses, and carrying harquebusiers, pikes, ammunition, barrels of powders and other necessities of war. Other military supplies were loaded into the *Lyon* and sent to Edinburgh by water, passing around the north of Scotland. Some of the land convoy was sent to Edinburgh, while the rest accompanied de Lorges to Stirling, where he was met by the Queen Mother, Cardinal and Governor. De Lorges also brought with him the *Order of St Michael*, one of the highest honors in France, which he conveyed to the Earls of Angus, Argyll and Huntley.[48] The Stirling convention of June 26th, 1545, accepted an offer from Francis I, through his commander, to assist the Scots militarily with men at war, arms and horse, whether in defence of Scotland against English invasion or in the event of invasion by Scots of England.[49] Six Scottish war commissioners were also chosen, the Earls of Angus, Argyll, Huntley, Rothes, Bothwell and Glencairn. They were given mandate to organize defensive and offensive campaigns against the English.[50]

However, the true purpose of such a significant force landing in Scotland was to hinder any English attempt at invading France by diverting forces to the north. The Seigneur de Lorges also had a diplomatic mission, to learn about the situation with Lennox and the accusations made against him. He was also to investigate the accusations

Lennox made against the Governor, Cardinal and Queen Mother in his writings to the King of France. As de Lorges was a bitter enemy of Lennox from his time in France, his appointment had been suggested by the Guise advisers of the King, who wanted the Queen Mother and Cardinal cleared of accusations made by Lennox.[51]

Whilst the French were settling in Scotland, on June 20th it was reported that the Earl of Ross, 'Donald of the Isles' and his supporters, now in allegiance to King of England, were 'burning, harrying, slaying' across the lands of Queen Mary's liege subjects. A proclamation was sent out against Ross and followers accusing them of treason, and threatening to use French men and resources to enforce their 'utter ruin and destruction'.[52] There were also reports that Ross during the spring had landed in Ireland, with the purpose of linking with a French contingent and supporting Gerald Fitzgerald in his claim as Earl of Kildare. This would have been a danger to English security in Ireland, and possibly Ross was putting himself out for tender to the highest bidder hoping that the French would pay him to go raiding anywhere else but Scotland. However the Deputy of Ireland learned from the Earl of Tyrone that Ross's purpose was to offer his services to Henry, and serve him in attacking Argyll and the lords of Scotland.[53]

On July 28th on the Isle of Ellenarne on Islay, Ross was elected by 17 chiefs to the Lordship of the Isles. The spring raids were obviously a show of power to impress the clans. Allegiance with the Scottish government was renounced, allegiance to England was offered and Lennox was recognised as second person of the realm of Scotland. The Council of the Isles gave leave for Patrick MacLean, brother of Hector Mor, who was also described as Baillie of Incholm and Justice Clerk of the South Isle, and Rory MacLean, Bishop-elect of the Isles, both to travel to England and to negotiate as commissioners with King Henry. They were to forward Ross's offer to serve him in his wars against Scotland under the command of Lennox. Rory MacLean would later be replaced by the Dean of Morvern.

The army of Ross gathered in Carrickfergus and at Greyfriars church on August 5th he wrote to Henry repeating the oaths taken. The Deputy of Ireland, writing to Henry six days later, stated that Ross had had a meeting with Lennox's servants on the Isles. He further reported that 4,000 warriors had accompanied Ross to Carrickfergus, with 200 galleys ready to take them to Scotland. 3,000 of them were described as tall men with chain mail, long swords, longbows and a few firearms, while the other 1,000 were mariners. Ross asked for 1,000 crowns to pay his men for a month. The Deputy could only supply 500 crowns, part of which was made up of victuals. Ross had another 4,000 men in Scotland harassing Argyll and Huntley.[54]

The Commissioners of Ross arrived in Dublin in August, and then travelled across to Woking. Here they made a request with the Privy Council to meet with Lennox, who was in Newcastle with Hereford.[55] On September 4th the Commissioners met with the Privy Council to discuss certain articles of the proposal forwarded by Henry. They agreed to waste the lands and properties of Huntley and Argyll and allies, and if feasible commit destruction as far as Stirling. 8,000 men were promised, on condition that Lennox campaigned within Scotland.[56] They also promised not to make agreement with Huntley and Argyll unless agreed by Ross, Lord MacLean, the Captain of Clanranald, or other chiefs. Here Hector Mor MacLean was mentioned as second after Ross, and John Moidart, the Captain of Clanranald, as third. This was the same Moidart who had been part of the rising in 1544, resulting in the defeat and death of Lord Lovat.

At the meeting it was agreed to grant Ross a pension of 2,000 crowns and payment for 3,000 men for two months, the rest to be paid by Ross and his adherents. They reported that Ross had already received 1,400 crowns, and that the Scots had approached him to negotiate, which he refused as he considered the Scots the true enemies of the Gaels. The payment of 1,400 crowns is not noted in any records and may have been for the recent Scottish raids in June. The commissioners stated that they were not after Henry's money, which suggests they had been enduring this accusation. They added that each chief would offer three crowns to Henry's one. They also agreed that Lennox would go to Ireland and meet with the Earl of Ormond, who would supply 2,000 gallowglass and kerns. They intended sailing to Dumbarton and capturing it.[57] However Lennox would be delayed in going to Ireland, as at Hereford's request he remained in Newcastle because of events on the border.[58]

In Scotland a joint Scottish/French army was preparing to invade England. A council meeting in Linlithgow, July 25th, attempted to remedy a common problem of armies on the march, in that the Scots in search for food and supplies would raid fellow Scots. The governor ordered letters to be sent out and posted at market crosses across the land, that any Scot raiding the subjects of the Queen would be tried as criminals. Special justice courts were to be set by the justice clerk to investigate any such crimes. The areas that the army passed through were to be supplied by inhabitants, who were instructed to cut and store corn. Oxen were pressed into military service to pull the artillery.[59]

Hereford prepared for the invasion by ordering the three wardens of the Western, Middle and Eastern Marches to mobilize 2,000 men, who would join with 1,000 of the bishopric of Durham and 150 Italian footmen at Berwick. The Spanish mercenaries were placed at Morpeth and Alnwick to defend against possibly siege, and a reserve force of foreign professionals were left in Newcastle and Durham. A levy would be raised from Yorkshire if necessary. Hereford seemed to believe the Western March was the purpose of the Scots, and French ships were supposedly planning to land men off the coasts.[60]

On August 9th 1545, 30,000 Scots, including 3,000 French, assembled at Faunrig Muir. They passed into England and basing themselves around Wark, sent out raiding parties to burn Cornwall, Tilmouth, Edderslie, Brantston and several other towns. On August 10th they burned Tweedsdale, Grendonrig, Newbiggins and Dunues. They were not able to capture any strongholds because of the 'great gallantry' of Spanish and Italian garrisons, which were able to resist Scottish attacks. Calderwood stated that whilst Lorges and Lord Hume wanted to take the army further south, Arran and the Cardinal claimed that they did not have sufficient artillery or siege equipment to attack castles. This contradicted a request later that month by the Cardinal for £600 expenses due to him for taking the artillery from Edinburgh to the borders and back, so maybe they were reluctant to attempt a siege so deep into English territory.

On August 13th the Scots returned home with little achieved. There are no details on why the army returned so soon. Tytler, quoting the *Diurnal of Occurrences* and comparing it to a similar claim made regarding the failed siege of Coldingham in 1544, believed that Sir George Douglas had somehow managed to sow divisions within the army, to the extent that it turned back. How this was done is not known.[61]

A ciphered message sent to Hereford by Angus, Sir George Douglas, Cassilis and Marshal Errol from Peebles on August 16th made the claim that they had ensured that the invasion was a failure. Once again no details were given. The letter stated that the Queen Mother, the Cardinal and Montgomery with Huntley's support conceived the idea of the invasion for purpose of besieging houses belonging to the King, and holding them until a bargain or agreement was reached.[62] When examining the structure of the Scottish army that invaded, we see that Angus, Marshall Errol, Glencairn, Cassilis, Lord Gray, Glamis and Yester were in the vanguard; Huntley and others were in the rear, whilst Arran and the French were in the middle. Lord Seton held one wing, whilst Buccleuch and riders from Teviotdale and Liddlesdale were on the other. Like the siege of Coldingham there would have been a great deal of distrust and jealously within the army.[63]

The intentions of Angus and his party in the event of an attack from the English forces would have been uncertain. Fraser suggested that Angus and his associate's dealings with the English may have had the permission of the Scottish government, and cited a later letter of authorization from Mary of Guise and the Governor to Scott of Buccleuch, dated September 26th 1547, in which he was allowed to 'intercommune with the protector and council of England, and such other Englishmen as he please for the safety of his kin, friends and servants, from the hardship and destruction of the Englishmen in time coming'. A further important instruction was added, in which whenever the Queen Mother or governor demanded, Scott of Buccleuch must 'renounce all bands, contracts and writings made to the Englishmen'. Buccleuch was allowed to become an 'assured Scot' only until he was called by the Scottish government to turn against the English. It is tempting to think Angus, Sir George Douglas and others of their faction were similarly employed by the Scottish government, however it is also likely that they were playing all sides until a clear winner emerged.[64]

It should also be considered that the Douglas motivation was to destroy the authority and credibility of Beaton, if we are to assume they considered him an enemy. This would mean sabotaging any attempt to develop a successful French military presence on the borders which would benefit Beaton, and which would have undermined the ability of the border lords to administer their own regions. So if dealing with the English to betray the Scots, the Red Douglas faction and allies were looking after their own local interests. It is necessary to look beyond the themes of nationalism and patriotism and take into context the international aspect, with French and English money flowing into Scotland, and numerous alliances forming and breaking up as the dynamics of the power relationships kept changing.

The Red Douglas had a vast army of adherents, and whilst there were noble causes to fight for that inspired the raising of armies and the performing of heroic exploits, the head of this family had to ensure he retained the loyalty of his followers by victories. Whether military, diplomatic or political, victories were expected to lead to prestige and material gain. In explanation to a porter after his large following had pushed through Edinburgh Town gate in 1555, Angus said he had had to put up with his men's 'unruliness', and he gave the impression that they were with him all the time, not through his choice but through their determination to stay close to and protect a feudal provider. On another occasion when he was preparing to ward himself freely to jail under crown instruction, his men stopped him from doing so as their prestige was guaranteed by his freedom, whilst shame would come with his imprisonment. It was these resourceful and violent bands of men whose loyalty Angus had to ensure,[65] if he was to be successful in the aristocratic politics of Scotland.

A parliamentary session at Edinburgh on September 2nd raised the issue of the threat from the west coasts, which in many respects was as dangerous as the threat from the south. Summons of treason were made against Lennox[66] and his brother Robert, Bishop of Caithness,[67] and a number of chiefs and captains of the Highlands and Islands who had joined Lennox, such as the MacLeods, McNeils, MacLeans, Allansons, MacKinnons and other clans.[68] Proclamations against Lennox were posted at the market crosses of Renfrew, Ayr, Lanark and other places where Lennox might be, calling him to attend parliament and answer the charges.[69]

The English retaliation led by Hereford was a series of raids between 8th-23rd September.[70] One unfortunate victim was Lord Home, who on September 9th had been granted £300 by the Lord Governor and council for the upkeep of his castle, as 'he having no goods left undestroyed to furnish it'. As a Scot not 'assured' his lands and estates were consistently targeted by assured Scots and English raids. During Hereford's invasion nearly all of Hume's lands and possessions in Berwickshire and Roxburghshire right up to the walls of Hume Castle were wasted and plundered.[71]

Hereford had instructed Angus and his faction to join him. He received a reply that they wanted to know his strategy, and when they did not receive a suitable reply they declined the invitation.[72] If Hereford had been attempting something beyond a series of raids and some type of concrete political action they might have joined. However they may have been trying to learn Hereford's plans. Hereford's raids also allowed the English to consolidate a grip on three strategic strongholds on the West March. Lord Maxwell, once a trustee of the English but now distrusted, had been imprisoned in the Tower of London since May 1544. He was offered freedom if he would put on the Red Cross of England as an assured Scot and command Caerlaverlock, Threave and Lochmaben castles in the name of Henry. Maxwell took personal command of Caerlaverlock whilst two sons commanded the other two.[73] He must have deposed his eldest son Robert, Master of Maxwell, who on June 30th after offering up pledges to the Scots was given command of those three strongholds to defend against the English. Arran would not sit idle. Warned by Lord Hume of the coming invasion, he sent his messenger William Hardy during early

September to deliver letters to Linlithgow, Edinburgh, Haddington and Kelso calling on all able men to ready themselves to resist.

When the town of Kelso was occupied by the English army a Scottish garrison composed of monks decided to hold out within the abbey. Hereford sent his Spanish mercenaries to assault the place and they were vigorously repulsed. On hearing of the siege Arran led a convoy of artillery southwards on September 12th. However he was not joined by sufficient forces and by September 20th he had ordered that the fiery cross be passed about Stirling so as to bring men to confront Hereford. At Kelso the English brought up cannon and artillery, and whilst the Spanish fired their harquebusiers at the occupants, a breach was affected and the abbey stormed. The defenders were overcome and slaughtered. The town of Kelso was torched and the abbey demolished. The raiders also visited and burned Melrose, Dryburgh and Jedburgh, and ensured that the surrounding communities and lands were wasted. However the raiders had caused so much devastation that there were no victuals or supplies to feed the army, so Hereford left Scotland by September 23rd, having destroyed fortresses, abbeys, friar houses, market towns, villages, towers, hospitals and other places to the recorded number of 287.[74]

Cardinal Beaton would write to Francis I of France stating that Hereford had invaded after the French and Scottish armies had disbanded, and Hereford's series of raids had lasted too short a time for the armies to successfully remobilize and confront him.[75] According to one account Arran did raise a force of 10,000 which invaded

England and advanced towards Norham, however at the first sign of resistance Angus advised withdrawing, which it did.[76] A letter from Thomas Erskine, the Commendator of Dryburgh, to the Queen Mother mentions a raid of September 15th, which was not led by Arran but by Lord Hume, the Earls of Bothwell and Dryburgh and the Commendator of Jedburgh. Dryburgh stated that Angus and Sir George were not involved in the raid. Lord Hume was expected to meet with the Queen Mother, and his account of the raid would imply that the Douglas had made deals with the English.

Dryburgh was the son of John, 5th Lord Erskine, keeper of Stirling Castle and a Guardian of Queen Mary. Lord Hume was a committed foe of the English, and although he had some territorial disputes with Sir George Douglas, she had no reason to distrust his account. Reading between the lines there may have been two invasions on the East March, the first led by Bothwell, the second by Arran. Angus and Sir George may have sent a warning to the English which caused the Scots under Hume to be repulsed in Northumberland, and they may have used their influence to cause the Arran muster to withdraw before Norham.[77]

At a parliamentary session formed in Linlithgow on October 1st, the destruction wrought by Hereford, the mustering of troops and defending the realm became a priority. A thousand horsemen were to be raised and financed by taxation, and the troops were to be divided amongst different captains, such as Alexander Hume at Lauder, the Kerrs of Cessford and Ferniehurst, the laird of Buccleuch, Douglas of Cavers, and other borderers.[78] £6,000 was to be provided monthly.[79] The disadvantages of the feudal muster in respect to speed of mobilizing are to be addressed through a contracted force of experienced borderers.

After the Hereford invasion Lennox finally made his way to Ireland, arriving in Carrickfergus during late October and finding the bulk of the army had faded away. Lennox may have had difficulty raising troops from his own estates as lands in Lennox and on the isles of Loch Lomond had been granted with two charters to the fourth Earl of Argyll, dated October 5th, 1545. At Carrickfergus his forces amounted to 1,500 kerns and 400 gallowglass, all natives of Ireland, the rest archers and harquebusiers. Donald, impatient after awaiting Lennox and concerned about his followers on the mainland, had travelled across the waters to Scotland. Those that were left, being short of wages and supplies, began to disperse.

Another reason for the failure was given as the misappropriation of the expected wages. A convoy had been sent from Henry to pay the army in Ireland in gold. On reaching the Isle of Mull, Hector Mor McLean took responsibility for the convoy. This must have been agreed by Lennox and the Council, and it would have repercussions, as when Maclean arrived in Carrickfergus some of the gold was missing, causing anger and accusations amongst the army, to the extent that many without pay left the army. The Irish council had also complained that they were having problems providing provisions. It is also possible that Duvyvaig's neutrality worked in favour of the Scottish government, and would have weakened Ross's cause in Ireland. Argyll also may have also used his influence with Irish lords and the gallowglass and kern captains to further undermine that cause.[80]

Maclean has been accused of deliberately taking some money to sabotage the expedition and of acting for Argyll, with whom he had entered into bond of manrent in May 1543. It is said he was a spy, or even an agent provocateur, getting close to Lennox so as to damage him. After Ross's death, MacLean's daughter Katherine would marry the Earl of Argyll, at Kilmartin, Argyll on December 12th 1545, which would bond Maclean closer to the seat of government power. Although there is no proof that MacLean was a government agent, the following year Maclean would be pardoned for past treasons and would enter into a bond of manrent with the Queen Mother, a significant honor. Possibly Maclean was an opportunist, who, having a landed and political stake in the Western Isles, would want to get close to individuals like Ross who were threatening major political and social changes.[81]

Back in mainland Scotland during October, there were reports from one of the Queen Mother's bodyguards, Alexander Shaw of Easter and Wester Sauchie,[82] that Arran and the Cardinal were once more intriguing against the Queen Mother. They were both supportive of a marriage between the young Queen and Arran's son, and they were to arrange a meeting at Hamilton with Angus and Sir George Douglas to persuade them to support the plan.[83] John Somerville and James Douglas of Drumlanrig set out to disrupt the meeting, successfully it seems, although the details and the methods employed are unknown.[84] Sir George Douglas had met with the English agent Brunstane, possibly to pass on details of these marriage plans.[85] It appears that Brunstane had already been informed of these proposals by sources unknown, as on October 6th from

Ormiston House he sent a ciphered letter to Henry VIII in which he reported that the Cardinal was planning to go to France with Montgomery and raise a larger French army whilst promoting the idea of marriage between Queen Mary and Arran's son. He also wanted to have the Queen and Queen Mother lodged in St Andrews Castle,[86] suggesting to the Queen Mother that whilst he was away in France it would be the safest place for her and her daughter. Beaton also would claim to Arran that lodging her in St Andrew's would keep her secure until the marriage between Queen Mary and Arran's son was finalized.[87] Beaton was playing the Queen Mother and Lord Governor to his own advantage, and his proposition to place the young Queen in his own castle would effectively put him in control of her destiny, whilst still holding Arran's son hostage. Nevertheless despite Beaton's ambitions it seems a ridiculous proposition to make, considering that the Queen Mother and Queen were secure in Stirling and protected by a formidable castle and a loyal bodyguard. So it is unlikely she would freely surrender herself to Beaton, or that she could be forced.

Here we have an example of a four-way spying war between the Queen Mother on one side and the Cardinal, the Lord Governor and the Douglas faction on the other sides. All sides have intelligence networks which they use to pursue political agendas and undermine the others' conspiracies. The bodyguards of the Queen Mother are being used as a sort of security service, and Alexander Shaw, recruited by Erskine, is able to gather up information on the movements and activities of several powerful players. The Queen Mother also seemingly has the formidable Douglas of Drumlanrig and Somerville supporting her.

For the Cardinal, his access to political power was through holding Arran's son hostage, and this was an advantage he did not want to lose. Promoting a successful marriage agreement would further bolster his influence and power. The Cardinal and Governor also needed to win some victories on the battlefield, and towards the end of the year they began to win back strategic prizes. Later in the month of November the Queen Mother would receive more information regarding the Cardinal's marriage plans for her daughter. He now planned in the New Year to go to France to gain support for the proposals, and her informant advised her to be wary of him.[88]

In early November, with Hereford back across the border in England and Lennox in Ireland, Arran ordered the men of Nithsdale, Galloway, Cunningham and Kyle to go to Dumfries by November 4th and march on Caerlaverlock Castle. Guns were taken out of Edinburgh castle and supplies from Hamilton. The army and a large siege train marched to the castle and retook it by November 8th. During that month Threave and Lochmaben castles were also taken. Robert, Lord Maxwell was captured and housed in Dumfries Castle.[89] His son Robert, the Master of Maxwell, was once more installed as captain of these castles. The next target was Dumbarton, with Arran and the Cardinal joining Huntley and Argyll in laying siege to the castle. On November 17th Lennox with Ormond took the remainder of the men towards Dumbarton, and some time was taken up chasing some French ships. He also sent his brother, the Bishop-elect of Caithness, to approach Stirling, the captain of Dumbarton, and try to persuade him to surrender the castle. Stirling claimed to hold the castle for the young queen and would only hand it to her when she came of age.

The Cardinal decided to try to turn Caithness away from his brother. At the September 2nd Parliament Caithness had been summoned for treason, but the Cardinal at the October 1st session had raised a protest, stating that Caithness could only be tried by ecclesiastical court and not civil court, and only by men chosen by the Pope. The Cardinal, acting with Huntley, appeared to offer to support Caithness in the restoration of his see if he would betray his brother, which he did. Stirling was finally persuaded to hand the castle over to Arran through money offered by the Cardinal and Huntley.[90] Stirling would later be pardoned for raids, robberies and other criminal activities committed against the surrounding country whilst he was captain,[91] and he was especially thanked for holding against the English.[92]

John Maxwell along with James Gordon, Laird of Lochivar, and the Johnstones, led a raid into England. Several towns were burned and prisoners and livestock taken. The success of the Scots in taking the Western March castles and Dumbarton further north had compelled many assured Scots to switch allegiance away from England, an act which Lesley says led to their pledges being hanged in Carlisle. At Kelso a French garrison joined with the borderers to raid the East and Middle Marches, causing 'great damage'.[93] Maxwell's brother Robert had less luck. As Warden of the West March and new keeper of Lochmaben Castle, he led a raid towards Stranleheugh in England along with Lochivar, the Johnstones and a number of Frenchmen. They were set upon at a small strait called the 'Yellow Silkhead at Wauchopdale' and 140 of them, including the Master of Maxwell, were captured.[94]

Lennox learned of the surrender of Dumbarton and although his movements immediately afterwards are unknown, he met with Ross and returned to Ireland. Ross died at Drogheda from a fever and Lennox and Henry paid for his funeral in Ireland at the cost of £400. Deprived of a Lord of the Isles, the chiefs chose a new leader, James MacDonald of Duvyvaig and the Glens. There was opposition from clan chiefs, who decided to reconcile with the Scottish government.[95]

On the 24th of January 1546, Duvyvaig, writing from Ardnamurchan, asked Henry VIII for money and ships so that he could wage war against the Scottish Government. This letter was delivered to the Irish council and deputy in Dublin by a group which included Alain Maclean, brother of Hector Mor. There is no recorded reply by Henry of Duvivaig's offer; possibly he was distracted, more likely he was disillusioned, as so much gold and time had been spent on an expedition that achieved no benefits.[96]

References: (1) (HP, vol.2 (395), pp.538-539. The Privy Council to Shrewsbury and others, 1st Jan, 1545). (2) (Fraser, p.269) (3) (HP, vol.2 (386), pp.528-533. Shrewsbury to Sadler and Henry VIII, 18th Dec, 1544). (4) (HP, vol.2 (350), pp.493-496. Shrewsbury and others to Henry VIII, 3rd Nov, 1544). (5) (HP, vol.2 (330), pp.474-475. Shrewsbury and others to Henry VIII, 4th Oct 1544). (6) (Merriman, pp.186-188). (7) (CSPS, Mary Queen of Scots to Charles V, 11th Nov/19th Nov, 1544), (8) (Henry VIII?, 30th Dec, 1544). (9) (CSPS, Chapuys and Van der Delft to Emperor, Jan 3rd, 1545). (10) (CSPS, The Doge and Senate to the Venetian Ambassador in Constantinople, Jan 23rd, 1545). (11) (CSPS, Van der Delft to Emperor, Jan 13th, to Jan 19th, 1545). (12) (Herkless & Hannay, pp.19-20). (13) (MacDonald Fraser, pp.259-260), (14) (HP, vol.2 (411), pp.557-558. Shrewsbury Tunsdale and Sadler to Henry VIII, 24th Feb, 1545). (15) (HP, vol.2 (411), pp.557-558, Shrewsbury Tunsdale and Sadler to Henry VIII, 24th Feb, 1545). (16) (Fraser. 269-270). (17) (HP, vol.2 (413), pp.559-560. Shrewsbury, &c., to Henry VIII, 27th Feb, 1545). (18) (Paterson, pp.180-183). (19) (Calderwood, pp. 181-182). (20) (Fraser, pp.260-261). (21) (Calderwood, pp. 181-182. Eddington, p.15). (22) (HP, vol.2 (414), pp.561-563. Shrewsbury, &c, to Henry VIII, 1st March, 1545). (23) (HP, vol.2 (422), pp.572-574. Shrewsbury and Others to Henry VIII, March 8th, 1545) (24) (CSPS, Chapuys to Secretary Joos Baves, 10 March, 1545). (25) (The Doge and Senate to Venetian Ambassador to Turkey). (26) (CSPS, St Mauris to Fransico de Los Cobos Fransico, May 7th, 1545). (27) (CSPS, Queen Regent to Chapuys and de Delft, March 8th, 1545). (28) (CSPS, Van der Delft to Queen Dowager, June 1st 1545). (29) (CSPS, St Mauris to Fransico de Los Cobos Fransico, May 7th, 1545). (30) (CSPS, Queen Dowager to Chapuys, April 10th, 1545). (31) (CSPS, Imperial Ambassador in France to Emperor, April 12th, 1545). (32) (RPCS, July 29th, 1545 (19)). (33) (Merriman, pp.150-152). (34) (Merriman, pp.150-152). (35) (Cathcart, Alison, (Oct, 2012), Scottish Historical Review, Vol XCI, 2:, no 232, pp.239-264). (36) (Byrne, Kevin. (1997), Colkitta, House of Lochar, Argyll, pp.14-16. Maclean-Bristol, pp.116-122), (37) (CSPS, Imperial Ambassador in France to Fransico de L) (38) (Herkless, Cardinal Beaton, p.281). (39) (Tytler, pp.325-328). (40) (Holinshed, pp.543-544). (41) (Tytler, pp.325-328. LP, The discourse of John Foster, 4th July, 1545). (42) (SP, vol.5, p.436). (43) (RSPC, vol.1, July, 1545, pp.11-13). (44) (RSPC, vol.1, July, 1545, pp.11-13). (45) (Imperial Ambassador in France to Fransico de Los Cobos Fransico, March 31st, 1545). (46) (Thomson, p.65). (47) (Marshall, p.60). (48) (ALHTS, vol.8, pp.lxiii-lxix, pp.378-385. Thomson, p.65, Marshal, p.60-61). (49) (RPS, 1545/6/2). (50) (RPS, 1545/6/3). (51) (Calderwood, pp. 182-183). (52) (RPCS, June 20th, 1545). (53) (LP, preface, Aug-Dec, 1545. MacLean-Bristol, pp 116-122). (54) (LP, preface, Aug-Dec, 1545. MacLean-Bristol, pp 116-122). (55) (LP, The Privy Council, 23rd August, 1545). (56) (LP, The Commissioner of the Earl of Ross to Henry VIII, Sept 4th, 1545). (57) (LP, Preface, August-Dec, 1545). (58) (Tytler, . 328-330). (59) (ALHTS, vol.8, pp.lxxii-lxxiii. RPCS, 1545 (24). (60) (LP, Hertford, Tunstall and Sadler to

Paget, 6th August 1545). (61) (Calderwood, pp.183-185. RPCS, August, 1545, (25). Tytler, pp.326-328). (62) (LP, Angus and others to Hereford and others, 16th August, 1545). (63) (Tytler. pp.326-328). (64) (Fraser, pp.274-275). (65) (Fraser, pp.282-283), (66) (RPS, 1545/9/2/6), (67) (RPS,1545/9/2/5), (68) (RPS, 1545/9/2/8). (69) (RPS, 1545/9/28/20). (70) (CP, Invasion of Scotland, Sept 23rd, 1545). (71) (SP, vol.4, pp.459-460). (72) (Tytler, p.330). (73) (Tytler, pp.335). (74) (ALHTS, vol.8, pp.404-409. CP, Invasion of Scotland, Sept 23rd, 1545. RPCS, June 30th, 1545, p.9. Tytler, pp.329-333). (75) (SCML, Cardinal Beaton to Francis I, 5th Oct, 1545). (76) (Tytler, pp.330-331). (77) (SCML, 16th-20th Sept, 1545, (CV), pp.142-143). (78) (RPS, 1545/9/28/39). (79) (RPS, 1545/9/28/42). (80) (Cathcart, p.260. Gregory, pp. 174-175. Maclean-Bristol, pp.116-123. SP, vol.1, p.339). (81) (Cathcart, p.258. Maclean-Bristol, pp.116-123. Tytler, pp.336-338). (82) (RPCS, vol.1, p.11), (83) (SCML, 16th Oct, 1545, 'Alexander Shaw of Sauchie to the Queen-Dowager', CVII, pp. 145-146). (84) (SCML, 21st Oct 1545, CVIII, CIX, 'John Somerville to the Queen-Dowager', 'James Douglas of Drumlanrig' pp.147-148). (85) (SCML, 16th Oct, 1545, CVII, 'Alexander Shaw to the Queen-Dowager', pp. 145-146). (86) (Tytler, pp.333-335), (87) (Herricks, pp.21-22). (88) (SCML, CXII, 29th November, 1545, 'Lord Fleming to the Queen Dowager, pp.150-152). (89) (ALHTS, vol.8, pp.lxxiv-lxxvi. Tytler, pp.335). (90) (LP, preface, Aug-Oct, 1545. Maclean-Bristol, pp.116-122. Merriman, pp.151-152. RPS, 1545/9/28/13. Tytler, pp.336-339). (91) (RPCS, July/Aug, 1546, (66)). (92) (RPCS, March 19th, 1547, (123)). (93) (Lesley, pp.191-192). (94) (Calderwood, pp.184-185). (95) (Gregory, pp.176-178. LP, preface, Aug-Oct, 1545. Maclean-Bristol, pp.116-122. Merriman, pp.151-152, RPS, 1545/9/28/13,Tytler, pp.336-339). (96) (Cathcart, p.258. Gregory, pp. 178-179. Maclean-Bristol, pp. 116-123. Tytler, pp.336-338).

St Andrew's Castle, the scene of the 1546 assassination of Cardinal Beaton and the subsequent siege of 1546-47. In the autumn of 1546 Protestant Scots would attempt to run the blockade and enter the castle through an entrance cut into the east wall facing the sea. A fierce naval battle ensued resulting in ships being overturned, and a hundred men 'slain and drowned' (Lesley, pp. 192-193).

The picturesque Nith valley and river overlooked from the Drumlanrig Estates. The Battle of Drumlanrig, Feb 1548 was technically not a battle but a series of sharp skirmishes and running fights that spread from Drumlanrig into Durrisderer and south to Dalswinton and Dumfries. The Lord Wharton had intended to devastate the lands of James Douglas, Laird of Drumlanrig and lure him out of his castle stronghold. However, Wharton fell into a trap when the Earl of Angus and Johnnie Maxwell, and 'assured Scots' in the ranks of the English army turned against their paymasters. Nithsdale and Dumfries was recovered for the Scottish Crown. It was the first Scottish victory since Pinkie.

The remains of Sanquhar Castle, once an important stronghold in the Nithsdale valley.

St Mary's Church, Haddington. On July 9th 1548, during the siege of Haddington, a cannon shell hit the church just as Mary of Guise and her entourage were paying a visit. Although Mary survived, several of her household and 16 of her gentlemen were killed.

Linlithgow Palace. Here during the summer of 1543, the Earl of Lennox rescued Mary of Guise and the infant Mary Queen of Scots from the clutches of James Hamilton, Earl of Arran.

The Earl of Lennox fortified Glasgow Cathedral in 1544. After the battle of Glasgow Muir on March 16th 1544, the victorious Earl of Arran captured Glasgow from Lennox and the Earl of Glencairn, and laid siege to Glasgow Castle and the Cathedral on 26th March 1544. When the garrison surrendered Arran had 16-18 leaders hanged. Lennox and Glencairn escaped to Dumbarton Castle (Engraving by John Slezer, 1693).

James Hamilton, 2nd Earl of Arran, Duke of Chatelherault (c. 1519-1575). Arran was maligned by John Knox as an 'inconstant Governor' (Knox's History), yet it should be noted that he began his career as Governor of Scotland at the age 23/24, and had to match his youthful inexperience against some of the sharpest minds in Scotland. He had to negotiate through political and religious upheavals that were sweeping across Western Europe, and he would change political allegiances and religious ideology whenever it suited, especially if it served the interests of his own family's dynastic ambitions. He showed himself skilled at diplomacy and political opportunism, and despite the slaughter at Pinkie and other disasters, he did during his eleven years as governor distinguish himself as a military organiser, managing to raise nearly 30 military musters and ensure that Scotland could keep fighting. His late intervention in 1560 contributed to the defeat of Mary of Guise and her French army, and paved the way for a Reformation Parliament. (portrait believed painted in the 1570s by Arnold Bronckorst.)

Matthew Stewart, Earl of Lennox. Cardinal Beaton was largely responsible for inviting the Earl of Lennox to Scotland in 1543, to use him as a counterbalance to the Earl of Arran and as a rival Second Person of the Realm after Queen Mary. The plan worked, in that Arran changed sides and joined the pro-French party, whilst a bitter and disgruntled Lennox joined the pro-English party.

ARCHIBALD
DOUGLASS EARL OF
ANGUS.

MARGARET
QUEEN DOWAGER OF
SCOTLAND.

Queen Margaret Tudor and Archibald, Earl of Angus. In 1514 Archibald, leader of the Red Douglases, would marry Margaret, the widow of King James IV, less than a year after the King's death at Flodden. They would later divorce and Archibald and his brother Sir George Douglas would be condemned as traitors and exiled to England. With the help of Henry VIII of England, they would continue to conspire to regain their lands in Scotland. Whilst Archibald gained a formidable reputation as a soldier and border raider, George would be known for excelling at the dark arts of murder, abduction, black propaganda and corruption. His reputation was known not just to the English court of Henry VIII but internationally amongst the French and Imperial courts.

A reconstruction of how Dunoon Castle might have looked in 1544 by the artist Andrew Spratt. The Earl of Lennox in the autumn of 1544 had failed in his attempt to possess Dumbarton Castle. His fleet then sailed past Dunoon and was fired on by guns from the castle. This led to Lennox and his English auxiliaries burning Dunoon and rampaging through Argyll. The Earl of Argyll fought several bloody skirmishes with Lennox, before the latter returned to England his ships laden with plunder (illustration: Andrew Spratt).

Mary of Guise, Queen of Scotland, and Queen Regent of Scotland (1515-1560). This French princess and widow of James V fought a long, hard battle to protect her daughter, the future Mary, Queen of Scots, against the ambitions of Kings and Earls. She would also outfox some of the most ruthless individuals amongst the Scottish nobility and clergy. Whilst upholding Scottish interests during the devastating 'Rough Wooing' by Henry VIII, she was overall a promoter of French hegemony, believing that through French influence Scotland would prosper and France would gain a significant foothold to threaten England. In this latter ambition she failed. Being pressured by her powerful brothers in France to crush Protestant dissent in Scotland, she succeeded in alienating those nobles who would have served her for the price of tolerance. It was the one major policy mistake she made during her career. When she finally passed away in Edinburgh castle, 1560, she was joined at her bedside by many of the Scottish nobles who had recently fought against her. Many weeped when she died, acknowledging no doubt her importance to Scottish history (Illustration: Corneille de Lyon).

After her escape from Linlithgow Palace in 1543, Mary of Guise made Stirling Castle stronghold the main residence of herself and her infant daughter, Mary, Queen of Scots. During her political struggles with the Governor of Scotland, Stirling would hold alternate parliaments to that of Edinburgh.

Edinburgh Castle was the site of many sieges and battles during the minority of Mary Queen of Scots.

The mighty castle of Tantallon, perched on the Lothian coast and overlooking the sea entrance into the Firth of Forth. During the 1544 invasion of Scotland this important stronghold was held by James Douglas, son of Sir George Douglas. Whilst his father, his uncle, the Earl of Angus and other relatives were held captive by the Governor of Scotland and Cardinal Beaton, Douglas was prepared to hand over the castle to English forces in return for help in getting his kinsmen released.

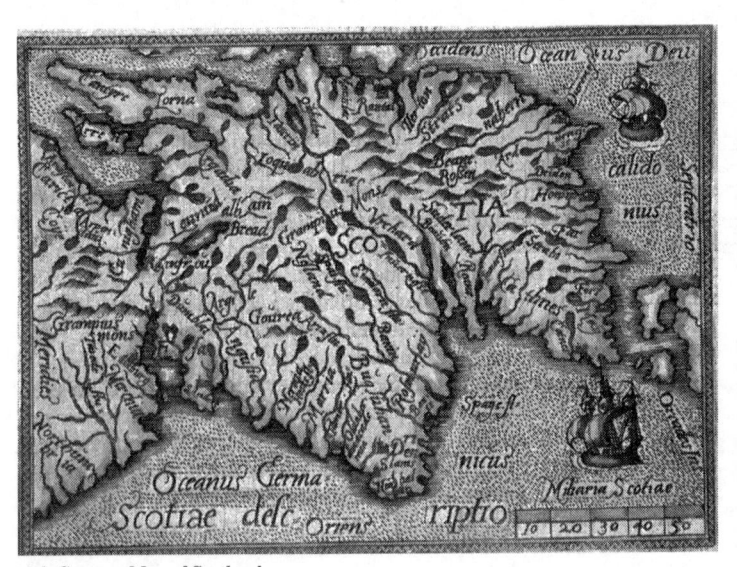

16th Century Map of Scotland

Chapter Five

To pardon the unpardonable deed

By early 1546 Cardinal Beaton had cancelled his plans to go to France, possibly because the Queen Mother was not prepared to leave Stirling Castle for St Andrews, and she was also openly promoting the Abbot of Paisley for the Bishopric of Dunkeld, which in turn could threaten Beaton's influence on Arran. On January 8th in Edinburgh eight cardinals were invited to make a settlement of the issue, and to decide whether Paisley or Robert Crichton were rightful nominees. By August Paisley would become known as Bishop-elect when sitting at parliament.[1] Cardinal Beaton decided to exert his ecclesiastical authority by summoning a convention of the clergy at Blackfriars Church in Edinburgh in mid-January.

One issue of importance was the recent invasion by Hereford and the destruction of the abbeys of Melrose, Jedburgh, Kelso, and Dryburgh and numerous other churches and monasteries. To repair the damage a contribution of £13,000 was to be levied for benefices above £40 in annul value.[2] There was also a discussion on the state of religion within Scotland and what means and methods should be employed in stemming the rise of the reformation there.[3] The convention could also be described as political, as it would be aimed against those powerful nobles that supported the reformation. The meeting was broken up when it was learned that George Wishart, the Preacher, was in Leith. The Cardinal and the Governor would gather forces to confront him and his followers.

In late 1545 whilst in Dundee, George Wishart was invited to Edinburgh by the Earl of Cassilis, along with some gentlemen of Kyle. They wanted Wishart to debate with the bishops, and the barons of Lothian would offer protection. On accepting the invitation Wishart travelled to Montrose, then Invergowrie, reaching Leith by December 1545. During a rally at Inveresk, Sir George Douglas was reportedly so overwhelmed by Wishart that he gave his support for the reformation. Whilst at Leith the Cardinal and Arran arrived in Edinburgh with armed force, which compelled Wishart to move to West Lothian with Crichton of Brunstane and Cockburn of Ormiston. He arrived in Haddington to preach. John Knox was a member of the party that joined Wishart, described as a bodyguard or sword bearer. The group included Hugh Douglas of Longniddry and John Sandilands of Calder. Wishart was disappointed at the numbers that came to see him preach, which were only a few hundred. He then set out for the house of Ormiston, with the Laird of Ormiston, Calder, and the Laird of Brunstane.[4]

With the associations of Wishart with men like the English agent Brunstane and several prominent Scottish reformers like Cassilis amongst others, Wishart was being used to stir up a reformation movement within Scotland to challenge the Catholic clergy, and especially Cardinal Beaton. However the small crowds in Haddington indicated that he did not at present have enough popular support. Possibly the reason that Wishart advised Knox to leave his company, stating 'one is sufficient for one sacrifice', was because he suspected that there would be a hostile attempt against him.

The Earl of Bothwell, the feudal power in that area, had been observing the movements of Wishart and the party. At midnight after Wishart's arrival at the House of Ormiston, Bothwell surrounded the place with armed forces and demanded the surrender of the preacher. The Cardinal and the Governor were also nearby with armed men. Bothwell managed to get Wishart to surrender to him under promise that he would not hand him over to Cardinal or Governor, and would keep him until he could assure his freedom and safety. Ormiston, Brunstane and Calder pledged to enter into bonds of manrent with Bothwell, and would persuade other Lothian barons to do the same if Bothwell fulfilled his pledge in defending Wishart. He then took him to Hailes Castle. Cardinal Beaton sent troops to capture the men at Ormiston. Brunstane escaped, but Calder and Ormiston were captured and imprisoned in Edinburgh castle.[5]

Bothwell had been long suspected as someone with

Protestant sympathies, however at a council meeting at Edinburgh on the 19th of January, he promised to hand over Wishart to Arran.[6] He would be rewarded several days later with ratification of the feudal casualties of the estates of the deceased Lord Saltoun, which entailed being granted a lump sum.[7] Bothwell had clearly used Wishart for financial and territorial gain. Once Wishart was in Arran's power, instead of trying him under civil law, Beaton persuaded him to allow an ecclesiastical trial.[8] Wishart was taken by Beaton and lodged in St Andrew's Castle. The Cardinal summoned all the clergy and bishops, including his rival the Bishop of Glasgow, to St Andrews for the trial, which was held at Abbey Church on the 28th of February. Arran had been expected to be present but Beaton pushed through with the trial before he arrived. Wishart was found guilty of heresy on March 1st. With a civil judge present with the authority to administer executions, Wishart was burned at the stake in St Andrews.[9]

Afterwards the Cardinal concentrated his mind on his own security. His illegitimate daughter Margaret, gifted with a large dowry, married David Lindsay, master of Crawford. An extravagant marriage was hosted at Finhaven Castle. This granted Beaton powerful territorial allies with the Crawford Lindsays, and he may have believed he needed them. He had a dispute with the Leslie family, especially with Norman Leslie, Master of Rothes over unfulfilled promises regarding land rights. Leslie was treated so contemptuously that he went to John Leslie, his uncle, and an assassination plot started up which would add other participants with various grudges against the Cardinal.[10]

After Easter the Cardinal went to Edinburgh to hold a

synod, and Knox would write that the Earl of Angus was intending to attempt some type of action against him. No details are given of the attempt except that the Cardinal was contemptuous afterwards, boasting that he was near untouchable, that he had the Governor's son in his power and that France was his chief sponsor. Sir James Melville wrote that Angus and Sir George Douglas would stir up Norman Leslie, Master of Rothes, John Lesley of Parkhill and Kirkcaldy, Laird of Grange to assassinate the Cardinal.[11] If this is true then the Douglas would have been aware that the public mood was turning against the Cardinal, with people were beginning to be drawn to the reformed religion through hatred of Beaton and the cruel execution of Wishart. As the new opinions increased so would the propaganda of which the noble reformers had the funds and means to distribute widely. Added to his perceived cruelty was his failure to address those grievances that were alienating many from the old religion, such as vice and corrupt practices. Within the nation his acts served to divide the population and sharpen religious divisions.[12]

It was reported on the Continent that marriage negotiations were being forwarded by the French for the marriage of Mary, Queen of Scots with the son of Arran. The Scots were supporting this as they wanted to be ruled by a native, and Arran was close in succession after Queen Mary to the crown of Scotland. There was little hostility between Scotland and England except for criminal raids and thefts across borders. The Scots were only prepared to fight if the French provided money and arms.[13] With the Earl of Hereford sailing for Boulogne he took with him all the German, Italian, Spanish and other foreign troops from the borders of Scotland. There were 1,500 to 1,800 Spanish troops.[14]

On the seas Scottish piracy was increasing. Scots were operating out of Breton ports and attacking Spanish shipping. The French apparently ordered them out of Normandy, and complaints were made to the Dauphin and the King, with the result that the Scots were ordered to surrender the Spanish prizes.[15] The Scottish pirates or privateers were also joining with English and French to target Spanish shipping, a problem addressed to the Emperor due to the serious disruption of trade routes.[16]

On the borders Wharton reported that English reivers were lifting cattle and taking them to Scotland so as to blame the Scots. He accuses the borderers of Liddlesdale, whether English or Scots, for being behind these raids. Wharton also said that there was not much more damage that could be done to the Scottish borderers. The 'women, children and impotent creatures' were what remained, and during the night they sowed seeds on the ground, and would quickly repair any burned or damaged dwellings. The writer, whilst pitying the borderers, who 'endure pain that no Englishman can suffer the like', gave witness to their endurance. There were also reports that the Earl of Angus was preparing to raid, and had 2,000 contracted troops at Melrose and Peebles paid for by French money. Sir George Douglas was now an important adviser to the Queen Mother,[17] which indicates that she was drawing further from the Cardinal and Governor. It appears also that with Angus receiving French money some type of understanding had been reached with the Queen Mother and the Douglas faction. No doubt she would have known how they had conspired with the English and possibly disrupted and undermined the planned summer and autumn invasions of 1545, but she would also be aware of how effective they could be on the battlefield if they were on side.

During late May the Justice-clerk was ordered to call assured Scots of the Merse and Teviotdale to the nearest Justice Courts and restore their loyalties to the Scottish Government. At this council meeting in Edinburgh, Arran and the Cardinal were present, whilst Angus, Cassilis, Glencairn and all the Protestant nobles were absent except Lord Maxwell. Angus as noted above was at either Peebles or Melrose preparing actions against the English, yet the absence of protestant lords could signify growing opposition to the Cardinal after the burning of Wishart. Of the Earls only Errol attended.[18]

The Cardinal would return to Fife, apparently having concerns about the possibility of an English invasion and an attempt on the sea coast. He called on the nobles and gentlemen of Fife to meet him at Falkland. Whether these concerns were real or contrived, it is also believed that he was using the gathering to slay or capture the Leslies, the Kirkcaldys of Grange, the Laird of Raith, Sir James Learmouth, Provost of St Andrews, and others who favoured the reformation of religion in Scotland.[19] The meeting was scheduled for a Monday, but a group of 16 men of Fife forced their way into St Andrew's castle on the early morning of Saturday May 29th. They were John Leslie, brother of Norman, the master of Rothes, William Kirkcaldy, the younger of Grange, James Melville and Peter Carmichael, and other gentlemen of Fife. Entry was achieved when the drawbridge was lowered to allow in builders and masons.

The raiders compelled the builders and other occupants to leave and then cornered Beaton in his chambers. Whilst Leslie and the Cardinal argued through the door, which had been barricaded with furniture and chests, hot coals were placed next to it and it was put on fire. The door opened and the raiders stabbed Beaton to death. His body was hung outside the castle so that the people could be certain he was dead. He was then thrown into the castle dung heap. The small group decided to hold the castle. They would later be joined by 150 fresh recruits, including Norman Leslie.[20] In the Cardinal's chamber were found letters and proof that he was planning to kill or capture Norman Leslie, Sheriff of Fife and Master of Rothes, John Leslie, the Laird of Kirkcaldy, and Sir James Learmouth.[21]

The Privy Council met in Stirling on 3rd-5th June. It was agreed that with the slaying of Beaton and the dangers of internal and religious conflict, an endeavour had to be made to forge a united front. All the parties, including Angus and his faction, were to reject the English marriage proposals. Huntley was appointed chancellor,[22] and Arran's brother, the Abbot of Paisley and Bishop-elect of Dunkeld, was granted the temporalities of St Andrews, effectively granting him the revenues and powers of the Archbishop.[23] For the Lord-Governor the death of the Cardinal had its advantages, as it eliminated an individual who held the ecclesiastical power to question his legitimacy, and who used his son as hostage to exert influence over him. His son was still hostage now the killers of Beaton had him, but he must have been hopeful of securing him by negotiations.[24]

On June 10th the three estates assembled in Edinburgh. A compromise was reached between the rival factions, in that those that had entered into bonds with Henry VIII to support marriage between Edward and Mary, and those that entered into bonds in respect of supporting or opposing a proposed contract of marriage between Arran's son and the young Queen, renounced these obligations before Arran and the Queen Mother. Twenty peers were chosen for Arran's Privy Council, whilst four peers would be selected each month to act as his secret council.[25]

During the spring of 1546, James MacDonald of Duvyvaig, who previously through his neutrality had assisted the Scottish government, now decided to attack the west coasts. Claiming the title of Lord of the Isles, he wasted Ayrshire and burned Saltcoats. At the Treaty of Ardrossan on the 18th of June, Argyll and Duvyvaig made peace. Duvyvaig agreed to renounce his claim to Lordship of the Isles in return for some deals regarding land, the Rhinns of Islay, for example, which had been contested between the MacLeans and MacDonalds would pass to him. Duvyvaig would also marry Argyll's sister Agnes. These important Campbell marriage alliances with the MacLeans of Duart and the MacDonalds of Duvyvaig and the Glens would have a profound effect on Irish politics. The MacLeans and MacDonalds would provide large numbers of mercenaries for the Irish wars during the latter half of 16th century.[26]

The Anglo-French Treaty of Ardres, or Campi, was concluded on June 7th 1546, and Scotland was to be comprehended into the peace. Alexander Crichton of Brunstane, although summoned by the Scottish parliament to answer charges for treason,[27] would find when attending that this process was dropped. Possibly because of his strong English connections, which would be useful in diplomacy, the charges were 'deserted at this time until they be further advised' or temporarily forgotten.[28] He would be asked to accompany Lord Ruthven, the secretary David Paniter and the Abbot of Paisley to London to finalize the treaty after the Scottish parliament ratified it on 14th August.[29]

Whilst the comprehension was declared throughout the realm, the English wardens interpreted it not as peace but as 'abstaining from war during the King of England's pleasure'. Whilst no lasting peace was declared by Henry, there was a lull in direct warfare, although there were still raids across the borders and the stirring up of reformation within Scotland. During the parliament, although the Scots did not directly accuse Henry of having a part in the assassination of Beaton, a statement was made regarding the relationship between Henry and the killers in which 'he confided most trustily, his employees, servants and household men'. The Scots asked that he should not receive these men into his protection.[30]

Arran, at the instigation of Gavin Dunbar, Archbishop of Glasgow, was prepared to open negotiations with the Castilians. In return for releasing Arran's son and surrendering St Andrew's Castle, instruments would be sought with the Pope so that a papal absolution could be granted to Norman Leslie and his company for the killing of Beaton.[31] The Castilians had sent certain articles to be considered by parliament. John Hamilton, now Bishop-elect of Dunkeld, Sir George Douglas and Lord Ruthven visited St Andrews with answers to the articles; however the Castilians apparently did not intend to satisfy the conditions of the articles, which they themselves had produced. Paisley, Douglas and Ruthven returned to the parliament.[32] The offer of remission was rejected, as the garrison was expecting to receive victuals by sea and was still in contact with Henry VIII.[33]

As already noted, Sir James Melville would state that Sir George Douglas and Angus had encouraged the Fife men to murder Beaton. If that was true then they were the first to betray them when they voted that the Castle of St Andrews should be besieged.[34] As a possible incentive for Angus's support against the Castilians, his sixteen-year-old natural son George was to be offered the vacant Abbacy of Arbroath, which would give access to revenue worth £1,000 per year.[35] The Queen Mother would appoint him to the Abbey on 13th Dec, 1546, after which he was known as the Postulate of Arbroath.[36] He would also be accused of kidnapping Master Archibald Beaton, taking him to Tantallon Castle and robbing him of money, gold and silver. He was cleared of the charge when Beaton 'of his own free will' said that he had not been plundered and the accusation was wrong.[37]

Whilst there were debates on how to deal with the occupiers of St Andrew's Castle, Arran was faced with another siege situation. In June the Bishop of Caithness, with a handful of helpers, took control of Dumbarton Castle. Arran quickly called a muster and ordered Glencairn, Lord Somerville and others to join him whilst sending for Argyll to bring in artillery and cannon from the west. The siege of Dumbarton lasted until July, although there are no details of whether it was surrendered or stormed, or what happened to Caithness and the defenders at that time.

Arran next focused his attention on St Andrews. An army was raised and Arran during August proceeded to lay siege to St Andrews Castle. He introduced a measure by which the country was divided into four districts, with each to take a turn in prosecuting the siege.[38] The siege would prove a difficult task, with castle walls strong enough to resist the Scottish artillery. An assault from land was too difficult, and there was small chance of success by a sea assault. Starving the occupants was the best strategy; although the Scottish navy did not have a large enough presence or the necessary ships to successfully blockade the castle. Henry would give his support to the besieged, despite the recent peace, and allow English ships to supply the Protestants.[39] To negotiate terms Kirkcaldy of Grange would travel to London, reaching it by the end of August.[40] Kirkcaldy would receive £200 from the English crown, and pensions for the Castilians for holding the castle and part reward for murdering Beaton. Agreement was made that in return for relief, the besieged would retain the Governor's son as hostage and they would continue to support the marriage treaty with England. The Parliament of Scotland, concerned about the Master of Arran being handed over to England, passed an act on August 14th depriving him of his place in the royal succession until he was freed.[41]

The Lord-Governor felt that he needed to earn some time with the English. After being granted a safe conduct, a delegation was to be sent to the English court, headed by his brother Dunkeld. However, when word reached the Scottish court that English ships were near the Scottish coasts, it was decided that Dunkeld would remain and Paniter would instead lead the envoys.[42] Relief did reach St Andrews by September,[43] although there were losses, when English ships transporting Kirkcaldy and carrying supplies were attacked by Scottish vessels as they tried to enter the castle through a passage cut into the east wall facing the sea. The fact that an attempt was to be made was known by the Governor, who sent word to Linlithgow, Stirling, Strathearn and Menteith for the people to be ready at short notice to go to St Andrews and repulse an incursion by the English sea convoy. Ships and boats, even fishing vessels were gathered.[44] Lesley stated that the Scots managed to overturn some of the ships and that a hundred were 'slain and drowned'.[45] Arran tried other methods to win the siege, exporting Ayrshire miners to dig a tunnel under the wall, an endeavour that failed because the besiegers dug a countermine, resulting in a bloody fight underground when both sides met. During October there were further warnings of English ships attempting to breach the blockade, and besides sailors and ships from St Monans, a larger ship, possibly the *Lyon*, was stationed to patrol the nearby waters.[46]

The Queen Dowager of Hungary mentioned the peace treaty between France and England and the inclusion of Scotland. In her opinion the treaty was ambiguous and technically the Scots were still at war with the Empire, as the Empire was not mentioned in the treaty. All shipping captures were fair game, and the Emperor stated that he would negotiate with the Scots if compensation was paid for shipping losses. The Scots stated that since the Emperor had declared war on Scotland then a new treaty needed to be made, and until then there was no need to pay compensation. She believed both the Scottish and English were temporizing. The Scots were apparently boasting that they wanted no peace with the Empire now they had peace with England. The Scottish embassy to London was viewed as a delaying tactic in respect to the siege of St Andrews.[47] Observed by French and Imperial diplomats, a meeting on November 27th became heated, with the English reaching the opinion that the Scots were just haggling to waste time. There was also a belief that Arran was sharing in the plunder from the piracy.[48] With no peaceful and just solution appearing, the Emperor prepared a naval fleet to protect shipping against the Scots.[49] However the Queen of Hungary continued to negotiate with the Scots in respect of restitution for Scottish piracy against Spanish and Flemish shipping.[50]

By December, the castle walls of St Andrews, although strong, had been weakened by the sustained five-month bombardment. Arran had brought up two large guns, Crooked Mouth and Deaf Meg, as well as other pieces of artillery, to pound at the walls. The siege had been costly and time-consuming, yet the besieged were also low on supplies, a result possibly of the sea engagement in September. The defenders were also suffering from sickness, possible the pestilence which would appear in other parts of Scotland.[51] Arran and the counsel that assembled at St Andrews did not seem to be aware of this advantage, and were concerned that whilst the army was distracted by the siege the English could invade. They entered into negotiations with the garrison of St Andrews. Arran wanted it clear that he was prepared to continue, and would only withdraw under advice of the Queen Mother and counsel, and as long as it did not damage his honour.[52]

The offer of remission, which had been made in August and rejected, was reintroduced to the negotiations. This time the Castilians agreed that in return for calling off the siege the castle would not be handed over to England. They would surrender if Arran could arrange a papal absolution, called the 'Appointment'. None of the besieged would be tried by civil or church courts, and until then they would keep Arran's son. Both sides agreed, and both were playing for time.[53] The Castilians were ready to hold and applied to Henry for supplies and support. He was aware how symbolically important this Protestant occupation of Beaton's castle was. Arran used the truce to petition France for engineers skilled in the art of siege warfare.[54]

There were reports that Scottish ambassadors were at the English court, yet there was no sign of good relations between Scots and English. Mary de Guise was reported to be preparing to sail to Scotland, and the occupiers of St Andrews Castle had offered to surrender in return for remission and an absolution from the pope.[55] The Scots were still technically at war with the Empire, and the French King was trying to negotiate a peace between both. The Emperor wanted two points addressed in any future negotiations: redress of injuries caused to his subjects, and restoration of goods taken whilst victims were under safe conduct. There was also a dispute between the King of France and the Pope over Cardinal Beaton's funds in a Paris bank, which the Pope claimed as church possessions, whilst the French King wanted to hold the account for the Cardinal's heirs.[56]

There were tensions building between France and Empire, and an outbreak of war would drag in Scotland and England. The French king would send de Valrounne and Lorges to Brittany with 12 galleys and raise troops for an expedition.[57] There were also complaints that Scottish pirates were taking Spanish and Flemish goods and selling them at French courts. Whilst publicly the King of France and Mary of Guise disowned these pirates, with the French King stating that once Scots entered into a treaty of peace he would hang the pirates and have the goods restored, other opinions stated that the French were using the Scots to trouble the Emperor until he negotiated peace.[58] Certainly the Queen Mother and Arran were supporting the economic warfare against imperial shipping. They granted letters of marque to the likes of the privateer Andrew Roberts of Leith, and the captain of the *Lioness*, allowing him to prey on Portuguese shipping and other enemies of Scotland.[59] Several months later John Cochrane and Alexander Hay, captain and master of the *Michael*, were also given licence to attack the enemies of Scotland.[60]

Articles of agreement between Henry VIII and holders of St Andrews were written up, agreeing not to surrender the castle without Henry's consent.[61] When Henry VIII died on 28th January 1547 negotiations continued with Somerset, the Lord Protector. Henry Balnaves travelled to Berwick from the Castle of St Andrews to meet with Somerset.[62] Norman Leslie was asked to remain at court, and Balnaves, after an audience with Somerset, was instructed to return to Scotland with £1,180,[63] and promised further support and money. He was to instruct the nobility to turn against Arran and the Queen Mother and once more support the marriage treaty. Somerset was determined to renew hostilities with Scotland, despite the Treaty of Campi.[64]

In April there were rumours circulating that Henry VIII had been poisoned. Leonard Gayton, who had been a prisoner in France at Montreuil, had returned to England

and informed Lord Grey that three different prisoners, two who would be executed, had informed him that the French had arranged for the English king to be poisoned. The story goes that Henry was to be asked to surrender Boulogne, and if he did not he was going to be administered a poison which would take six weeks to kill him and which only a special antidote would cure. Two Italians were to travel to England and give the poison to 'a certain great man about the King' who would give it to the King, then to Prince Edward and Princess Mary. In the confusion that the deaths would cause in England the Dauphin would land an army at Tynemouth, join the Scots and invade England, or alternatively besiege Boulogne if an offer of money was refused.

One of the informants was a former servant of the Queen Mother of Scotland who was discovered to be a spy working for Henry VIII, although his name is not given. Lord Grey, in writing to the Lord Protector, stated that this story was confirmed by another called Poussin, who the previous Christmas before Henry's death had also been aware of the poison plot, and also added that several powerful men in the council were in favour with France.[65]

There is no evidence that Henry was poisoned; it is likely he died of natural causes, with severe weight problems and various illnesses. There may have been a poison plot, although the fact that Gayton spoke to three people in prison who revealed the plot should itself seem suspicious if the details were so widely known. What he was told could have been part of an elaborate scheme to spread misinformation and create suspicion within the King's council whilst Henry was alive. After Henry's death and Clayton's freedom from French prison the details of a possible poisoning and treason within the council re-emerged. No doubt it would have been investigated, but the lack of any further records suggests that nothing of serious interest was discovered. The English were becoming more aware of the many layered webs of distortions and half-truths that the French would frequently spin out in their propaganda campaigns.

After the armistice with the Castilians, the Governor had sent Paniter to France to request skilled engineers, arms, money and a renewal of the Scots-Franco alliance. As Henry VIII had used the Treaty of Campi as a lull in the fighting and not a full peace, they advised the French to increase the size of their fleets.[66] The Lord Governor also sent John Hay, a nephew of Cardinal Beaton, to the French court to propose a marriage between Arran's son and Queen Mary, and as an alternative to a French proposal for a marriage treaty between Scotland and Denmark, one of France's important allies. The Queen Mother sent John Erskine, the Abbot of Dryburgh, to France, to learn what he could about these plans and disrupt those that were unfavourable to the Queen Mother.[67]

King Francis I of France passed away soon after Henry VIII, and was succeeded by Henry II. In response to the pleadings of Paniter, the French ambassador D'Osell was sent to Scotland to renew the alliance and treaties between Scotland and France. D'Osell would enjoy a strong relationship with the Queen Mother and would become an important politician in the ensuing years.[68] Through him she would be able to win French support against Arran and his supporters, and take more control of the destiny of her daughter. As Stewart of Cardonald, a Scot in English pay would report, there were sharp divisions between the Queen Mother and Lord Governor over possession of the Queen. The Lord Governor next intended to send his brother, the Bishop-elect of Dunkeld to France with the purpose of promoting his marriage proposal, and Dunkeld was supposedly interested in acquiring the Bishopric of Mirepoix, which had formerly belonged to Beaton. Politics in Scotland would conspire to sabotage this intention and Dunkeld would remain in Scotland having to deal with local and national matters.[69]

During the truce, the garrison of St Andrews, with no army outside to oppose them, began to raid the surrounding districts, becoming the 'terror of their neighbourhood'. John Rough, the former chaplain of the Lord Governor, had joined the Castilians, but apparently disgusted by their 'debauched and dissolute lives' he left the castle to preach in the town. John Knox, when he learned that the crimes of the garrison were being associated with the reformed religion, decided to enter the castle and denounce them. There were those in the garrison who did not approve of the criminal activities of their associates and were glad of the moral voice of Knox, who would become public preacher to the congregation. The Master of Arran, whilst a royal hostage in St Andrews would have been subjected to the oratory of Knox, and this would have influenced his conversion in late years.[70]

During 1547 there was a growing determination to organize the government against the criminality and rebellion within the realm, with the Governor and the Lords of Council intending to punish all offenders, and not grant any 'remission', or 'relaxation'.[71] There was also violent opposition to the officers of government, where heralds, messengers, and other officials were being assaulted and humiliated. The stability of the country was being challenged by growing lawless bands,[72] and even the religious establishment was threatened by the 'heresies of Luther'.[73] The names of the accused heretics were to be passed to the council, so that they could be arrested and tried under the laws of the land.[74]

The government also sought to put a halt to feuds between the mighty lords. Sir George Douglas and Lord George Hume were involved in a conflict over the castles, lands and rights to Cocksburnpath. The Privy Council called on them to follow legal means to resolve the issue. They did not ask them to go to the Court of Justice but instead brought evidence of their claims to the Governor and Privy Council, who would rule on the matter. According to the council, 'concord... between all parties' was important for the country, so instead of becoming a matter to be settled by a judicial court, it was a matter of national security to be settled by the lords.[75] In July the matter was ruled in favour of Douglas.[76]

On the borders there was constant daily and nightly activity from reivers with 'slaughters, murders, and oppressions', and the council employed the Master of Maxwell and several lairds and their retainers to base themselves at Lochmaben for a month and stop the raids.[77] The Earl of Angus was given letters with authority to muster the men of Clydesdale and Tweeddale and direct them to lie close to the Tweed near Peebles. The Laird of Drumlanrig was ordered to take 100 horsemen and lie near Moffat.[78] Another measure for defence was introduced when it was learned that the English were planning a land and sea invasion. A system of bales was to be used whereby in the event of a navy being spotted off the coasts, a bale on top a hill would be set alight, and this would alert a nearby spotter on a hill, who would light another bale. The system extended from Abbots Head, where Sir George Douglas was given responsibility, and carried through to Dowhill near Fast Castle, then Dounhill near Dunbar, then Northberwicklaw, Dounprendarlaw, then Arthur's Seat at Edinburgh, then finally Burniscraig near Linlithgow.[79]

Both Scotland and England were preparing for hostilities to break out. The Protector stated that he would not consider continuing peace with Scots without consultation with the Emperor. In London, certain assured Scots were having secret meetings with the Protector, and obviously the Scottish ambassadors were aware of this.[80] On the Continent the English were sending out contradictory opinions regarding the peace with Scotland, and whilst the French stated that the Scots were not included, the English were saying they were, which was the opposite to what the Protector was saying. At this time Boulogne was being fortified by the English, which was also a breach of the treaty.[81]

There were accusations that Scots were involved in the Desmond rebellion which broke out in Ireland.[82] In June English deputies would claim that 6,000 Scots had raided Ireland, whilst Scottish ambassadors retorted that the Irish rose up themselves. Whilst on the Continent M. d'Etampes was supposedly sent to Brittany to raise 6,000 troops for a Scottish expedition.[83] The ambassador of the Emperor had audience with the Protector and learned that the Scots would not be included in treaty, as 18,000 Scots with 7,000 'savages' had taken Langholm.

This campaign was in response to a massive plundering raid of the western borders by 5,000 English, which began to turn into a military invasion as strongholds were taken and occupied by English troops. This was a clear breach of the truce. The Governor assembled an army at Peebles and advanced south. Langholm Tower had been betrayed to English forces by a Scottish spy. With a train comprising two falcon guns from Edinburgh Castle and ten carts of ammunition, bullets and other necessities, the Governor reached Langholm by mid-July. After a four-day siege and the bombardment by cannon shots, Langholm was retaken, and then razed to the ground with gunpowder. The Protector would use the Scottish response as an excuse to make war on Scotland by land and sea. He would also claim that the French had been making demands on Scots for command of two fortresses with reminders of the large amounts of French money spent. The Protector believed that the French wanted a foothold in Scotland,[84] and he made preparations to send the navy and an army to Scotland.

During June, the 'absolution' arrived from Rome. When the garrison within the castle of St Andrews was offered the papal dispensation, they refused it due to the terms used to describe the death of the cardinal, *'remittimus irremissibly'*, 'we pardon the unpardonable deed'. This was not in their opinion an absolute remission. It is also clear that they were refusing in order to buy more time, and would be aware that Somerset was preparing to march into Scotland with a large army.[85] Fifteen French galleys arrived at St Andrews on the 29th of June, led by Leone Strozzi. King Henry II of France would claim that this was not a breach of the treaty with England as the castle was held by rebel Scots and no

English were involved.[86] Arran broke off from the campaign against the English and returned to St Andrews to assist the French.[87]

The French brought 4,000 foot which had been raised in Brittany along with a contingent of horse, siege equipment and artillery.[88] For three weeks the castle was bombarded from sea and from land, until the besieged made terms with Arran and the French. They surrendered on July 31st, 1547. They were offered the chance to enter French service or be shipped to a country of their choice, but not Scotland. Although these terms seemed reasonable, the French went back on the arrangement, and some of the Castilians were sent to prisons in France, while others, such as the preacher John Knox, were sentenced to become galley slaves.[89] Within the castle of St Andrews the French found a great deal of wealth stored by the dead Cardinal. They loaded it into their ships and took it back to France.[90] A Scottish fleet reportedly attacked the Isle of Man, where a 'dreadful command' had been given by Arran, the details not given.[91]

Somerset's army mobilized at Newcastle. He received a visit from a number of barons and lairds from the Lothians and Berwickshire, led by the Armstrong Laird of Mangerton, who pledged to serve the Protector in return for their lands being saved from devastation.[92] Somerset had apparently issued a statement on September 2nd in which he was not intending to end Scotland's independence but wanted a peaceful conclusion of the marriage treaty negotiated in 1543. Further versions proclaimed that if the Scots would agree to keep Queen Mary in Scotland until she was old enough to decide for herself whether to marry, the English would withdraw from Scotland. These conciliatory messages were not passed to the populace, and instead the Lord Governor and Dunkeld would distribute a story which was more threatening and insulting.[93]

Somerset's army of 10,000 entered Scotland on the 2nd of September, advancing along the coast in sight of the English fleet. Within the ranks were Italian and Spanish mercenaries, experienced at war with the latest military tactics and innovations.[94] Arran quickly mobilized an army at Edinburgh.[95] The English army stopped when they reached the 'Peath', a deep ravine six miles in length. The banks were so steep that a crossing would have to be done by following paths that sloped. It would have been here that the Scots could have hindered the advance of the English. Another opportunity to obstruct the advance was lost when the army managed to cross the Tyne by a narrow bridge, whilst wagons and carriages forded the river. The only opposition met was by Dandy Kerr and a small squadron of horse. This absence of resistance was attributed to the fact that the lands that Somerset had passed through belonged to the forty Berwickshire and Lothian barons serving him.[96]

On the 8th of September 1547, at Monkton Hill, Arran introduced a statute in which descendants and heirs of anybody killed in battle with the English would receive special privileges and exemptions.[97] As the armies advanced towards each other, on the 9th there was a skirmish between Scots and English horse, where the latter led by Lord Hume came off worse. Severely wounded, he would later die in Edinburgh castle, whilst his son, the future Lord Home, was captured. The English managed to take possession of the Castle of Hume.[98] Arran assembled his army on the north side of the Esk, near Musselburgh, whilst Somerset occupied the crest of the sloping hill on the south side of the Esk. The English army was in a dangerous position and could not engage the Scots, who were in a strong defensive array. Not being able to engage, the option of withdrawing was also dangerous. They could not wait indefinitely due to lack of provisions, so the advantage was with the Scots, who only had to wait.[99] The English also had a fleet of ships shadowing the army, and two galleys were sent close to shore where their cannon could do the most damage against the flanks of the Scottish army.

On September 10th was fought the Battle of Pinkie. Somerset had learned that the Scots were going to hold their defensive position and wait for the English to attack or retreat. He decided to reposition his army so that the higher ground of the hill of Inveresk could be commanded; from here ordinance could be placed and shots fired into the Scottish camp. Somerset could then hope to dislodge the Scots.[100] Believing the English were preparing to retreat, Arran had the trumpets blown and ordered an advance against the English. The Scots advanced in three divisions across the river, the first made up of pikemen led by Angus, the second by Huntley and the third by Arran. There was also a division led by Argyll.[101] Angus and Sir George Douglas were on horseback directing their infantry. They went at a slow pace, with Angus intending to give the English the opportunity to withdraw; thereby the Scots would have the advantage in attacking the rear. They possibly did not appreciate that the English were moving to take a heightened position in order to bombard the Scots. Arran wanted an immediate attack and sent a message ordering Angus to speed up, which he disregarded. Arran sent another command threatening treason, and this time Angus obeyed.[102]

Somerset, observing the advance of the Scots, prepared to engage and repositioned the artillery and the divisions. As the vanguard of Angus's pikemen climbed the hill they drove back horse and foot led by Lord Grey, and then was assaulted with Somerset's cannon positioned on hilltops. The cannon from the ships fired into the ranks of Arran and Huntley, and whilst Angus would have expected these two divisions to advance and relieve the pressure on his own division, they either withdrew from the north, away from the cannon fire, or held back. Knox accused both Arran and Huntley of holding back because Angus's division was filled with 'professors of the Evangel', and decided that both Scottish and English Protestants should fight it out. Although this sounds like post-reformation propaganda, it is clear that the destruction caused by the galley guns disrupted the capacity of the Scots to retain their structure.

Confusion spread throughout the ranks.[103] Angus attempted to maneuver his division away from the cannon, while at the same time his pikemen were assaulted by the fire of the harquebusiers of the foreign troops, some of them mounted, such as the Spanish mercenaries led by the famous Pedro de Gamba. Others on foot advanced forward and fired into the vanguard. This movement of Angus's, allied to the retreat of Highlanders from the north, gave the impression that the Scots were retreating, and this caused mass panic. The army began to disintegrate. The English, elated and encouraged, gave chase. For five hours they pursued with 'great fury, slaying cruelly great numbers', reportedly 15,000. The victors believed that this battle, won by 'the grace of God alone', now gave them 'the whole of Scotland by the hollow of their hand'.[104]

Angus and Sir George, on horseback, managed to escape. The former would arrive at Stirling and blame Arran and Huntley for their failure to support his division. After reporting his version of events he would return to his castle of Tantallon whilst Sir George went to Dalkeith. Godscroft says that the Queen Mother was not unhappy with the discomfort of Arran as it weakened the power of the Hamiltons. This view of the Queen Mother sounds unlikely, for there was nothing positive for her or Scotland in this defeat. The Hamiltons may have been humbled but they were needed to help raise fresh forces, and Arran and his brother would show great energy in the next few months as they tried to turn the situation away from a total defeat.[105]

The defence of Scotland also had to be reassessed, and the Queen Mother would push for stronger French involvement. This would suit her political aims and was also practical and pragmatic. The English had large resources in manpower and money to call upon, from home and abroad, and especially from the Empire. They were also adapting the latest European technological and military breakthroughs to their campaign, including the latest architectural innovations in castle and fortress designs. To match them the Scots needed French manpower, knowledge and money, and the Queen Mother would negotiate to bring this about.

From Pinkie to Edinburgh the land was strewn with dead Scots.[106] The English were recalled and gathered at Edmondstone Edge, where a great roar chilled the hearts of the citizens of Edinburgh as the victors celebrated . The English, having collected the spoils of the battlefield and stripped the dead of armour and weapons, marched towards Leith, where they encamped. The horsemen entered the town, whilst footmen remained outside. During that time the army did not stray too far from the camp.[107] The Earl of Bothwell arrived at the camp and gave his submission.[108] Bothwell had been detained prior to Pinkie because of treasonous correspondence with England. He was released after the battle. The followed year, September 3rd 1548, he would renounce allegiance to Scotland and adhere to England.[109]

The Earl of Huntley had been captured, along with other nobles and gentry. He would be taken to England. Amongst the dead were the Lords Cathcart, Elphinstone, Fleming, the Masters of Buchan, Livingstone, Methven, Ogilvy, Erskine, Graham and Ross, the chief of the MacFarlanes and Gordon of Lochivar. The bodies were gathered up by the people of the surrounding villages and placed in lime pits. The government paid twenty-two shillings to two men to get carts and bury the dead within two days. In England it was celebrated as a fantastic victory, and in London huge bonfires were lit in celebration.[110]

Around the same period and as a diversion to the march of Somerset, the Earls of Lennox and Wharton, with 5,000 men, went up the Western March. They took Castlemilk, and wasted the country including Annandale. At the Church in Annan, an officer called Lyon, with the Master of Maxwell and Lairds of Johnston and Cockpool, made a desperate defence until the besiegers allowed them to honourably withdraw. The church at Annan was then blown up with gunpowder.[111] Throughout Annandale the borderers offered their allegiance to the English crown. It was also reported that 'secret articles' were signed by the usual suspects such as Angus, Glencairn, Cassilis, the Lords Maxwell, Boyd, Gray, Cranston, and Sir George Douglas, although in context we should conclude that some or many did so to protect their lands. Whilst English power overcame the Scots in this campaign there was great anger at the methods used to promote a marriage.[112] The Earl of Huntley, when asked by Somerset why he opposed the union, replied that he had 'no objection to the match, but to the manner of wooing', which gave the war the term the 'rough wooing'.[113] But there was also anger at Arran, and on one occasion in Edinburgh he was chased into a church by widowed women armed with stones. As Lord Governor he was chief figurehead for blame.

There were other allegations regarding causes for the defeat, which reached the ears of the Queen-Dowager of Hungary. According to the Imperial Ambassador in London, as early as September 19th it was reported that Sir George Douglas had provided assistance to the English army.[114] It is difficult to prove this allegation; however the slow pace of Angus's advance at Pinkie, where Arran had to order him to speed up under threat of treason, may be down to the Scots offering to give the English an opportunity to withdraw, making it easier to attack them. And perhaps this is what Sir George advised, since he was with Angus in the vanguard. This plan seems to have backfired, because it allowed the English, who were marching to Inveresk Hill, the necessary time to prepare their forces against the Scots. So Sir George Douglas may not have been intentionally helping the English, but if it had been his advice to advance at a slow pace then this could have assisted the English.

After Pinkie, Somerset had an opportunity to use his military advantage to push for favourable terms with the defeated. Yet he made no attempt to occupy Leith or Edinburgh or advance to Stirling, held by the Queen Mother. This stronghold was where Arran and a number of nobles had fled to. It is believed that Somerset was concerned with intrigues made against him in the council back in England, and instead of attempting to gain from the Scots he only stayed until September 18th before marching back to England. It was reported that Arran did make an attempt to treat with Somerset but received the reply that he would not do so without consent from the Emperor, as the Empire was still at war with Scotland.[115]

However Arran was possibly also playing for time until Queen Mary was moved from Stirling to Inchmahome under the guardianship of Lord Erskine and Lord Livingston. Whilst Somerset had dangerous enemies in England who were plotting against him, Lesley believes that Somerset withdrew because the Queen Mother had proclamations sent across the country to raise another army. As Somerset had not been able to capture Edinburgh, and bringing in supplies to a vast army would have been a hazard,[116] he decided on a strategy of occupying captured strongholds and erecting fortifications.

Upon withdrawing, Leith was plundered and set on fire, and the fleet burned Kinghorn and several villages along the Fife coast. A garrison was placed on the isle of Inch Colm, where the vacant monastery was fortified. The fleet captured the castle at Broughty Craig on the mouth of the

Tay.[117] The English ships bombarded the castle until they gained entrance due to the compliance of Patrick, the 4th Lord Gray. English troops under Dudley occupied the castle, strengthening the defences.[118] Requesting the use of artillery from Stirling Castle, Arran led a force to lay siege to Broughty Craig, an effort that failed, leading to the death of Gavin Hamilton and the desertion of the ordinance. The English constructed a fort on a nearby hill overlooking nearby Dundee, which became a base for raids across the surrounding area and for bombarding Dundee with artillery.[119] Arran visited Dundee, where he made arrangements with burgesses for raising funds for defence.[120]

Returning to Stirling, Arran called a meeting of nobles and prelates. The clergy anticipated that a war tax would have to be raised to contribute to the retaking of places captured by the English. To harass the garrison of Broughty Craig, the Burgh of Dundee and the prelates were to fund 100 harquebusiers and 100 pikemen. The barons and gentry in the sheriffdoms of Perth, Forfar and Kincardin were responsible for funding 100 horsemen, led by Master James Halliburton. The Abbot of Inch Colm agreed to pay £500 to Arran to pay for soldiers to help in the recovery of the abbey. Instructions were sent to the holders of Hailes, Dunbar and Edinburgh castle not to surrender to English forces or to suspect Scots, with an obligation that Arran would provide troops for the castle's relief if the English attempted to lay siege.[121] Another attempt was made on Broughty Craig when Argyll arrived with a few thousand of his men, including a regiment of 150 professional soldiers, paid the immense wage of £300 by the government.[122] However the

Scots were beaten off during an attack. Despite this the ships off the coast had no water, and within the castle munitions were low.[123]

Somerset marched through the Merse and Teviotdale, receiving submissions from the chief men and the surrender of strongholds. The Lairds of Cessford, Ferniehurst, Ormiston, Mellerstrain and others submitted.[124] Scott of Buccleuch had apparently been granted a license from Arran and the Queen to enter into assurances with the English so as to protect his lands, property and adherents. Part of the agreement was at an opportune time as Buccleuch was to renounce assurances with English and fight for the Queen, and it is likely that other Scots made similar licences under these conditions.[125]

Roxburgh was taken, repaired and garrisoned, with Somerset showing his work ethic by picking up a spade to dig. It was later learned that before Somerset left for England there had been some negotiations, where Arran asked for safe conduct to be granted for deputies to go to Newcastle and negotiate. This the protector granted before withdrawing. Once the army withdrew, Arran decided not to send the deputies, content no doubt in having Somerset out the country.[126] With Somerset in England, another council meeting was called at Stirling by Arran. It was decided that another army should be raised and a request made for fresh aid from France. The French ambassador D'Osell suggested with the compliance of the Queen Mother that the young Queen should be sent to France and an offer made to marry her to the Dauphin. Arran was reluctant, as he had hoped that his own son would become the husband of Queen Mary. However he would prove himself open to negotiations in respect of France winning his support for the betrothal. D'Osell would leave Scotland for France on November 16th, to negotiate with Henry of France. Queen Mary was moved to Dumbarton Castle.[127]

Despite the disastrous military setbacks in Scotland, in Flanders there were complaints that Mary of Guise, Arran and the Council members had been benefiting financially from the piracy against imperial subjects. There were obvious difficulties in recovering goods or getting compensation through the Scottish courts, and there had been sales in Scotland and sequestrations, and possibly the monies had been used in the latest wars.[128] From the English side Somerset was asking the Emperor to compel the people of Flanders, Holland and the Low Countries to continue to wage war against the Scots. However the conflict had so far resulted in losses for his subjects through piracy and loss of trade and for economic reasons there was hope that peace could be negotiated between the two sides.[129]

The Scottish envoy Adam Paniter approached the Imperial representative, St Mauris, in Paris during November with regard to a possible treaty between the Scots and the Emperor, without taking into consideration the opinions of the English. St Mauris stated that the Scots had not made good on claims for restitution due to piracy, so it was difficult for the Emperor to negotiate under these conditions. Paniter replied that restitution was reliant on proof of misdeeds. He also alleged that Scots who had become naturalized English, and French pirates, were also responsible for piracy and were blaming the Scots. The Scottish ambassador reminded St Mauris that Scotland and the Low Countries had been valued friends and partners until the Emperor sided with the King of England. He also made it plain that the people of Scotland were 'burning to avenge the ignominy they had suffered', and 'even if deserted and abandoned by all the world', they would still fight.[130]

The imperial representative in London however was concerned about the nature of possible peace negotiations between Scotland and England, where the Emperor's demands for reparations for Scottish piracy against his subjects may be sidelined so that England could gain control of its northern neighbour. Such a deal would not balance out the fact that the Empire entered the war against Scotland at Henry VIII's request with heavy economic losses. The Protector, whilst stating that no treaty would be agreed with the Scots without agreement from the Emperor, also revealed that the peace negotiations instigated by Arran appeared to have been temporizing, as he had in his possession a document sent to the Scots ambassador in France with instructions to demand from the French King men, munitions and money. He had also been informed that France was sending a commander called Chapelle to Scotland with captains specializing in engineering and fortifications. Foreign professionals were more used in the wars between Scotland and England as both sides sought to catch up with modern developments in war technology, and the English warned that the French were preparing major interventions in Scotland. Several Italian and French captains had been sent to instruct Scots in fortifications and in demolishing castles.[131] An Italian, Captain Ubaldino, would be sent to Scotland by the French King to instruct

Scots on skills in fortifications and demolishing castles, and he was granted access to all fortresses. Merriman gave a detailed account of the work that Ubaldino did in adding defensive spurs to Edinburgh and Stirling Castles, whilst adding continental modifications to Dunbar Castle on the east coast, which made it a formidable tormentor of the English occupied zones. Pietro Strozzi, who led Italian mercenaries to Scotland, would also introduce continental innovations to the reconstruction of Leith. During Ubaldini's time in Scotland the Queen Mother would keep up frequent correspondence regarding his activities, as well as learning the importance of fortifications.[132]

On December 12th Lennox led another raid up the West March. Angus and William Cunningham, Earl of Glencairn, had promised 2,000 horse and companies of foot if he would ride to meet them in Scotland. He travelled to Dumfries and found that only 300 men were waiting to join him. John, the Master of Maxwell, some gentlemen of Nithsdale and Glencairn were at Dumfries to negotiate with Lennox. Glencairn handed Lennox two letters from James Douglas of Drumlanrig which offered to assist Lennox in his enterprise, but only if he brought Scotsmen. If he brought Englishmen he would raise the country against him. He believed that a trap was being set for him whereby he was to be delivered to the Queen Mother and Arran.[133]

Lennox instead ordered them detained. He then sent 600 horsemen under the command of Wharton's son Henry northward on a midnight raid in order to lure out James Douglas, Laird of Drumlanrig. They burned and looted his lands. Drumlanrig held back until the following day as they were withdrawing with a large number of livestock and goods, then he attacked the invaders, driving them across the river Nith. They recovered and counter-attacked as Drumlanrig was fording the river and after a hard encounter succeeded in routing his company. Afterwards many of the people of Galloway offered assurances to the English. It is not clear what happened to the Master of Maxwell, but it seems he entered into an assurance with the English warden Wharton and offered up pledges.[134] The fate of Glencairn is not known, although he would die in March 1548, to be succeeded by his son Alexander as fourth Earl of Glencairn.

Seigneur de la Chapelle arrived in Scotland with his company and assured Mary of Guise and Arran that the French King was prepared to offer significant amounts of men and money.[135] He also brought to Arran an offer from the King of France that in return for supporting the marriage between Queen Mary and the Dauphin he would receive the French dukedom of Chatelherault. This would be worth £5,000, and as an added incentive his son could marry a Frenchwomen of high nobility.[136] Chapelle joined the siege of Broughty Craig, where the principle Scottish commander, Argyll, had secretly entered into an assurance with the English commander, Dudley.[137]

Chapelle and Argyll advanced towards Dundee, and Gray abandoned the town. A sea captain sent to parley with Argyll managed to use the opportunity to slip into Dundee, taking the artillery back to Broughty Craig. Argyll gave proclamation that all burgesses in Dundee should stay indoors under threat of the gallows. They did so, under condition that they were pardoned for previous acts in support of the English. There was a fight outside Broughty

Craig in which the assured Scots and English forced Argyll and Chapelle's men to withdraw.[138] However Tytler accused Argyll of receiving a bribe of 1,000 crowns. Lord Grey would produce a receipt for the Lord Protector as proof of this alleged payment. Argyll would withdraw his men on 5th February.[139]

References: (1) (Dowden, John, 1912, 'The Bishops of Scotland, pp.88-89). (2) (Belleshiem, vol.11, 'The History of the Catholic Church of Scotland', pp.169-170). (3) (Walsh, James, 1874, 'The History of the Catholic Church of Scotland', pp. 263-264). (4) (Knox, pp.56-59). (5) (Knox, pp.59-60). (6) (RPCS, January 19th 1546, p.20). (7) (RPCS, January 23rd, 1546, pp.20-21). (8) (Thomson, p. 70). (9) (Thomson, p. 70). (10) (Thomson, pp.71-72). (11) (Calderwood, pp.220-221. Knox, p.66. Melville, pp.19-20). (12) (Grub, George, 1861, 'Ecclesiastical History of Scotland, pp.28-29. Melville, pp.19-20). (13) (CSP, Spain, March 1546, 11-20). (15) (CSP, Spain, St Mauris to Cobos, April 1st - April 6th, 1546). (16) (CSPS, Prince Philip to Emperor, 9th May, 1546). (17) (LP, preface, January-August 1546). (18) (RPCS, May 23rd, 1546, p.23). (19) (Calderwood, pp. 221-222). (20) (Thomson, pp.71-74). (21) (Calderwood, 221-222). (22) (Hume-Brown, pp.20-21), (23) (Lesley, p. 193. Merriman, p.213). (24) (Herkless & Hannay, pp.30-31). (25) (RPCS. June 5th, 1546 (47). RPCS, June 11th, 1546, (52). Tytler, Mary, pp.3-4). (26) (Maclean-Bristol, pp.116-122. Roberts, p.9. Tytler, pp.336-338). (27) (RSP, July 4th, 1546) (28) (RSP, July 14th, 1546). (29) (RSP, August 14th, 1546). (29) (RSP, August 14th, 1546). (31) (RPS, 25th July 1546). (32) (RPS, August 14th, 1546). (33) (Thomson, p.74). (34) (Calderwood, p.224-225. Melville, pp.19-20), (35) (Thomson, p.74). (36) (RPCS, Dec 13th, 1546, (106)). (37) (RPCS, 1546, p.55). (38) (ALHTS, vol.8, pp.lxxx-lxxxi, pp.460-471. Hume-Brown, p.20). (39) (Tytler, Mary. pp.5-7). (40) (Merriman, p.216, Tytler, pp.6-7). (41) (ODNB, vol.24, pp. 833-835. Tytler, pp.6-7. Walsh, p.270-271). (42) (Herkless & Hannay, pp.33-34). (43) (Merriman, p.216). (44) (ALHTS, vol.8, pp.lxxxi-lxxxii. Calderwood, pp.225-226). (45) (Lesley, p.192-193). (46)

(ALHTS, vol.9, pp. xiv-xix. ODNB, vol.24, pp.827-833). (47) (CSP, Spain, Queen Dowager to Van der Delft, Sept 14th, 1546/ Merriman, pp. 195-205, pp.218-221). (48) (Herkless & Hannay, pp.33-34. SP, Spain, Queen Dowager to the Emperor, 25th Sept, 1546). (49) (CSP, Spain, Van der Delft to Queen Dowager, Oct 7th, 1546). (50) (CSP, Spain, Emperor to Prince Philip, Oct 14th, 1546). (51) (ALHTS, vol.9, pp. xvi-xix. Tytler, p.7). (52) (RPCS, 1546, 106,107). (53) (Hume-Brown, pp.21). (54) (Thomson, pp.71-78). (55) (CSP, Spain, Van der Delft to Emperor, Jan 23rd, 1547). (56) (St Mauris to King of the Romans, Jan?, 1547). (57) (St Mauris to the King of the Romans, Feb 15th, 1547). (58) (CSP, St Mauris to King of Romans, Feb?, 1547). (59) (SCML, Mary Queen of Scotland, Jan 15th, 1547). (60) (SCML, Mary Queen of Scotland, May 11th, 1547). (61) (CSP, Spain, Feb, 1547). (62) (CSP, Spain, April 18th, 1547). (63) (Walsh, p.271). (64) (Tytler, pp. 11-12). (65) (CSP, Calais Papers: April 1547', 1547-1553, pp. 323-337). (66) (Tytler, pp.8-10). (67) (Herkless & Hannay, pp.34-35). (68) (Tytler, pp.10-11). (69) (Herkless, pp.35-36). (70) (Keith, p.127. Luckock, pp.124-125. ODNB, vol.24, pp.833-835). (71) (RPCS, March 17th, 1547, 110). (72) (RPCS, March 17th, 1547, 111), (73) (RPCS, March 19th, 1547, 117). (74) (RPCS, March 19th, 1547, 118). (75) (RPCS, March 28th, 1547, 124). (76) (RPCS, July 24th, 1547, 135). (77) (RPCS, May 3rd, 1547, 129). (78) (RPCS, May 3rd, 1547, 130). (79) (RPCS, May 20th, 1547, 131. (80) (CSP, Spain, Van der Delft to Emperor, June 16th, 1547). (81) (Merriman, pp.218-221. CSP, Spain, Van der Delft to Emperor, 17th June, 1547). (82) (CSP, Spain, Van de Delft to Emperor, 29th May, 1547). (83) (CSP, Spain, St Mauris to Prince Philip, 29th June, 1547). (84) (ALHTS, vol.9, pp. xvi-xix. Lesley, pp.193-194. Tytler, pp.12-13. Van der Delft to Emperor, 24th July, 1547). (85) (Thomson, pp.75-77). (86) (CSP, Spain, St Mauris to Prince Philip, 15th August, 1547). (87) (Tytler, pp.14-15). (88) (CSP, Spain, St Mauris to Prince Philip, 10th Aug, 1547). (89) (Thomson, pp.76-77). (90) (CSP, Spain, Van der Delft to Prince Philip, 18th Aug, 1547). (91) (CSP, Spain, Sept 1st, 1547). (92) (Tytler, pp.20-22). (93) (Herkless & Hannay, pp.38-39). (94) (Scott, pp.415-416). (95) (Knox, p.83-84). (96) (Tytler, pp.20-23). (97) (ERS, Exchequer rolls of Scotland, 1513-1556). (98) (Knox, pp.84, Patterson, pp.193-194). (99)

(Calderwood, pp. 246-247, Scott, pp.416-417). (100) (Holinshed, pp.550-551. Tytler, pp.26-27). (101) (Knox, pp.85. Tytler, pp.26-27). (102) (Calderwood, p.247. Hume, pp.119-123) (103) (Knox, pp. 85-87). (104) (CSPS, Van der Delft to the Queen Dowager, 19th Sept, 1547. Lesley, pp.198-199, Paterson, pp.196-197). (105) (Hume, pp.119-123). (106) (Scott, pp.416-417). (107) (Lesley, pp. 199-200). (108) (Tytler, p.34). (109) (SP, vol2, pp.157-163). (110) (ALHTS, vol.9, pp. xxi-xxii. Paterson, pp.198-199). (111) (Tytler, pp.34-36). (112) (Tytler, pp.37-39). (113) (Thomson, p.85). (114) (CSP, Spain, Van der Delft to the Queen-Dowager, September 19th, 1547). (115) (CSP, Spain, Van der Delft to Queen Dowager, Sept 22nd, 1547). (116) (Lesley, pp.200-201, Tytler, pp.36-37). (117) Thomson, pp.80-87). (118) (Lesley, pp.200-202, Tytler, pp.34-35). (119) (Knox, pp. 87-88). (120) (SCML, 31st Dec, 1547, CXLIX). (121) (RPCS, vol 1, 140. Lesley, pp.90-92). (122) (ALHTS, vol.9, pp. xxv-xxvi. CSPF, Grey to Somerset, Nov 21st, 1547). (123) (CSPF, Sir Andrew Dudley to Earl of Warwick, Nov 30th, 1547). (124) (Tytler pp. 35-36). (125) (Hume, History of the House of Douglas). (126) (CSPS, Van der Delft to Emperor, 18th.CSPS, Van der Delft to Prince Philip, 21st Oct, 1547). (127) (Merriman, pp. 300-301, Thomson, pp. 80-87). (128) (CP, Spain, Flemish council to Van der Delft, Nov 3rd, 1547). (129) (Lesley, pp.201-202). (130) (CSP, Spain, St Mauris to Queen Dowager of Hungary, Nov? 1547). (131) (CSPS, Van der Delft to the Emperor's Council, Dec 12th, 1547. CSPS, St Mauris to Queen Dowager, Dec 15th, 1547). (132) (CSPS, A Patent in Latin, Feb 5th 1548 Merriman, pp.320-330). (133) (Holinshed, pp.553-554). (134) (Calderwood, pp.250-252. Holinshed, pp, 554-555). (135) (CSPS, Flemish Council of State, Jan 22nd, 1548). (136) (Merriman, pp.300-301). (137) (CSPF, Grey to Somerset, Feb, 9th, 1548). (138) (CSP, Spain, Van der Delft to Emperor, Feb 23rd, 1548). (Tytler, pp.38-40).

Chapter Six

The Frenchman's grave

During February 1548, Lords Wharton and Lennox were preparing for another invasion of Scotland by the West March, with the aim of targeting the lands of Douglas of Drumlanrig and the other Scots not assured to England. They were expecting to join up with John, Master of Maxwell and Angus. He had 700 horse, not including the 500 assured Scots, and 4,000 foot. Wharton however had been set up. Maxwell had offered to help Lennox to invade Scotland along with Wharton. Upon hearing this Arran offered his rich ward the Herries heiress in return for Maxwell changing sides. This bid was successful and Maxwell with his assured Scots would join Wharton and await an opportunity to turn on the English Warden.[1] Angus was said to have sent letters to both Wharton and Lennox, reiterating his support for the 'godly cause' and asking that Wharton should not attack the lands he had targeted as the people were loyal. He wrote to Lennox 'as a father to a son'.[2] Despite this Angus was expected to join the invasion.

Wharton marched through Nithsdale in two bodies, his son Henry commanding the horse along with John Maxwell, whilst he and Lennox commanded the foot. He came into sight of Angus and his forces, which then apparently turned around and advanced away from Wharton. Enraged, Wharton set out to devastate the country. He divided his forces, with his son galloping forward with the horse and burning and wasting around Durrisdeer. Lord Wharton's foot pursued Angus to Drumlanrig, and here Angus and the Laird of Drumlanrig attacked Wharton, forcing him to hurriedly ride away. Both the Laird of Drumlanrig with his horse and Angus, now joined with a fresh contingent of foot, made their way to Durrisdeer to engage the son of the Warden. As Henry Wharton's troops were firing the town Angus and Drumlanrig advanced on them. At a given signal Maxwell lifted a black flag on a spear and the assured Scots turned on the English, who, assailed from within their own ranks, were overcome and routed. The Scottish horse and foot then made after the foot of the Lord Wharton and caught them near Dalwilston. Whilst Lennox fled on horse the Warden stayed to fight. The English were in danger of suffering serious losses when suddenly the Scots were attacked by a body of English horse, who having fled the fighting at Durrisdeer, regrouped and rode in to assist the Warden. The Scots were taken by surprise and scattered, and 400 were said to have lost their lives in the fighting, and by drowning in the Nith.[3] Wharton managed to escape to Dumfries and then to Carlisle. Maxwell and his friends had provided pledges to ensure loyalty, and Wharton intended to hang 14 of these hostages. He tempered this punishment due to protests from Scottish allies, and hanged three instead. Soon after this engagement Maxwell would recapture Dumfries.[4]

Along the Eastern March Lord Grey of Wilton led a force of 1,000 horsemen from Berwick to Haddington, the force including the lairds of Ormiston and Brunstane. Buccleuch shadowed the force, which he put at the improbable number of 10,000. He believed that Grey was going to attack those Scots not assured to England, and Buccleuch's plan was to wait for an opportunity to ambush him. However news of Wharton's defeat caused Grey to quickly withdraw back to Berwick.[5] Arran assembled an army and advanced to retake and raze the strongholds of Saltoun, Ormiston and Brunstane, belonging to several of the important assured Scots. When one garrison held out against him Arran had them all hanged.[6] The demolishing of the Houses of Ormiston and Brunstane may have been sweet retribution, as during January both had offered to capture the Lord Governor and Dunkeld whilst they were in Edinburgh.[7]

On the Continent the Emperor learned with some accuracy that Lord Wharton had been defeated by the Earl of Angus on the Western March, with assured Scots changing sides during the battle The report of the battle became distorted when it reached the French King and council, where they were informed that Arran had defeated an army of 9-10,000 led by Lennox, in which 3,000 had been captured and slain.[8] Whilst such Scottish victories were celebrated by the French nobility, the wars were not popular with the French people, and especially in Brittany where there was anger amongst the commoners because of the oppressive levies that the French king was enacting to fight wars in Scotland. Popular opinion was for better relations with the English.[9] One obstacle to better relations was the English occupation of Boulogne, which was a humiliation to the French. The French King offered to give the English 400,000 crowns in return for Boulogne and the surrender of French occupied Scottish places.[10]

The mercenaries, such as the Spanish, were frequently employed by the English, especially in garrison duty, yet there were complaints with respect to the rate of pay.[11] It appears that the Spanish garrison at Hume Castle was instigated by Mary of Guise to rebel and hand the castle to the Scots, although the attempt failed.[12] Lord Hume and his son had contracted to hand over the castle to the Queen Mother, Governor and the French, until hostilities ceased. His own resources had been spent during the constant raiding and wasting of his lands.[13]

On his return to Berwick, Lord Grey asked Sir George Douglas to meet him. Douglas sent a messenger to Grey stating that he could not visit him as Arran was intending to lay siege to his castle of Dalkeith, although there is no evidence that he was intending this.[14] It is clear that Douglas was still playing all sides against each other, and Lord Grey would learn that he was intriguing with the French and had handed over a son as hostage.

Grey would return to Scotland and occupy Haddington on the 18th of April, 1548, which was then fortified. The new English fort at Haddington was quadrilateral, protected by deep trenches, a wall of turf, ramparts and breastworks.

Bastions were constructed at each corner, defended by artillery and javelins, with protected openings from which harquebusiers could fire from. Behind the walls there were more trenches and protective turrets and curtains covering the dungeon. It was a continental design and one reason why the Scots needed French engineering skills to help overcome such structures. Once the fortifications at Haddingdon and Lauder were completed he laid waste to the surrounding districts of Musselburgh and Dalkeith. Lord Grey sent a force to Dalkeith; Sir George was at the village with 25-30 men and made an effort to defend it, but they were quickly overcome and slain. Sir George escaped with a servant and Dalkeith was then captured.[15]

Angus, who was in Dalkeith Castle, also escaped, but Sir George's son James, the future Earl of Morton, was wounded in the leg and captured. Apparently prior to this engagement Sir George Douglas forwarded to Lord Grey a plan in which he offered to guide 6,000 men through Scotland to where Mary of Guise was residing so that she could be captured. The Lord Protector told Grey to ignore the plan as it was possibly an attempt to lure the English into a trap. He advised Grey to stay in friendly contact with Sir George Douglas until there was an opportunity to deal with his duplicity. Through contact with Lennox, Douglas asked Lord Grey for favourable treatment of his captives. Lord Grey left a garrison of 2,000 foot and 500 horse at Haddington and travelled to Berwick.[16]

Sir George Douglas was later reported at Elphison with the Queen Mother, the Governor, Dunkeld and several French representatives, so he was correct in implying to Grey that he could get close to the Queen Mother, although it could also mean he was acting as an agent for the Scottish government. There was a call to all assured Scots to return to allegiance to the Queen and Governor, with the offer of full restitution and full pardons. Sir George Douglas, with his vast intelligence network in southern Scotland, would be the perfect man to act as go-between in such offers, and considering his past treachery, he would also be an example to the assured Scots of the government's commitment to forgive. The success of this offer is reflected in the fact that assured Scots between Berwick and Edinburgh had reportedly received victuals from the French, and that the Laird of Buccleuch, Dandy Kerr, the lairds of Melstane and Blacula and some of the Humes were receiving French wages and supporting French garrisons on their lands.[17]

The Governor was anxious about the future prospects of his son, and whilst his son was a more unlikely prospect for marrying the Queen Mary, he was loath to let her leave the country. The Queen Mother was opposed to the marriage and according to the Earl of Huntley she had put her opposition into words in a letter, and also asked the Gordons to help her to escape to France. Huntley had agreed to help the Queen Mother to negotiate her daughter's marriage to a French noble, in return for the French King paying off his ransom to the English, granting a pension, and for him gaining the Earldoms of Orkney, Ross and Moray. Huntley painted a picture of a Queen Mother in fear of her safety and desperate to flee Scotland. The Governor decided to enter into negotiations with England, and surprisingly used Huntley as mediator. Huntley agreed and used the occasion to inform Lord Grey of the politics swirling around the issue of the marriage.

The Governor was being placed under pressure from France and was looking for alternative deals with England. The King of France was demanding that in return for French soldiers, money and aid, Arran should hand over his son as hostage, a quite terrible prospect considering his son had just been liberated from the Castilians. The French King also wanted custody of Edinburgh, Dumbarton and Dunbar Castles.[18]

On June 16th 1548 the French fleet entered the Firth of Forth and 6,000 troops, under the command of Andre de Montalembert, Sire D'Esse, with Germans under the command of the Rhinegrave. They disembarked at Leith. The fleet flew the flag of Scotland so that Henry II could claim that the sailing was not done under his permission, since France and England were technically at peace.[19] The French were joined by Arran with 5,000 troops. All the towns and villages from as far as Stirling and Selkirk were to provide corn, and mines were to provide coal, which no doubt piled further hardship on the people.

Dunbar was handed over to the French, but the Scots stayed in command of Edinburgh until their allies could prove how effective they could be against the English, although the French were allowed to fortify Leith. The newcomers almost immediately began to mobilize around Haddington, and an initial skirmish between French and English outside Haddington left fifty French dead. Nevertheless there were fears that the English could find themselves surrounded within the town as the forces of their opponents increased.[20]

At a nearby abbey a parliament was assembled to discuss a treaty of alliance. Here they voted to implement the Treaty of Haddington on July 7th, whereby in return for French assistance against the English, Queen Mary would marry the Dauphin. There were safeguards written into the treaty, whereby the Dauphin and the French would uphold the realm's 'same freedom, liberties and laws as has been by all kings of Scotland in times past'. Knox would claim that the vote was won by bribes, flattery and the presence of French soldiers acting as parliamentary Officers of Arms. He also described Queen Mary as being 'sold' to France, and the French considering themselves 'masters in all parts of Scotland'. It was also agreed that the young Queen would travel to France and be educated there.[21]

Arran would later be offered the title of Duke of Chatelherault, an area in Poitou, which he would be granted on the day Queen Mary reached majority and he resigned as Governor. He would gain not only a dukedom in the French nobility but extensive lands and possessions worth 10,000 livres tournois per annum. He was also gifted a palace in Paris. This ensured that Arran, with his huge wealth and power would be committed to supporting the interests of Queen Mary. His son, who would become known as the Earl of Arran, was to be invited as a guest of the French court, although technically a hostage. There was also a promise that his son would be offered a French marriage. There were reports that Arran, now calling himself Duke of Chatelherault despite not yet confirmed in this title, would also give his other two sons to ensure he continued the war against the English. The Master of Arran would be sent to France during that summer. After the assembly, the Queen Mother had a narrow escape whilst touring the Scottish and French camps outside Haddington during the night of July 9th 1548. A cannon from the town fired towards her, and whilst she escaped physical harm, sixteen of her male attendants were killed, as well as other members of her household being injured and wounded.[22]

Around Haddington, although there were no major battles, the skirmishing was intense as described by the Spanish captain Gambo. In one encounter Spanish mounted harquebusiers alongside border horsemen engaged French horse, which withdrew and lured them into a line of entrenched harquebusiers, which in turn drove away the borderers. Although Gambo claimed that he had eventually gained the upper hand, this type of skirmishing allied with siege warfare developed into a war of attrition which took its toll, physically and psychologically, on the besieged.[23] There were also accounts of atrocities committed by both sides, with Scots buying English prisoners from French so as to kill them. Desertions were also a concern, especially during the siege of Haddington. In one example of measures taken by the Governor against deserters he authorized Archibald Hamilton of Roploch to arrest and punish anyone within the barony of Lesmahagow who failed to attend the muster at Haddington, or left before the period of duty was concluded. Similar acts would have been passed across the country.[24]

The news that Queen Mary was to be sent to France had long compelled England to prepare fresh forces for an invasion. This new Scottish/French alliance must have been degrading to the English powers, for despite all the money and manpower spent on war their aim of a marriage union was to be usurped by the French.[25] After attending the funeral of her attendants killed at Haddington, the Queen

Mother, accompanied by Chatelherault, travelled to Dumbarton to see her daughter arrive from Leith, then set off for France on August 7th. She reached Brittany in two weeks.[26] She sailed in the company of her four attendants of the same age called the Four Maries; Marie Livingston, Marie Seton, Marie Fleming and Marie Beaton, with her guardians Lord Erskine and Livingston, her governor Lady Fleming and her half-brother, Lord James, amongst others. They arrived at Brest on August 13th, having successfully avoided an English fleet out to intercept them.[27]

When King Henry first met Mary he declared her 'the most perfect child he had ever seen'. She was to be housed and educated in the royal châteaux of Blois, Chambord and Fontainebleau and introduced to the art and culture of the Renaissance. She would learn different languages, French, Latin, Italian, Spanish and Greek, and enjoy courtly pursuits such as music, dancing, singing and writing and reciting poetry, as well as outdoor pursuits like horse riding and hunting. Henry would treat her as his own daughter, whilst her Guise uncles saw her as not just as a future monarch of Scotland but also a potential Queen of France. Queen Mary would develop a friendship with François, the Dauphin of France, who was of a similar age. He was the eldest child of Henry and Catherine de Medici. Although François was unhealthy and suffered illnesses great affection grow between the two, and there was an expectation, especially from the Guise family, that they would marry and unite Scotland and France through union.[28]

With Queen Mary safely in France, Henry II sent a messenger to Somerset and the English council announcing that as the father of the Queen's husband he now considered Scotland to be part of his dominions. He instructed the English to stop waging war against the Scots and withdraw from the occupied zones.[28]

During the month of August the siege of Haddington was reinforced. The French daily pounded the English defences with cannon; hardly a house was left undamaged, and several ramparts were taken. The English, whilst defending vigorously, were preparing for fresh assaults. They then apparently experienced a moment of good luck when there were reports that D'Esse and the Governor were in severe disagreement, with the former blaming the latter for having lost 300 French gentlemen. The circumstances of this accusation are not recorded, but it may allude to some costly military decision made by Chatelherault that led to French losses.

The Governor withdrew his Scottish forces, and the French themselves withdrew to a nearby hill. At Berwick, where Lord Grey was stationed, this news compelled him to act quickly and he ordered a force of 2,000 lance led by Sir Robert Bowes, Sir Henry Wharton and Sir Thomas Palmer, and including mounted harquebusiers led by the Spaniard Gambo, to set out and deliver a convoy of ammunition to Haddington. Once they drew close to Haddington the horse continued whilst a strong body of infantry was left to defend a pass. A scouting force of 200 horse was sent forward and met no opposition, gaining entry into Haddington. They then returned to the main body of horse.

The English then spied French cavalry on a nearby hill and set off to engage. They skirmished with the French, who withdrew and lured the English to a position on the other side of the hill, where they were set on by a strong body of infantry. The English lost up to 500 and the rest were driven to Haddingdon. Bowes and Palmer were captured. It is said that the assured Scots in the English party tore off their red crosses and replaced them with white crosses, and English survivors considered this the reason they lost the battle. It was also believed that the French withdrawal from the siege had been a stratagem to lure the English into a trap, with English spies being bribed with French coin to spread false information. The nature of this increasingly unpopular war made it difficult for Sir John Wilford, the commander of Haddington, to get English recruits. Somerset had to hire 3,000 Germans to serve in Scotland, led by Commander Kurt Pennick.[29]

At the beginning of September the Earl of Shrewsbury marched into Scotland with an army of 22,000, including 7,000 horse. Prior to this a number of summonses were sent out across Scotland calling for all available men to muster at Gladsmuir on August 20th, 1548. The siege had been weakened due to men leaving for the harvests, as well as a significant number of desertions. The Governor's reported recent falling-out with the French may have also discouraged many Scots. The magistrates of Stirling, Linlithgow and Edinburgh were called on to seek out and arrest deserters, and ferrymen were ordered not to allow suspected deserters to cross over the waters and return home. The remaining besieging forces withdrew to Edinburgh and positioned itself themselves in such a manner that the English army could not attack the town or successfully engage the Scot-Franco forces. The withdrawal however allowed the town of Haddington to receive provisions and troops.[30]

Dunbar Castle was an important stronghold on the East Coast. Refortified by the Governor during 1544-47, it was handed over to the French command as part of an agreement with the incoming forces, and due to the significance of being able to bring in supplies from the sea. Dunbar was then strengthened through the work of the Italian engineer Umbaldino, and became a major threat to the English occupation by targeting land supply routes to Haddington. Before reaching Haddington Shrewsbury had made an attempt on the castle which failed. He destroyed Dunbar town, and placed 3,000 Germans in Haddington before returning to England. These mercenaries would then be dispersed about the forts and castles under occupation. A fleet of ships in support of the land invasion and under command of Lord Clinton landed on the coast of Fife, and upon making a descent on St Monans was set upon and driven back with heavy losses by a force led by the Laird of Wemyss.[31]

There was no end to the protracted warfare and skirmishing that went on during early October. Chatelherault decided to make an attempt on Jedburgh, which was garrisoned by Spanish troops. Holinshed has D'Esse leading this campaign, although he may have mistook this for a campaign that D'Esse led the following year. Although many of Holinshed's details of the campaign can be confirmed, contemporary reports placed the Governor as commander. The Governor had Walter Kerr, Laird of Ferniehurst, and Mark Kerr, Laird of Cessford, arrested and thrown into Edinburgh Castle. The reason for this would be their links with the English forces and their employment as assured Scots. Sir Walter Scott of Buccleuch, who had also been under assurance from the English, changed sides and joined with Chatelherault. His own clan was feuding with the Kerrs and he may have suggested the arrests as a necessary measure if the Governor was to have success in travelling so far south from Edinburgh.

The army advanced to Jedburgh, and managed to drive off the defenders, who retired to Kelso. Cessford's brother rode to Roxburgh and informed Lord Grey of this attack. In response Lord Grey sent forward a party of light horse who surprised a body of Scots positioned around Ancrum and forced them to disperse into the surrounding woods. The Scots, aware that Lord Grey was following on with a larger force, withdrew to Peebles, where there were calls for more Scots to join them. Lord Grey, with the support of the Kerrs, proceeded to attack those lands belonging to Buccleuch and his adherents, burning Hawick and communities along the Teviot, Borthwick, Slitrig, Ettrick and Yarrow water, and even burning to death the aged dowager Lady Buccleuch in the tower of Catslack. When Grey and his raiders returned across the border, it appears that the Spanish had fully withdrawn from Jedburgh. The Scots returned to Edinburgh.

English captains with German mercenaries, led by Kurt Pennick, attacked Angus's castle of Tantallon, where the occupiers, possessing significant amounts of powder, defended themselves fiercely with cannon and firearms. The English wasted the surrounding areas, and burned a town belonging to Angus called Redsyde. They also burned villages and hamlets around Dunbar. On October 7th a captain from Haddington advanced towards Dalkeith, which Sir George Douglas appeared to have recovered, and burned the town whilst shooting cannon at the castle walls. The captain then apparently marched down the Esk, plundering and burning communities only a few leagues from Edinburgh. Two other raids were recorded coming out of Haddington.[32] The Lord of Borthwick was reportedly shadowing the raiders with a large force of 4,000 foot and 500 horse, yet was not able to stop the destruction, and the town of Borthwick itself was burned.[33]

Whilst the Governor had marched south to Jedburgh,[34] the French billeted inside Edinburgh were antagonizing the locals by reportedly behaving as if Scotland was now a province and possession reliant on French aid and soldiers. There had also been a delay in money crossing from France to pay the wages of the French troops and mercenaries, which was causing the allies to plunder and pillage their hosts. During one argument in which a French soldier tried to take a culverin from an Edinburgh citizen, a scuffle broke out between citizens and soldiers. Two French soldiers were killed and the rest chased down Niddrey road. The Chief Magistrate, Provost and Captain of the Castle, James Hamilton of Stenhouse, intervened, arresting two French soldiers and taking them to jail. Around 60 French came out of D'Esses's lodging and attacked and kill the Provost and over twenty other men, including some town burgesses and two other men called Hamilton. Over thirty Scots were wounded by shot and bullets as the French fired indiscriminately at doors and windows, and at any sign of movement.

The citizens began to organize a force to tackle the French. Chatelherault, having returned from the enterprise at Jedburgh, determined to support the Scots if the French did not submit themselves to justice. The Queen Mother, with the French Ambassador, offered to negotiate between D'Esse and the Governor. They came up with a proposal; that as a form of compensation the French should attempt a feat of arms and capture Haddington. All parties agreed to this.[35]

The French, led by D'Esse, marched out of the city and joined with the forces of the Rhinegrave at Musselburgh. Some of the townspeople locked the gates behind them and began to seek out Frenchmen, and those that were found were killed and their bodies hidden. Whilst this was occurring the French attempted a midnight raid on Haddington, with Scottish helpers successfully slaying the sentries. They advanced to force the gate and enter the town, and were enjoying initial success when premature cries of victory alerted the English. The defenders grabbed weapons and attempted to organize a defence against the raid. A French spy in the employ of the English stopped his compatriots as they passed through the gate and entered a narrow pathway. He fired two cannon positioned to target the gate entrance and killed and wounds over forty with an explosive mix of grapeshot. The French attempted several times to storm the gates but were repulsed as the English organized their cannons and fired more grapeshot into the advancing French, causing hundreds of casualties. The English foot soldiers then managed to push out the French, who retreated to Edinburgh.

Chatelherault was having a late meal when he heard about the assault against Haddington, and perceiving that they had been successful in capturing the town he quickly put on his armour and with as many horse as he could gather he rode to join the fight. A short way from Haddington he saw French and Germans in retreat. He then decided to return to Edinburgh.

The attack and the defeat were treated as a form of penance by the Scots. Chatelherault however was still incensed at the deaths of his Hamilton kin and the Edinburgh burgesses and townspeople by the French, and would refuse to address D'Esse and the Rhinegrave when they arrived at his Edinburgh home after their retreat from Haddington. The next day he would meet with them in council and reprimand both for spoiling and wasting the country they had promised to save. The Governor also promised to make enquiries about the fight between the Scots and French and ensure that those guilty are punished. One of the ringleaders was hanged at the Market Cross. D'Esse and the Rhinegrave, recognising that lack of wages was causing the French and Germans to oppress the Scots, decided to pawn and sell their jewels, chains and plates, and use their own wages to pay their men. Fortunately payment eventually arrived from France.[36]

The war was costly to the French crown, with King Henry sending 200,000 crowns to pay for winter expenses to his French army, and also to pay pensions to those Scots nobles whom he needed to stay loyal. Henry also reportedly borrowed a million in gold from merchants, on which he had to pay interest of 16 per cent. The King also had Chatelherault's eldest son as a type of hostage, although he was a member of the court, well educated, and was assigned a lucrative 10,000 francs a year post at Guyenne, leading a troop of Scots Guards. The Governor's other son David was also invited to France. Whilst Chatelherault had some distrust of the French, and the death of his kinsman Hamilton of Stenhouse could have led to a serious split between Scots and French, the fact that the King of France had promised the dukedom of Chatelherault, as well as holding his son, although comfortably, ensured that he kept 'firm in his own devotion, and willing to foster it amongst the other Scottish lords'.

Adam Paniter was well rewarded by Henry for his part in the marriage negotiations involving Queen Mary and the Dauphin of France, and especially the role he had played in winning support amongst the Scots nobility, pensions and bribery being the language of his diplomacy. Amongst the chief powers it was accepted that the Dauphin would become King of Scotland and his father Protector of Scotland. The young Queen was well received in France wherever she travelled, and King Henry by all reports was fond of her and proud to call her his daughter.[37]

Sporadic warfare still provided winter sport for the warriors on all sides. As an indicator of the Queen Mother's diplomacy and conciliatory skills, in December 1548 the Protestant Earl of Cassilis and former ally of England was made Lieutenant of the South in the name of the Queen and Governor, with the French King paying for the upkeep of companies of light horse. Cassilis's role was to harass the garrisons of Haddington, Hume, Lauder, Dunglas, Roxburgh and others, whilst disrupting and blocking the supply lines and routes to and from these places. On December 3rd the Earl of Angus and the Rhinegrave with 50 lances and 200 light horse engaged in fierce skirmishing outside Broughty Craig, with the English gaining the upper hand. Hume Castle was taken by the Scots in a night assault on December 26th 1548. In retaliation the English burned the town and surrounding districts, and there is an opinion that this was counter-productive and angered the assured Scots. A request was made to the Protector to grant further assurances so as to stop these Scots from turning against the English. The Protector considered circulating a document across Scotland, where he invited all Scots having lands within the English-occupied districts to return to those lands and possessions, and to enjoy English protection if they recognised English authority. The Protector acknowledged in a private interview with the secretary of the Imperial Ambassador that the lands under occupation were wasted and spoiled, with the Scots launching continuous raids. Food and supplies were being brought in from outside, and the Protector believed he needed loyal Scots to remain within the occupied areas and assist in bringing in provisions. The Protector however, after consideration, did not mass circulate the document.[38]

There were reports that a campaign was about to begin, as the French were fortifying Musselburgh Church and lords and nobles were assembling in Edinburgh. Ships were also being made ready. Further reports stated that French troops had landed in the west with more money to tempt the assured Scots away from loyalty to England. This tactic worked with Kerr of Cessford and Kerr of Ferniehurst, who, having been arrested by Arran in October 1548, and housed in Edinburgh Castle, were released in January 1549, and paraded around Edinburgh by John Hamilton, Bishop-Elect of Dunkeld. They were offered 500 horse and 500 foot to prosecute war against England from their base of Teviotdale.[39] Their support would also allow the French to occupy Jedburgh, an important site for threatening supplies into England and further encircling the occupiers. In February 1549 a Scots-French force of 1,500 foot and 500 horse led by D'Esse laid siege to the Kerr stronghold of Ferniehurst Castle on the right bank of the river Jed near Jedburgh. A tunnel was dug under the walls and the castle was stormed. The English surrendered to the French commander; however a captain had his head cut off by a Scot who accused him of mistreating his wife and daughters. The Scots massacred the surrendered defenders, even buying prisoners off the French, with one claiming 'I sold the Scots a prisoner for a small horse'.

D'Esse next led his forces to Jedburgh and from there sent out raiding parties into England. Villages and communities were spoiled and burned, and Cornwall and Ford Castles were captured and razed to the ground. Here there were a number of sharp skirmishes in which the Scots and French gained the upper hand. The English gathered a larger force, which set out from Roxburgh to tackle the raiders at Jedburgh. D'Esse was not able to give battle or defend the poorly-fortified and supplied Jedburgh, and withdrew to Melrose, then further north out of harm's way.[40]

On the Continent there were reports that the French King was intending to send more troops and make up the total in Scotland to 10,000, whilst the Protector warned the French that he would consider it his right to capture as many French as he could if they intended to sail to Scotland. He made ready 20-25 armed vessels to block the passage of the French. In France the people considered Scotland 'the Frenchman's grave', and thought the Scots 'fatten their barren country with Frenchmen's bones'. There were reports of many desertions amongst the soldiers being readied to sail for Scotland. The war was costing the French King a great deal of money, with the Scots refusing to pay more than agreed. There was also a stream of Scots nobles petitioning for pensions to keep them loyal and out of the financial clutches of the English. The Scots also jealously guarded the Castle of Edinburgh, only allowing a few French access into the structure, even if in the company of the Queen Mother. Suspicions amongst the French in Scotland were that the English were using bribery to win over certain Scottish nobles.

The Protector also claimed to have 4,000 Germans under Kurt Pennick stationed in various garrisons in the occupied areas. The Emperor apparently gave the Protector permission to raise another 16,000 foot and 3,000 horse from Germany to be used in Scotland and possibly against French interests in Guyenne. This muster would include 5,000 raised from Saxony with the assistance of the Bishop of Arras, and 500 Low Germans who were to be transported in secret, in groups of ten. Harquebusiers, fuses and ammunition, as well as other war equipment and supplies, were also to be acquired. However it was reported that rather than 4,000 German mercenaries as the Protector claimed there were only 2,000, and the winter had had a heavy toll on those German mercenaries and Spanish under Kurt Pennick. A third are said to have succumbed to disease, the pest or plague, hunger and the cold, and many were sent to London with no prospect of returning. Those remaining 'wish themselves well out of such a poor country'. Kurt Pennick sent an envoy to Ostend to recruit men in what developed into a contest with the French to tempt mercenaries to fight in the Scottish wars.[41]

Adding to these military setbacks, the English crown and nobility were beset with suspicion and distrust, as a plot was discovered during January 1549. The Protector's brother Lord Seymour, High Admiral of England, was accused of planning to murder the young King Edward and all his close relatives, and also his own brother the Protector. Seymour apparently wanted to make himself King, and a search of his home uncovered 200,000 silver crowns. At his trial the following March he was condemned to death by parliament. Although the charge of attempting to murder Edward was dropped, it was found that he had planned to kill his brother, and through marrying Lady Elizabeth, the late King's daughter, he hoped eventually to claim the crown for himself. He was also accused of recruiting 400 nobles to his cause, and of being in the pay of the King of France, and as Admiral of England he was in a position to allow Mary, Queen of Scots to safely reach France.[42]

In Scotland the prospects for the besieged within and around Haddington were not so great, since the horse were described as 'feeble', and there was difficulty in recruiting men for a steadily unpopular war. Spanish and German levies that had sailed from Holland were expected but had not yet reached Broughty Craig. As the siege of Haddington began to tighten, the Scots began to recover ground. The English were pushed out of Roxburgh, and the lines between Haddington and Dunbar were blocked to the extent that it was difficult to receive supplies from the coast. Whilst attempting to open up communications Sir John Wilford was captured.[43]

The French commander D'Esse, unpopular in Scotland, was due to be replaced by Thermes. In June, before leaving for France with a joint Scots/French company, he decided to mount a maritime raid on the Island of Inchkeith on the Firth of Forth opposite Leith. The English, with Italian mercenaries, had occupied the isle a few weeks before. This occupation was for the purpose of harassing French and Scottish shipping in the Firth of Forth and as a base to attack Leith and Edinburgh, as well as the coastal settlements. The Protector believed it would give England a major strategic advantage along the east coasts of Scotland, especially if the English were planning another invasion. The Queen Mother also understood the dangers of this occupation and was at the forefront of persuading the French to recapture the Island. She personally put her name to this expedition, organizing and encouraging the Scots and French to mobilize at Leith whilst gathering together as many boats and sea transports as possible. These operations were attempted in secret and throughout the night.

At the break of dawn Mary addressed the assembled soldiers with an encouraging speech in which she reminded the French that 'we have a God who has brought you from France to preserve this realm from destruction and ruin!'. She and her ladies then cheered and wave on the French and Scots as they boarded. The French galleys distracted the Island defenders with cannon shot, allowing the troops to land on Inchkeith. They were met by heavy fire from harquebusiers and arrows, yet despite losses the English, alongside Italian troops, were pushed back to their stronghold and constrained within a small area with little hope of supply or rescue. Their offer of surrender was accepted. The banners won at this engagement were presented to the King of France when D'Esse returned to France, and he rewarded the soldiers with money and pensions. Elsewhere the Scots and French continued to make steady ground. The German garrison at Coldingham was overcome and put to the sword.[44]

On the open seas the pirates were blamed by neutral powers for preying on their shipping and people. Christian, King of Denmark, would complain of the piracy in Danish waters,[45] and argue that the pirates were attacking Danish merchants because they were trading with Scots, which angered the English, and were also trading with the English, which angered the Scots. He was concerned that he would not be able to pull back his people from seeking redress for the 'atrocities' committed against them. An unnamed French pirate was preying off the Spanish coasts whilst claiming to be a subject of the Scottish Princess, with the proceeds being brought into French ports. The young Mary's household had been reduced earlier in the year due to lowering of expenses and now she had been living with the daughters of King Henry. It is possible that a ship had been outfitted and a privateer recruited to try and gain some extra income for the little Queen. Possibly her mother or even the King provided the funding for an enterprise that would have added a little romance and adventure to her name.[46]

The new French commander, Thermes, arrived with 1,000 foot, 100 men-at-arms and 200 light horse at Dumbarton on June 23rd, 1549. With the advice of the Governor he constructed a fort at Aberlady, and employed troops around Haddington to ensure no supplies could safely get in. On the English side Lord Grey retired and was replaced by the Earl of Rutland. The English garrisons were increased by German mercenaries, and a field army was based at Dunglas. Rutland attempted a siege of Hume castle which was given up. He then unleashed his forces to devastating effect by wasting the lands and possessions of those former assured Scots now accepting French pay, especially Teviotdale. When an army of English and Germans advanced towards Thermes encamped around Haddington, Thermes, through skilled manoeuvring, managed to force his enemy to withdraw.[47]

On the Continent Henry II declared war on England on August 9th 1549, and the French would renew attempts to capture Boulogne, directing more military resources. Rebellions and politics in England during the summer of 1549 would also have a bearing on relations with Scotland. Rebellions in Norfolk, Devon and Cornwall were put down with extreme severity by 1,500 German and Italian mercenaries bound for Scotland. Reports during September stated that a body of Spanish troops stationed at Coldingham near Berwick had been attacked in their lodgings by French forces and German mercenaries, and their commander Julian captured. The Imperial and Venetian records stated that this was an important engagement, with many infantry and cavalry lost and the rest of the army routed. As this was another attempt to bring troops into Haddington, it was believed that England would not be able to hold the stronghold for long.

An army of 6,000 English and Germans was raised to bring the garrison out of Haddington, led by Lord Rutlin. Their advance was so sudden that they surprised the French encampment around Haddington, yet failed through being overcautious to press their advantage, allowing the French to withdraw their forces to safety. Scots horse that had been shadowing the English army managed to raid and plunder the German baggage train as they advanced in formation towards the retreating French. Whilst the English force managed to bring victuals into Haddington, the place was riddled with plague. Lord Rutlin would lead the surviving garrison, munitions and equipment out of Haddington on September 19th, and then burn the town before marching to England. With Haddington abandoned the Governor, Queen Mother, and Thermes quickly had it occupied.[48]

Despite these successes there were still reported tensions between the Governor and the Queen Mother, with Chatelherault now becoming weary of the French and wanting them out of Edinburgh. He decided to winter in the capital, as he feared there might be a revolt of the townspeople against the French if he was absent. He may also have worried that the French might try to take over Edinburgh Castle. The Queen Mother was also weary of the Governor, and allied with Sir George Douglas she sought to get him to visit France. The French King would invite Chatelherault to France, to officially confirm him as Duke, and no doubt bestow other rewards or bribes. Chatelherault declined this offer, at the insistence of his brother Dunkeld and the Hamilton clan, who believed the Queen Mother wanted the Governor out of Scotland so that she with her French cohorts could take over the government. George Douglas, whom Chatelherault distrusted, wanted the Governor out of Scotland simply because he was a dangerous and powerful rival, and also it was in Douglas's nature to play powerful factions off against each other.[49]

Faction fighting within England would result in Somerset being ousted as protector by the Council in October 1549. An attempt to call up the people to support him ended up with the Council, now dominated by his rival Warwick, throwing him into the Tower of London. Although he would be released in February and returned to the council, English momentum in the conflicts in France and Scotland was slowing down. By late 1549 the English could see that they could not win this war.[50]

Fast Castle was taken during November by stratagem, and there were plans to capture the other occupied strongholds. The war dragged on into 1550. The English and French began to negotiate for peace until Broughty Craig was stormed and taken during mid-February by a joint Scottish-French force. In late March £4,000 was raised from the clergy and prelates, and musters called from Edinburgh to prepare to advance to the West Marches with the intention of refortifying Annan, while another muster led by the Governor laid siege to Lauder and possibly Dunglas. On March 31st Lauder was stormed by Chatelherault, and as he reached the inner court it was learned that France and England had negotiated a peace treaty at Boulogne, March 28th 1550, which included the Scots.

The war in Scotland was ended, and a proclamation of peace was made in Edinburgh on April 20th, 1550. The English agree to withdraw from Scottish territory and destroy all fortifications. They were allowed to hold on to Roxburgh and Eyemouth until the Anglo-Scottish Treaty of Norham, 10 June 1551, and both were demolished. In consultation with the French the Scots agree to retain Inveresk and Luffness. Inchholm, Inchgarvie and Montrose were to be razed, and also Lauder and Dunglass towards the border. It was also suggested that the French could continue to garrison Dunbar, Blackness, Broughty Craig and Inchkeith, and besides these troops another 1,000 French were asked to remain behind as a safeguard until peace was concluded. For the Governor the continued presence of the French troops would have seemed a double-edged sword. Whilst it was necessary to discourage any English breach of the treaty, it also allowed France to retain a foothold, and offered some added muscle to the Queen Mother's own ambitions for Scotland.[51]

On April 20th at Edinburgh the Earl of Cassilis was discharged from his commission as Lieutenant of the South, absolved from any wrongdoing he may have done during his employment and thanked by the Queen Mother, Governor and Council for having done 'good, true and thankful service'. The activities which Cassilis had followed in harassing the occupied areas had contributed to the dire straits of the garrisons. Not only would it be dangerous for the occupiers to leave the castles, the supply trains and convoys would also be targeted. Cassilis would also have licence to attack assured Scots, and Lord Home, who commanded his own company of light horse, was given authority to seize, try and condemn assured Scots who had supplied Lauder with victuals and munitions. An operator like Cassilis or Hume would not only have to be competent captains, they would also need to know how to gather information and how to assess its worth, whether valuable or subterfuge. They were also up against experienced English captains with their own intelligence networks, and information was the coin they fought over to gain advantage in the battlefield.[52]

It has been estimated that between April 1544 and March 1550 Henry VIII and the Protector respectively spent £350,262 and £603,871 on the wars in Scotland, an incredible amount of money that gained nothing for England, and even cost them Boulogne. The cost in lives and blood was in itself staggering, and Scotland endured a level of destruction that had not been experienced since the Wars of Independence. Yet Scotland survived, and out of the war a new nation would begin to emerge and evolve.[53]

References: (1) (SP, vol.4, pp.411-412. Tytler, pp.40-42). (2) (Fraser, pp.279-280). (3) (Holinshed, pp.555-556). (4) (Paterson, p.201.SP, vol.4, pp409-410). (5) (Thomson, pp.80-87. SCML, 19th Feb, 1548, pp.217-219). (6) (Merriman, pp.305-306. Tytler, pp.41-42). (7) (Herkless & Hannay, pp.43-44). (8) (CSP, Spain, Van der Delft to Emperor, Feb 27th, 1548. CSPF, Dr Wotton to the Council, March 18th, 1548). (9) (CSPF, Dr Wotton to the Lord Protector, March 27th, 1548). (10) (CSP, Spain, March 20th, 1548). (11) (CSP, Spain, Van der Delft to the Emperor, Jan 22nd, 1548). (12) (CSP, Spain, Van der Delft to Emperor, March 22nd, 1548). (13) (SP, vol.4, pp.458-463). (14) (SCML, 15th March, 1548, pp.220-222). (15) (ALHTS, vol.9, pp. xxxii-xxxiii. CSP, Spain, Van der Delft to Emperor, April 23rd, 1548 Thomson, p.82). (16) (CSPS, 1547-1603, Vol 1, June 3rd 1548. Thomson, p.82). (17) (CSPF, Henry Johnes to Somerset, July 7th, 1548). (18) (Herkless & Hannay, pp.45-46). (19) (Calderwood, pp.255-256.Paterson, p.201. (Thomson, p.82). (20) (ALHTS, vol.9, pp. xxxii-xxxiii. CSPS, Van de Delft to the Emperor, July 7th 1548. CSPS, Van der Delft to Prince Philip, July 8t, 1548. Thomson, p.82). (21) (Knox, pp.89-91.Tytler, pp.44-45). (22) (CSPS, The Doge and Senate to Venetian Bailo at Constantinople, July 11th, 1548. Marshall, pp.68-70. ODNB, vol.24, pp.827-836). (23) (CSPF, Gamboa to Somerset, July 23rd, 1548). (24) (ER, vol.18, p.128. Tytler, pp.48-49). (25) (CSP, Spain, The Doge and Senate to Venetian Bailo at Constantinople, July 11th, 1548). (26) (Marshal, pp. 68-69). (27) (Thomson, p.83). (28) (Weir, pp.11-14). (28)

(Thomson, p.83). (29) (Holinshed, pp,557-558. Thomson, p.83. Tytler, pp.46-47. CSPS, Van der Delft to Emperor, end of August, 1548, & Sept 7th.). (30) (ALHTS, vol.9, pp. xxxiiv-xxxv. CSP, Spain, The Doge and Senate to the Bailo at Constantinople, 28th Sept, 1548. Thomson, p.83). (31) (Thomson, p.83. Tytler, pp.46-47). (32) (CSP, Spain, Van der Delft to Emperor, end of August, 1548. CSPS, Advice of events in Scotland, Oct 1st-9th, 1548. Eddington, pp.28-29. Lesley, pp.216-218). (33) (CSPS, Advice of events in Scotland, Oct 1st-9th, 1548). (34) (CSPS, Advice of events in Scotland, Oct 1st-9th, 1548. Thomson, pp.82-87). (35) (CSPS, Advice of events in Scotland, Oct 1st-9th, 1548. Stevenson, Thomas Fisher to Somerset, Oct 11th, 1548, pp.31-33). (36) (CSPS, Advice of events in Scotland, Oct 1st-9th, 1548. CSPS, Secretary Jehan Dubois to Loys Scors, Oct 24th, 1548. Lesley, pp.217-218. Thomson, pp.82-87. Stevenson, Thomas Fisher to Somerset, Oct 11th, 1548, pp.31-33). (37) (CSPS, St Mauris to the Emperor, Oct 24th, 1548). (38) (CSPF, Richard Maners to Somerset, Jan 9th, 1549. CSPS, Secretary Jehan Dubois to Loys Scors (Louis de Schore, President of the Flemish Council of State). Oct 4th, 1548.CSPS, St Mauris to the Emperor, Oct 24th, 1548. Eddngton, p.52. SP, vol.4, pp.458-460. RPSC, April 20th, 1550 (174), pp.98-99). (39) (CSPS, John Brende to the Protector, Jan 17th, 1549. CSPS, John Brende to the protector, Jan 19th, 1549.Eddington, pp.28-29). (40) (Eddington, pp.28-29. pp.33-35. Holinshed, pp.562-563) (41) (CSPS, Sir Ralph Bulwer to Somerset, Jan 20th, 1549. CSPS, St Mauris to Prince Philip, Jan 6th. CSPS, St Mauris to the Emperor, Jan 31st, 1549. CSPS, Van der Delft to the Emperor, March 19th, 1549..CSPS, St Mauris to the Emperor, April 5th 1549.). (42) (CSPS, The Emperor to Van der Delft, Jan 30th, 1549. CSPS, Van der Delft to the Emperor, March 19th, 1549). (43) (CSPS, John Brende to the protector, Jan 19th, 1549. Thomson, pp.82-87). (44) (CSPS, Van der Delft to the Emperor, July 3rd, 1549. CSPS, Simon Renard to the Emperor, July 18th, 1549. Holinshed, pp.562-564. Marshall, pp.69-70. Thomson, pp.82-87. Tytler, vol.6, pp.49-50). (45) (CSP, Spain, Albert Johanson, Counsel of Calenbery, July 5th, 1549). (46) (CSPF, Christian King of Denmark to King Edward VI, 16th July, 1549. CSPS, St Mauris to the Emperor, April, 5th, 1549. CSPS, The Emperor to the King and Queen of Bohemia, July 4th, 1549). (47) (Holinshed, pp.564-566. Thomson, vol.3, pp.84-85. Tytler, pp.49-50). (48) (Bindoff, pp.135-139. CSPS, Van der Delft to the Emperor, Sept 23rd, 1549. CSPV, Matteo Dandolo, Venetian Ambassador at Rome to the Signory, Sept 28th, 1549. Holinshed, pp.564-566.Lesley, pp.279-281. Paterson, p.203). (49) (Marshall, pp.69-70. Stevenson (ed.), Thomas Holcroft to Somerset, pp.47-50) (50) (Bindoff, pp.157-159). (51) (Holinshed, pp.564-566. Lesley, pp.279-281. Merriman, pp.345-348. RPCS, March 25th 1550, 144, 145. RPCS, April 20th 1550 150. RPCS, April 22nd, 1550, 159, 160, 161, 162. Tytler, pp.49-50). (52) (RPCS, April 3rd 1550, 147. RPCS, April 20th, 1550, 174) (53) (Merriman, pp.365-366).

Chapter Seven

Dangerous elevation

With victory against the English, Henry II, through the gold and blood that France had spent, now believed he had the right to consider Scotland a mere province, much like Brittany or Normandy. There was now a danger of Scotland being politically and militarily dominated by France.[1] The agent for this endeavour was the Queen Mother, who needed French support to bolster her own claims to the Governorship. Ironically Scottish success had not just relied on French-Catholic aid but on a coalition at times between Catholic and Protestants, supported by the Queen Mother. To ensure that Protestants did not once more join the English camp she would set out to develop good working relations with the reformers which might contradict her own devout Catholic upbringing and the opinion of her equally devout brothers in France. Yet the French crown understood this pragmatism. In July 1550 the Protestant prisoners in France known as the Castilians and slayers of Beaton were released by Henry II, and restored to their lands. This faction would align itself with the Queen Mother, and give her added leverage to challenge Chatelherault.[2]

Despite his power, Chatelherault would be accused by later writers of protecting injustice and cruelty. His brother John Hamilton, who became Archbishop of St Andrews in 1549, possessed a reputation for lechery which may have been propaganda from Protestant activists; nevertheless Robert Sempill, the father of one of the Archbishop's concubines, Lady Stenne, slayed Lord Sanquhar within sight of Chatelherault. The slayer was allowed to go free without arrest or trial.[3] He is said to have had three sons and three daughters, which in many ways made his capture of the moral high ground profoundly hypocritical.[4]

The Laird of Raith, John Melville, was executed for writing a letter to his son John Melville who was in England, an act that was considered treason by the Archbishop of St Andrews and the Abbot of Dunfermline, and grounds for forfeiture.[5] The letter was found in the House of Ormiston, captured and demolished by Chatelherault in February 1548,[6] and also the home of John Cockburn, the Laird of Ormiston, another accused of treason and now an exile in England. It was alleged that Ninian Cockburn, one of the accused who entered St Andrew's castle during the assassination of Cardinal Beaton, had some involvement in revealing the letter, possibly to win favour with Chatelherault or the Archbishop. Melville, himself described as an 'aged man', had a son and other close kin within St Andrew's castle during the siege. He had also been marked for death and forfeiture by Beaton, so this was a form of revenge against the surviving Castilians, as well as a source of profit for the Hamilton clan as the forfeited estates of Raith were passed to Chatelherault's illegitimate son David.[7]

Chatelherault also took part in a trial as lay judge, alongside the new Chancellor, the Earl of Huntley, against Adam Wallace, who was accused by the Bishop of St Andrews of heresy and of preaching without qualification from the church. According to Knox he and his wife would visit Alison Sandilands, the Lady Ormiston and wife of the exiled John Cockburn. Wallace had been employed as tutor to her children, yet he was accused of preaching that there was no purgatory and that praying to the 'Saints and for the Dead' was the same as worshipping idols. The mass was in his opinion an 'abomination before God'. He was arrested by the Bishop of St Andrews and taken to Winton in East Lothian, then taken to Edinburgh for trial. He had the audacity not to recognise the authority of the bishops or that of the Governor, citing the Bible as the only true source of judgment. Wallace was convicted of heresy and burned on Calton Hill.

In many ways his death paralleled that of George Wishart, and interestingly enough, like Wishart he was close to the Ormiston family. The only recorded person to speak against Wallace's death sentence was Alexander, 4th Earl of Glencairn, yet another link with Wishart through his father William, the 3rd Earl. Chatelherault, and the Archbishop used the trial of Wallace as a show of strength against the reformation, which was gathering in strength, and it was an attempt also to demoralize the Protestants in Scotland, whose allies in England were at peace with France. It also conveyed to France that Catholic power was now seeking to assert itself in Scotland.[8]

The Queen Mother's opinions about these oppressive measures are not known, although these types of acts would turn the people and the Protestant-minded against the Archbishop and Chatelherault. Her brother, the Cardinal of Lorraine, would request that the French King support the Archbishop of St Andrews to procure the papal Legate of Scotland, obviously an attempt to win him over,[9] yet the Queen Mother would have difficulties with the Hamilton family, who were the main obstacle to her gaining the Governorship from Chatelherault. She planned a visit to France so as to explain her difficulties and discuss with the French King and her family ways of politically defeating Chatelherault and forcing him to give up power. The bulk of the French forces had left Leith docks in May under great fanfare. She now lacked significant military backing; however Thermes and Chappell remained, and during the summer they toured Scotland, examining and strengthening the major fortresses, such as Dunbar, Edinburgh and Dumbarton, all the way north to Dunnotter. They stated that they had not known of any one nation containing so many castles.[10]

On September 1550 Thermes and Chappell were to embark for France from Newhaven, in a small fleet of ships commanded by Strozzi, Prior of Capua.[11] The Queen Mother planned to go with them to France. Although the reason she gave for the voyage was to visit her son and daughter, Chatelherault suspected, or had learned, that her true motivation was to recruit French political support against him. He intrigued to keep her in Scotland by engineering conflict with England.[12] The taking of an English ship by Scots could have caused a renewal of hostilities, but did not.[13] However, more dangerous to the Queen Mother's crossing to France was a sharp escalation of naval activity in Scottish waters by pirates from Flanders and the Low Countries. A fleet of warships was ordered to protect the coasts and waters of Scotland.[14]

Between July 4th-24th, ships from Zeeland had attacked Scottish shipping, raided the Isle of May and committed acts of 'inhuman cruelty', and Scots pirates had apparently retaliated against subjects of the Empire. The Queen Mother and Chatelherault had authorised Bassefontaine, the French ambassador in Bruges, to negotiate a truce with the Queen-Dowager of Hungary. A truce was agreed, to run to the following May.[15] Scottish piracy was becoming better organized. It was reported that over a hundred Scottish ships were sheltered in various English harbours, near Ipswich, Harwich, Southampton and Portsmouth. Their intention was to wage war against the Emperor. They formed profitable relations with the locals, and corrupt relations with civil and crown officials. There are no reports that they raided locally.

A John Haverton, described as a Scottish vice-admiral, was said to be in charge of the pirates. A captain John Green was also a well-known pirate. It is not known whether these pirates were sanctioned by the Scottish Government; their reported aim was to gain as much spoil as possible to make up for losses during the war with England, so many may have been disgruntled merchants. What is interesting is that the Scots were using English ports for shelter. Here national differences and prejudices were overcome by economic partnerships with the local administrations. Their tactics when sailing towards Spanish or Imperial waters were to stay close to the coast and travel from port to port; in this way they better avoided Spanish or English patrols.[16]

Perhaps more dangerous was the threat of open conflict between the Earl of Huntley on one side and the Earl of Cassilis, Sir George Douglas, James Douglas of Drumlanrig and Lord Robert Maxwell on the other side. Huntley was Lord Chancellor as well as Lieutenant of the North. A grant of the lands and earldom of Moray in February 13th 1549 had made Huntley feudal superior of the MacIntosh clan. During the month of August, Huntley arrested William MacIntosh of Dunnachtane, captain of the Glenhatten, and accused him of being part of a conspiracy. The source of information for this accusation was a kinsman, Lachlan MacIntosh. After some form of trial, William MacIntosh was found guilty, forfeited of his lands and then beheaded at Strathbogey, on August 23rd. This MacIntosh had powerful allies, such as the Earl of Cassilis, and open warfare was averted by the Queen Mother, who ordered the forfeitures reduced and lands restored to the MacIntoshes.[17]

The hostile parties representing Huntley and Cassilis were brought before the Queen Mother, Chatelherault and council in Edinburgh and ordered to cease hostilities and to ensure that friends, kin and adherents of the above nobles keep the peace.[18] The Queen Mother decided on an innovative method of contributing to peace in Scotland by taking Huntley, Cassilis, Sir George Douglas, Drumlanrig and Maxwell to France with her, along with the Earl of Sutherland, Lord Fleming, Earl Marshal, and the Bishops of Caithness and Galloway.[19] An English ambassador would conclude that the Queen Mother's intention in bringing this group to France was to allow the French to take control of all the castles and forts in Scotland whilst the above strong party of Scots was in France and unable to do anything to stop them.[20] It is also tempting to think that the burning of Adam Wallace may also have provoked anger against Huntley by the Protestants, and equally it was important to take the potential combatants out the country. The party left from Newhaven several days later and landed at Dieppe on September 19th. They travelled to the court of Rouen, where grand festivities were arranged.[21]

They stayed in Rouen over the winter, and it was here that the Queen Mother spent time with her children. Mary was nearly eight years of age, and her son Louis from her marriage to the Duke of Longuevelle was fourteen. Mary was an intelligent child who enjoyed education and learning and was able to speak several languages. She was exposed to the full splendor of the Renaissance, and her book collection revealed a mind willing to explore many subjects, whether history, geography, astronomy, theology, poetry or romance. She loved fine clothes and the games and pastimes of courtly life, but she also enjoyed outdoor pursuits, such as archery, croquet, horse riding, hawking and hunting. She may also been aware of the political machinations, corruption and loose morals that were part of court life; Henry for example would impregnate Queen Mary's governess.

The Queen Mother's brothers, the Duke of Guise and Cardinal of Lorraine, were ambitious and formidable politicians, and many tales and accusations would be laid against the Guise family, their ruthlessness and their use of poison to rid themselves of opponents. Their agenda was to gain power in France, and they saw Queen Mary as a route to the crown. Already there were plans that Queen Mary would marry her child companion François, the Dauphin of France. In France Mary would adopt the Stuart spelling of her surname. The Queen Mother would discuss with her Guise brothers how to gain the governorship of Scotland from Chatelherault. They offered her advice and support on the methods of gaining Scotland. The preservation of the Roman Catholic Church in Scotland was vital to French strategic interests,[22] yet with the strong and determined Scottish protestant party it was also vital to win them over.

As noted above, Henry II released the imprisoned Scottish Protestants, opening a door for the Queen Mother to win favour with this group and the wider protestant public.[23] Henry II had also since his crowning in 1547 shown a tolerance towards French Protestants and had appeared to be in favour of some measure of church reform, especially during his severe disputes with the Pope in 1551. However this would change when tours by bishops of their dioceses discovered how strong the growing protestant population was becoming within France, and how much of a threat this was. Before long he would reverse any tolerance towards French Protestants, or Huguenots as they were called, and introduce anti-heresy laws. Politically however he would also show blatant double standards when allying with German Protestants against Charles the Emperor, favouring Scottish Protestants whilst oppressing

French Huguenots.[24] The Scots Protestants, along with the Catholics visiting France, were promised that 'they should be richly rewarded for their good service' and the King of France bestowed the Order of St Michael on several lords, as well as expressing, along with his nobles, great affection for the Scots.[25]

Chatelherault appears to have been confirmed as Duke in 1550, as his son James was confirmed as Earl of Arran and Lord of Hamilton in the same year. In discussions with Henry II, the Queen Mother agreed that the confirmation of Duchy of Chatelherault, along with the prospect of his son receiving a valuable French bride and becoming a captain of the Scots Guards, were immense bribes that should ensure smooth transition of the governorship to the Queen Mother. However in the case of difficulties the King also discussed applying another type of pressure on Chatelherault, in respect of the crown revenues spent during his governorship, for which he would have to account once Queen Mary came of age. The possibility of remission would be offered only if he lowered himself from 'dangerous elevation'.[26]

To win the support of powerful parties within Scotland, the Queen Mother and Henry II agreed that the Earl of Huntley, who had married Chatelherault's daughter, was to be awarded with the earldom of Moray, and the son of the protestant Earl of Rothes, whose mother was a Hamilton, was to be made an earl. The Douglases were also to be rewarded, Angus to be reconfirmed as Earl, and James the son of Sir George Douglas to be confirmed as Earl of Morton. Other rewards were bestowed on potential supporters, and all were to be confirmed by the Queen when she came of age.

Adam Paniter, the Bishop of Ross and ambassador to France, Sir Robert Carnegie and Hamilton, Commendator of Kilwinning, were sent to Scotland to forward these matters to Chatelherault.[27] The Queen Mother also received favourable treatment from the King, 50,000 francs per year for her upkeep and 50,000 francs to spend as she thought fit.[28]

A new spy now infiltrated the company of the Queen Mother. Sir William Kirkcaldy of Grange had been one of the Castilians who had surrendered at St Andrews and been imprisoned in France. He apparently escaped Mont St Michael on January 6th 1549 with three others and travelled to England to meet John Knox.[29] In February 1551 Kirkcaldy was introduced to the English Ambassador in France, John Mason, by an individual called the 'secret agent'. Grange appears well informed on Scottish matters within the camp of the Queen Mother, and would be in contact with a few old associates and sympathizers amongst the protestant contingent, such as Sir George Douglas, Glencairn, Cassilis and others.[30]

Back in Scotland, the Scots and French were reportedly attempting to construct a fort on a hill near Berwick, a provocative act that forced the English garrison to send a contingent of horse and foot to disrupt the building. During November the Master of Erskine entered into talks with the English council in respect of contested lands around Berwick, but without any satisfactory outcome. Erskine travelled to France with Sinclair, President of the Session, before travelling to Flanders for peace negotiations during January. They successfully managed to finalize a treaty with the Emperor, where peace was made with the Low Countries and trade recommenced.[31]

Chatelherault set about repairing the towns damaged during the war, such as Dunbar, Haddington, Edinburgh and Dundee, which barely had any roofs due to artillery bombardments from the English when they garrisoned Broughty Craig. These were endeavours which credit Chatelherault; however he had to contend with a rival power within the realm. D'Osell, the French Ambassador, was effectively an independent commander of French forces stationed at Dunbar, Blackness, Broughty Craig, Inchkeith and elsewhere, accountable to the Governor in practice but accountably to the Queen Mother and France in truth. When Chatelherault held a Justice Ayre at Jedburgh in early 1551 he was accompanied by D'Osell and French troops.[32] The assertiveness of D'Osell would be indicative of the plans that the French had for Scotland, to learn from the Scots in order to supplant them in positions of authority.

The issue of the 'Debatable Land' on the borders became a source of contention between Scotland and England, as to how to divide it up. The question was what to do with it due to the lawless nature of the place and the dominance of border clans. This area north of Carlisle and the Roman Wall contained the Solway Moss. It also covered the southern entrances of Eskdale and Liddledale, the important stronghold of Langholm and the bridge at Gretna. The Armstrongs and Grahams were the chief raiding clans within the Debatable Land, and their reputation would attract the most desperate of outlaws and broken men.[33] In January Chatelherault appointed Sir Walter Scott of Branksholm as the law in Liddlesdale, and commanded him to act with reasonableness and fairness when interacting with the inhabitants and not to support any criminal acts committed by borderers, or profit from them. By this legislation he was expected to be incorruptible.[34]

The English however had a different opinion regarding Scottish interest in settling the area. Chatelherault had called a muster in Edinburgh with the purpose of marching to Liddlesdale and dealing with the border clans, although the five to six ships lying off the east coast did not make any tactical sense, as Liddlesdale can only be reached via the Irish Sea. So that fact and other information led the Captain of Berwick to warn Sir Robert Bowes that the town of Berwick was the real target. A warning was made to the French ambassador in London, who immediately dispatched a messenger to Scotland to put a stop to any such plan, if there was one.[35] Nevertheless Chatelherault did manage to oversee a meaningful peace with England, the Treaty of Norham of June 1551, in which his brother was a commissioner, ratified in September.[36]

During the summer King Henry, the Queen Mother, Queen Mary and their family and entourage travelled the towns and countryside of France. They went to Tours, Angers and Nantes, then visiting Orleans and Fountain, where all the Scots nobles met her. They then visited the Duke of Guise at Jamveille.[37] During this tour, according to Lesley, a plot was uncovered in which a member of the Scots Guards named Stewart or Stuart was planning to poison the young Queen of Scotland.[38] This individual approached some lords in England with his plan, who in turn threw him in prison and extradited him to France.[39] Stuart was said to be an archer of the Scots Guards. The idea of trying to offer his services to England is strange since it was not in their interests to see her killed, and as Fraser stated, they still lobbied for fulfilment of the Treaty of Greenwich.

The news of the plot caused the Queen Mother to become badly ill, and the English ambassador reports a rumour that some 'miscontented Scots' were responsible for the plot.[40] One Scot accused was the Earl of Lennox, living in retirement in Yorkshire with his wife, Lady Margaret Douglas, and his sons, Henry, Lord Darnley, and Charles. The archer's full name was Robert Stewart, and he planned to put poison in the pears that Queen Mary was fond of. Lennox obviously denied knowledge of this and even renounced his claim to the throne of Scotland. Lennox did have links with the Scots Guards in France, his brother John Stewart, Lord of Daubigny, being a captain. That however does not prove involvement.[41]

Once in France Robert Stewart was put to the torture, then hung, drawn and quartered.[42] Lesley stated that a man called James Henderson revealed the plot,[43] although the names of the men behind Stewart are not revealed. Possibly there were no other parties and Stewart was a lone opportunistic assassin looking to earn a large reward from the murder of a high-profile victim. Adding to the threat against her daughter, the Queen Mother would meet with terrible tragedy when her son, less than fifteen years of age, died of natural causes in her arms at Amiens.[44]

When the delegation of Pantier, Sir Robert Carnegie, and Hamilton, Commendator of Kilwinning, reached Scotland, they met Chatelherault and negotiated with him the terms of resignation offered by Henry II. Chatelherault agreed; the fact that there would be no accounting for all crown revenue spent during his tenure in office may have been a major incentive for acceptance. Another factor was his brother, the Archbishop Hamilton, who was bedridden and suffering from some form of fever and could not advise his brother.[45]

The Queen Mother attempted to sail directly to Scotland from Dieppe during September, but the route was blocked due to a falling out between France and the Empire, with the latter setting a naval blockade of the seaport. The Queen Mother managed to acquire a safe conduct from Edward VI, the young King of England. With this protection she reached Portsmouth on the 22nd of October. She was met by Lord Howard and the Earl of Southampton, who escorted her and her party to Hampton Court, where she was met by a large contingent of nobility. After a lavish and honourable reception she took royal barges down the Thames towards London. She was lodged in the Bishop of London's palace, and then travelled to Westminster, where she met the fourteen-year-old Edward. It may have been a strange experience for the Queen Mother to have an audience with a young boy who was around the same age as her dead son.

Pastimes and lavish entertainments were put on, and during them Edward asked the Queen Mother to reconsider allowing him to marry her daughter, stating that this had been promised by the Scottish government. He also added that whoever married Mary other than him would be considered an enemy of England. The Queen Mother replied that the nature of pursuing the fulfillment of the marriage treaty through warfare had compelled many of the nobles to seek support from France. She did agree to pass on his words to the King of France in order to learn his opinion.

After several more days of royal entertainment the

Queen Mother was escorted to the borders by the Duke of Northumberland, staying at different towns on the way. On arriving at the border she met with the Earl of Bothwell and Lord Hume and was conveyed to Edinburgh.[46] Bothwell had been declared a traitor in a council meeting of May 23rd, 1550, and he may have tried to use the journey to Edinburgh to win favour with the Queen Mother, but it would be after 1552 before he would be allowed to return to Scotland as a freeman.[47] The visit to England was a diplomatic success; it would have sent a message to Protestants in Scotland and England that she was possibly open to toleration.

Before she returned, Chatelherault had another change of political direction. His brother the Archbishop of St Andrews, having recovered from his illness, immediately set out to steel Chatelherault's mind against lamely handing over the office of governorship. Sir James Melville, whilst in France, related a story told to him that the Archbishop had recovered his health through the enchantments of an Italian magician called Cardanus, and confronting his brother, called him a 'very beast for quitting the government to her, seeing there was but a skittering lass between him and the crown'. Such were the elaborate embellishments used to produce continental propaganda against the Hamiltons, yet such stories helped feed the perception that only through defeating the Hamiltons could the French claim Scotland.

Chatelherault set about passing legislation which would win the support of the church with stronger laws against adultery, bigamy, blasphemy, swearing, lewd behaviour and there was to be censorship of the press, especially those publications that produced ballads, songs or stories perceived of a rude or amoral nature. Printers would need a licence from the Governor or the Queen Mother.[48] The government of Chatelherault was also concerned about political and reformist material being produced locally, and being widely spread across Scotland.[49]

When the Queen Mother arrived in Edinburgh in November she was met with great honour by Chatelherault.[50] She would learn that Chatelherault had changed his mind about giving up the governorship voluntarily. She could still use the issue of royal revenues he had spent to pressure him. He in turn would need to build up support amongst the nobility as well as gather up wealth. In 1552, with the encouragement of the Queen Mother and nobles, Chatelherault decided to hold Justice Ayres across the country and to put a halt to the many feuds and disturbances in the realm.[51] In March they sent commissioners to meet with their English counterparts at Lochmaben and settle disputes over the 'Debateable Land'.[52] There was also in the same month a request from the King of France for Scotland to support him in his growing dispute with Charles V, despite Scotland having successfully negotiated a treaty with the Empire in 1551.[53]

Henry had entered into an agreement with German protestant princes with the Treaty of Chambord and sent forces into Lorraine, capturing the cities of Metz, Toul and Verdun. The issue of supplying an army for Henry II was discussed by the Lords of the Great Council, and there was an acknowledgement of the military and monetary debt that Scotland owed France during the recent wars. They would send a message suggesting a peaceful course, and if that course was blocked they did agree that if war started they would send a sufficient number of soldiers to the Continent.[54] The French war against the Empire would give Chatelherault and the Queen Mother opportunities to rid themselves of troublemakers.

In 1552 the Archbishop of St Andrews published a work called 'Hamilton's catechism'. There is dispute about the true author of the work, possibly an English Dominican called Richard Marshall or a sub-prior of St Andrews called John Wynram. It is an exposition of Catholic doctrine which appears to be written to appeal to a broader audience, including Protestants. It is unusually silent on the subject of papal authority. The Council of Trent had set down the doctrine of justification by faith, yet the catechism does not fully confirm to that interpretation. The mass, which was a major bone of contention between Protestants and Catholics, was not considered a 'propitiatory sacrifice'. Having been part of the trial that burned Wallace in 1550, Hamilton the politician was changing his position and using the catechism to reach out to Protestants. The Queen Mother needed a coalition with the protestants of Scotland to stop them joining with England.[55] Through this catechism the Archbishop was possibly seeking to create some kind of common ground for which the different religious factions could work out their differences, or at least become more tolerant of each other. This is not to say that the catechism was produced to help justify Protestants fighting for Catholic France, but it may have contributed to an understanding, making their recruitment easier.

The Queen Mother and Chatelherault travelled to Aberdeen in the spring. Chatelherault would be accused of using Justice Ayres to extort bribes from the richer nobility whilst hanging thieves who could not afford a fine or composition. He certainly travelled extravagantly, employing a 'fule' for entertainment, the best cooks and musicians, and was accompanied by judges, clerks, messengers and barons from Lothian, Stirling, Perth and Fife.[56] The Queen Mother would use the journeys from town to town to learn more about the country and win friends, the more influential the better. She would also enter into secret agreements with clergy and nobles to get them to support her when she made her bid to become Governor and oust Chatelherault. The Bishop of Ross would urge the Governor to resign, and was met with refusal.[57] After a month in Aberdeen the party travelled to Inverness, arriving on July 19th. Clanranald and Clan Cameron refused to show, and Argyll and Huntley were respectively sent out to 'pass upon' them. The head of Clanranald, John Moidart, would enter into talks with Argyll and offer excuses why he could not come to Inverness, which resulted in a truce until the following February. Ewen Donaldson of Clan Cameron died during Huntley's pursuit, although how he died is not known.

They next travelled to Elgin, where Sir George Douglas died. He was worth £3,582. This Douglas was an individual to rank with any political intriguer in Scotland if not England, with the correspondence of Spanish, Imperial and Venetian ambassadors passing his name to the Continent in discussion of his exploits and machinations. He appears to have been sympathetic to the protestant religion, but his politics were shady and seemed defined by what would best benefit his family.

Scottish earls were similar to mini-kings, and in a

nation of competitors each earl sought to expand his lands and titles to increase power and influence as a means of surviving. Sir George understood this; his brother had married a widowed queen, and Angus kept a royal captive of James V, his stepson, just so that the Red Douglas clan could expand and benefit through royal patronage. The alliance with Henry VIII was convenient in that it gave the Red Douglases a lever to use against a weak and insecure government, and by exploiting the threat of English power they gained remission of their Scottish forfeitures. Yet they were also able to ally with anyone, whether the Queen Mother, Chatelherault, Cardinal Beaton, the English or the French, all dependent on the best gains on offer to the family. Their power and talents in war and politics made them important allies to whichever side could afford them. If Sir George left a living legacy it was in James, Earl of Morton, who would prove an able successor in political pragmatism and ruthlessness, and become like his father an important figure in 16th century Scottish history.

Chatelherault and the Queen Mother next travelled to Banff, then to Dundee and Perth, before going south to Glasgow, Langrig and Dumfries. They travelled to Edinburgh and the Lothians, and then to Jedburgh, where Chatelherault attempted to impose order by appointing skilled captains and wardens to the borders. He further brokered potential allies by knighting several captains, the Kerrs of Cessford, Ferniehurst, Scott of Buccleuch and others. The Kerrs were at feud with the Scotts, over the damage that the former, when assured to England, had inflicted on Buccleuch, his clan and adherents during 1548. Possibly by knighting the belligerents, Chatelherault and the Queen Mother hoped they would endeavour to settle their differences. The matter was taken up by the Court of Session in Edinburgh, but the Kerrs decided to sidestep the legal procedures and on October 1552, Sir Walter Scott of Buccleuch, veteran of Ancrum, Pinkie and numerous other battles, was cut down with swords by the Kerrs in the High Street of Edinburgh. Whilst Scott still had breath in his body two servants of the Kerrs returned to the bloody scene and finished him off.[58]

The killing of Buccleuch was a disaster for security on the borders as individuals prepared to take on the position were scarce. Chatelherault made a request for the Queen Mother, Argyll, Cassilis and Glencairn to meet at Edinburgh to discuss the problem.[59] The meeting resulted in Chatelherault calling a muster from across the south of Scotland to assemble at Jedburgh on Oct 27th. An artillery train with four falcons, each to be pulled by twelve horses, was raised, as well as two cartloads of powder and ammunition. Chatelherault pursued the Kerrs and their adherents, and they were so effectively set upon that they withdrew to 'woods and fells' and were left with 'na manner of thing to live on'. They sued for peace, and as a result they were given the option of serving in the French army which was preparing to fight against the Emperor. One hundred light horsemen were to be raised, and as a condition of their service the council agreed to ensure that their landed and titled rights and possessions would be protected. It was also stipulated that no one from the Scott clan was to be raised for France, to avoid the feud with the Kerrs being carried across the waters.[60]

Feuds were common, and destructive. The Lundys and

Fairnies were called to arbitrate their feuds with the Beatons, and the same was asked of the Montgomerys and Boyds.[61] The Master of Ruthven killed Charteris of Kinclaven because he was pursuing an action against him. Gentlemen were also adopting the rapier as a weapon of choice and duelling became frequent and fashionable. In Edinburgh, a special place called the Quarry Holes, which was quiet and out the way of the noisy streets and taverns, was used for settling differences.[62]

During the previous month, November, orders were sent out to raise enough footmen for an army. All able men between 16 and 60 years of age were to gather at the nearest burghs, where a fixed number would be chosen corresponding to one man per forty merks of land. Those without equipment were to be supplied. The burghs themselves were to raise 300 harquebusiers through taxation.[63] 400 hundred horsemen were to be raised from the borders, through a mix of taxation and voluntary contributions. Anyone avoiding making a contribution would be declared a rebel against the crown. The Earl of Cassilis would be Lieutenant-General of the army, and Lord Ruthven the Coronet of the footmen. Those travelling to France would have all legal involvements suspended whilst away, and for 12 days after they returned.[64] The Earl of Huntley was to raise two companies of Highland foot.[65]

In November Charles V led 6,000 troops to lay siege to Metz, captained by the Queen Mother's brother the Duke of Guise. She would express her joy in writing at the successes of her two brothers in the wars against the Empire, and this correspondence would be captured and sent to the Queen-Dowager of Hungary in Flanders. The Queen-Dowager wrote to the Emperor and reported on this successful piece of espionage, where three Englishmen under the employ of the Emperor attacked and robbed a French messenger travelling from France with letters from Scotland. The man was set upon in a village in France, and although he escaped to a church his assailants captured a bag full of letters. The assailants sent the Queen-Dowager the letters from the Queen Mother addressed to the King of France, which included a memoir from D'Osell.

The Queen Mother sent a messenger to the Queen-Dowager's court demanding that the correspondence should be returned, arguing that the bag belonged to Scotland. The Queen-Dowager countered that it was a French diplomatic bag and as the Empire was at war with France the contents were justified spoils. Despite the legal wrangling the contents of D'Osell's memoir were hinted at in the Queen-Dowager's correspondence to the Emperor. They implied that the Queen Mother and her French cohorts were intending to 'encroach' in Scotland and change some legislation and judicial laws, although the details were vague enough to be deniable. The material about Chatelherault and his brother the Archbishop of St Andrews was more openly hostile, and it was this that the Queen-Dowager suggested should be used to further the divisions between Chatelherault and the Queen Mother.

The Queen-Dowager invited the Court-Master of Scotland in Zeeland to see the letter as he was a dependent of Chatelherault. He in turn asked for the Queen-Dowager to write a letter asserting the contents of the letters and he would take it to Chatelherault, along with a written copy of the memoir. She advised that the memoir should not be shown to the Three Estates of Scotland, as French hostility towards Chatelherault and the Archbishop could encourage their enemies. The Queen-Dowager also reported from the captured correspondence that 5,000 foot and 500 horse led by the Earl of Cassilis were being made ready to travel to France.[66]

The contents would also reveal that the Queen Mother was conspiring in Ireland. It was learned that an Irishman called Charles Paris had been working as a message carrier between the French King and certain Irish princes and earls. Bringing letters from France to Ireland, he landed in Scotland. It was learned that he had been intending to travel to England with the letters until he was arrested by D'Osell in Scotland and incarcerated.[67]

Various powerful individuals would support the Queen Mother, such as Huntley, due to his Catholic, pro-French credentials. He would raise footmen for the Continental army but stay in Scotland. Cassillis, the leader of the Continental expedition, was in receipt of a French pension, yet he was a committed Protestant and offered support to the Queen Mother. Ruthven was also a committed Protestant, and whilst becoming Lord Ruthven on October 6th 1552, he was also provost of Perth, a town with a significant Protestant population.[68] Glencairn was another Protestant supporting the Queen Mother, and the recipient of a French pension. Angus appeared to support the Queen Mother during that period, although this would change.[69]

The Queen Mother understood that the support of the Protestants was important if she wished to undermine and replace Chatelherault. Pragmatically she recognised that the Protestants were an influential party and could not be ignored, and in France the Catholic monarchs had also come to an understanding with the Huguenot members of the aristocracy, which resulted in a moderation of state persecution. This tacit arrangement would break down in 1562 with the bloody and cruel Wars of Religion. Between Chatelherault and the Queen Mother the warfare was political in nature and they would outwardly portray cooperation. Whilst both would attend council meetings, they were gathering recruits to their cause wherever they could, and undermining each other at every opportunity.

Reports in January 1553 said that galleys in Normandy and Ponthieu were to be used to ship the Scottish army to France, the number stated as 3,000 foot and 1,000 horsemen. There was a question of whether Chatelherault would allow the army to leave unless it was chiefly made up of men siding with the Queen Mother, then, 'let the wolves devour and all hazards threaten them, rather than keep them at home to foment troubles and sedition.'[70] The war on the Continent may have also attracted protestant participation, since Henry II had allied with the Lutheran princes of Germany against the Empire. However there is no evidence that the army in its entirety was sent to the Continent.

The Kerrs did not go to the Continent. They were the subject of a council meeting in May 1553, when on the advice of Chatelherault it was thought more expedient not to persecute them and instead accept offers made to the Council, although the nature of 'offers' is not stated.[71] This leniency may be down to the reported quarrelling between the parties of the Queen Mother and Chatelherault, where it was said that the former was trying to replace

Chatelherault as Governor with her illegitimate stepson, James, Earl of Moray.[72] There are no accounts of direct fighting between the parties of the Queen Mother and those of Chatelherault,. They attended council meetings together up to September and gave the impression of a working government. Any warfare between the two, if it can be described as that, seems to have been through proxies, where those favour to one party attacked those who favoured the other.

Across the country there was the impression of a growing lawlessness and disorder, and even the experienced Master of Maxwell resigned as Warden of the West March on August 29th because of daily and nightly incursions of the English borderers.[72] By the autumn the raiding was so bad that the French ambassador in London complained to the English Privy Council and demanded a meeting of border commissioners. In the north the feuds between the Sinclair Earl of Caithness and the McKays, the Cummings and Dunbars and others were causing a breakdown in law and order.[73]

In England Edward IV died, and Mary Tudor became Queen of England. For the deposed Earl of Lennox living in exile in Yorkshire with his wife Margaret Douglas, the rise of the new Queen of England brought opportunities to once more get involved in intrigue and politics. Margaret was a friend of Queen Mary, and whilst Lennox had made a commitment to convert of Protestantism it was suspected that during the reign of Edward he and his wife secretly practised Roman Catholicism. Lennox was invited onto the English Privy Council, and during this period the advances of the English reformation were challenged by the conservative Catholicism of Mary. Many English Protestants sought safe havens in Scotland, whilst Scots who were preaching in English during the reigns of Edward returned to Scotland and spread their faith. The Queen Mother of Scotland was not vigorous in pursuing Protestants at that time, and men like William Harlow and John Willock, with some popular support and noble backing, were able to make significant contributions to reformed religion in Scotland.[74]

A report was spread that the French King had instigated an armed incursion of Scots into Ireland, which he denied, insisting that he respected the peace between Scotland and England and was supportive of the rule of Mary Tudor as Queen of England.[75] D'Osell, on his way to Scotland with several captains, assured the Queen of England that the French King wanted to keep the peace, and he handed her letters from him and the young Queen of Scotland. D'Osell was not a popular man in Scotland, and the Scots are said to have had enough of the French, with some seeking to get Chatelherault to use his power and oppose the marriage of Mary to the Dauphin.[76]

D'Osell returns to Scotland, followed by the Vidame of Chartres with a number of soldiers. The purpose was to take over the forts of Scotland. There was a fear that Queen Mary of England's intention to marry Philip of Spain would threaten French interests in Scotland. A rumour circulated that a promise had been made to the Queen by Philip offering Spanish troops to help conquer Scotland. It was believed that the French plan to occupy castles and forts would be opposed by the Scots. It is also possible that the French troops led by D'Osell and Vidame were using the excuse of an Anglo-Spanish marriage alliance to enter Scotland and apply pressure on Chatelherault to resign as governor. There were reports that he was stirring up the Scots against the French. Before the end of the year he let it be known that once Queen Mary reached 12 years of age he would step down. Until then he continued to rule as Governor, despite growing opposition.[77] These words of Chatelherault's, if indeed he said them, were probably to buy time. By the following year he had once more hardened his stance.

A Council meeting at Linlithgow, at which the Queen Mother was not present, was possibly made up of the 'nobility and foremost men' who were said to support Chatelherault. Unfortunately the names of the attendees were not listed. He sent the Bishop of Ross with a message to the King of France that his authority stemmed from the Three Estates, and his obligation was to remain governor until Mary married or returned to Scotland. Chatelherault reminded the King that his duty was to commit to Scotland's independence, which would include opposing not just the English but the French, a position taken by Argyll when the Queen Mother attempted to bring him to her side. This message reflected a fear across Scotland that the French were seeking to take over their country.[78]

From September 18th 1553 to January 22nd 1554, Chatelherault held council meetings in Edinburgh and Linlithgow without the Queen Mother, which suggests that by 1544 the Queen Mother and Chatelherault had split into separate political camps. It is not clear who his allies were, although in February he entered into a bond with Angus, who had practically retired from politics, yet his reported detestation of the Queen Mother may have tempted him to show his face.[79] The Earl of Bothwell had returned to Scotland by the end of November 1553 and was residing in Crichton Castle. As a Protestant, he may have found the new Catholic monarch in England too dangerous. He did in November 1552 write from Newcastle to the Queen Mother asking her to write to the French King,[80] and for the King to write to the Governor allowing him to return to Scotland and have his lands and titles restored. This suggests that it was Chatelherault who was opposing Bothwell's return. At Crichton Bothwell offered to serve the Queen Mother, although he stated that violent weather stopped him from 'such service as [his] will commands'.[81] The nature of this 'service' was not made clear.

Bothwell's rehabilitation may have had something to do with reports that a French army was coming to Scotland with the hostile intention of attacking the north of England. Thirty ships of war with large numbers of men supposedly meant for Scotland were said to be heading for an invasion of England. Bothwell's knowledge of northern England and his experience as an admiral and the sea coasts would have proved useful to the French. Throughout the following months the French plans became more ambitious. They intended to co-ordinate with Englishmen opposed to the Anglo-Spanish marriage alliance and to provide a fleet of 200 to set sail on April 20th and counter Spanish naval power. An army of Scots and French would be raised by the Vidame, once he arrived in Scotland, to invade the north of England.[82]

The plan came to nothing, and in Scotland it was reported that Chatelherault was gaining in strength and the

Scots were divided amongst themselves. The position of the Queen Mother, which was described as one of 'weakness' in a letter to Philip of Spain, compelled her to write to Lennox, offering to restore his lands and titles if he would join her against Chatelherault. It was an amazing about turn, yet Lennox considered the offer and if further enticed to enter Scotland he decided that he would betray her, contact Chatelherault and join him in driving the Queen Mother out of Scotland. He would also crown himself King. It was an ambitious project, and meant driving out the French also, as well as denying Chatelherault's own claims to the crown of Scotland. Lennox's plan was also discussed by Queen Mary Tudor and she was supportive, resulting in serious discussions regarding raising 200-300,000 crowns for the funding of an expedition.[83]

Here was a danger of Scotland being pulled into a civil war once more, with involvement by England, France and Spain. It is not known whether Chatelherault received any communication from Lennox, or learned of his plans. He would have no doubt learned about the Queen Mother's initial approach to Lennox, as it is possible the approach was not serious but was meant to put pressure on Chatelherault. If Lennox was to return with French support, Chatelherault could find himself cut out of the succession and replaced by Lennox as second person of the realm.[84]

There were other pressures as well. The young Queen Mary, having reached the age of twelve, had selected as her guardians the King of France and her uncles, the Duke of Guise and the Cardinal of Lorraine. They in turn devolved the guardianship to the Queen Mother.[85] This direct involvement of the Cardinal of Lorraine, and his influence in continental politics and religion, could threaten the Archbishop of St Andrews' position as leading prelate of Scotland. He obviously decided to sacrifice his political offices in Scotland to preserve his ecclesial standing, but first he would need to negotiate terms with the Queen Mother. He would resign as Lord Treasurer on March 5th 1554. In return for his resignation the Queen Mother released the Archbishop from his arrears of £31, 000.[86]

Whilst the Archbishop had been diligent in financial affairs during times of war, during peacetime he and his brother would use their power and prestige to fill the coffers of the Exchequer, and also reward themselves and family with gifts and favours. Realising that the Hamilton grip on power was loosening he had resigned the Abbey of Paisley to his nephew Claude. This was confirmed by Papal Bull in December 9th 1553, allowing the Hamilton clan to continue to benefit from the rich benefice. The Treasurer Accounts of November 1552 would reveal gaps between expenses and receipts, and the following year the Lord Treasurer was recompensed for these expenses by receiving the monies owed to the Exchequer by sheriffs, burghs and clergy for the defence of Scotland.

Justice Ayres, as already noted above, allowed both the Lord Governor and Lord Treasurer to accumulate wealth through imposing fines, and in the opinion of an Imperial envoy, he preferred the feuds and localized conflicts within Scotland, as they gave him opportunities to accumulate land and estates. The same envoy recounted how the Archbishop had profited from the sale of two captured Spanish ships, even though the proceeds were not legally his. Overall the two brothers were viewed as 'covetous and greedy' and this led to the Queen Mother gaining the necessary political support to oust them. She could not however oust the Archbishop from his ecclesiastical post, and throughout the years he would still be able to influence politics through religion.[87]

With the loss of his brother, Chatelherault had no choice but to give in to the Queen Mother's demands. In the Edinburgh parliament of April 12th, 1554, Chatelherault finally resigned as Governor. He was honored as 'ane noble and mychtie prince' who through his efforts to defend Queen Mary and Scotland from England, 'hes left free the haill realme'.

There is much truth in the praise that Chatelherault received. Whilst his switch from a Protestant reformer to a born-again Catholic in the autumn of 1543 reflected political opportunism and an instinct for survival, changing sides ensured his royal standing as second person of the realm and his continued employment as Governor. It also benefited his family, with powerful positions of authority, political, religious and military going to close family and kin. But once he had committed himself to the French alliance he was in the forefront of the battle against Henry VIII, the Emperor Charles, and the Lord Protector. As his legal discharge as Governor stated, he defended against an enemy 'who daily for the space of seven or eight years' invaded 'with fire and sword'. But he also cruelly persecuted Protestants, and it is this record of cruel intolerance that perplexes and baffles historians. In March 1543 Chatelherault had presided over one of the most radical and reforming parliaments in Scottish history, yet by the end of the year he had joined with Beaton in persecuting Protestants in Perthshire. The only explanation is that faced with alliance with an increasingly unstable Henry VIII, Chatelherault chose to side with Beaton as the best way of defending Scottish sovereignty and his own dynastic ambitions. In changing sides, and with his son a hostage of Beaton, Chatelherault seemingly surrendered his reforming sympathies to allow the more extreme forms of religious persecutions to flourish in Scotland. This is why Knox called him 'inconstant'.

Despite this dichotomy Holinshed's estimation that Chatelherault was 'faint hearted by nature' seems wrong when compared to the Governor's war record. From 1543 to 1550 he was responsible for calling and leading over twenty-five musters, as well as ordering military actions all over Scotland. He personally led at least 15 sieges, although he probably participated in more than that. Whilst the Scottish armies were technically weaker than the modernizing English army with their foreign mercenaries and better firepower, Chatelherault understood that by continuing to fight, the Scots ensured they were not defeated. The fact that he was able to call up so many musters despite the military and economic setbacks would have had a huge psychological effect on the English crown, never able to finish off the Scots no matter the manpower and money spent. Whilst his tactics on the battlefield are questioned, and Pinkie blackened his reputation amongst the people and future historians, he was hampered by damaging distrusts within the armies due to religious, local or national differences. When after the Hereford raids of 1544 the parliament of the Queen Mother called on Chatelherault to resign, against the odds he managed to retain his position, once more displaying his dogged determination. He made bad decisions, allowing his son to be retained as hostage by Beaton and later by the French King, which possibly weakened his ability to act independently.

The English had their assured Scots, and Chatelherault did not have the money or power to match the English purse until French gold took a more active role in the war. Chatelherault however was a good strategist and a good organizer, and he understood the best time to advance and the best time to withdraw. He poured money and time into strengthening castles such as Dunbar which, situated on the coast, was a vital link to the sea as well as a base for harassing land convoys during the English occupation. He also understood the significance of destroying strongholds so they could not be used by an enemy, especially in the hotly-contested borderlands. Despite his remarkable ability to mobilize armies he also realised that French help, expertise and money were needed to help the Scots overcome the new continental fortification designs being introduced into Scotland by the English. French help would be needed to capture these strongholds such as Haddington, and to build up and modernize Scottish castles such as Edinburgh and Stirling. French troops were also a counter to the foreign mercenaries that the English, with Imperial assistance, were bringing into Scotland. And of course the French navy was vital in countering English forces, and in supporting the Scottish privateers who were waging economic war against the Habsburg Empire and English shipping. French assistance was important against England, but Chatelherault would not allow the French to dominate Scotland, and in this balancing act considerable political skills were needed.

The discharge also acknowledges the part he played in 'pacifying the civil and internal conspiracies and insurrections', conceived by Scots against the power of the crown. Here the role of intelligence networks was important in uncovering dangerous plots and schemes. Chatelherault used bribery, patronage and force to undermine endeavours such as the 'Douglas Bond', various insurrections in the Highlands and Isles, the Castilians' alliance with Henry VIII, schemes by Lennox and numerous other political and religious plots. However he could also be very pragmatic, forgiving powerful enemies and using wealth and patronage to retain a pretence of loyalty. He also had a talent for making military gains through bribery and diplomacy. Throughout the war Chatelherault had displayed leadership, innovation, energy and resourcefulness.[88]

References: (1) (Lesley, pp.234-235). (2) (Knox, pp. 99-101. Thomson, p.91). (3) (Calderwood, pp.261-263). (4) (Herkless & Hannay, pp.52-53). (5) (Knox, p.93). (6) (RPCS, 143). (7) (Calderwood, pp.261-263. RPCS, 62). (8) (Knox, pp. 103-106. Thomson, pp.87-89). (9) (RPCS, April 22nd, 1550, 158). (10) (Lesley, pp.233-234). (11) (Tytler, p.51). (12) (Thomson, p.90). (13) (RPCS, June 27th, 1550, 181). (14) (RPCS, July 6th 1550, 184). (15) (CSP, Spain, The Queen Dowager of Hungary to the Emperor', August 1550, 16-31. CSP, Spain, Volume 1, pp. 156-167). (16) (CSP, Spain: June 1550, Volume 10: 1550-1552 pp. 108-118). (17) (Lesley, pp.235-236. SP, vol..4, pp.534-536). (18) (RPCS, Sept 5th, 1550, 189). (19) (Tytler, pp.50-52). (20) (CSPF,, June 1551, pp. 115-129). (21) (Tytler, pp.50-52). (22) (Tytler, pp.52-53). (23) (Knox, pp. 99-100). (24) (MacCulloch, pp.268-269. p.274). (25) (Knox, pp.106-107. Lesley, pp.256-257). (26) (Lesley, pp.237-238. ODNB, vol.24, pp.833-835. Tytler, pp.53-54). (27) (Lesley, pp.237-238. Thomson, pp.91).

(28) (CSPF, Mason and Pickering to the council, pp. 77-81). (29) (Knox, pp.96-97). (30) (CSPF, Sir John Mason to the Council, pp. 69-77). (31) (CSP, Spain: November 1550, pp. 184-192 Tytler, p.54). (32) (ODNB, vol.24, 827-833). (33) (Macdonald Fraser, 276-277). (34) (RPCS, Jan 7th, 1551, 194, 195). (35) (CSPF, The Council to Sir John Mason, February 1551, pp. 69-77). (36) (RPCS, Sept 3rd, 1551, 200). (37) (Lesley, p.239). (38) (Lesley, p.241). (39) (CSPF, June 1551, pp.115-129). (40) (CSPF, 'Sir John Mason to the Council', April 1551, pp. 81-98). (41) (ODNB, vol.52, 729-733). (42) (CSPF, Sir John Mason to the Council, April 1551, pp. 81-98). (43) (Lesley, p.239). (44) (Marshal, pp.74-75). (45) (Thomson, p.90). (46) (Lesley, pp.239-241). (47) (SCML, 20th Nov, 1552, CCXLIV, pp.362-363). (48) (Tytler, p.54-55). (49) (Thomson, p.93). (50) (Lesley, p.241). (51) (RPCS, Jan 27th, 1551, 204. Thomson, p.92). (52) (RPCS, March 20th, 1551, 207, 208). (53) (RPCS, March 20th, 1551, 206). (54) (MacCulloch, pp. 273-274. RPCS, March 20th, 1552, 206). (55) (Herkless & Hannay, pp.60-62. ODNB, vol.24, pp.863). (56) (ALHTS, vol.10, pp. xxviii-xxxiii. Gregory, pp.182-183. Lesley, pp.243-244. RPCS, April22nd, 1552, (125). Thomson, (ALHTS, vol.10, pp. xxxii-vvviv..Eddington, pp.15-16. Lesley, pp.243-244. RPCS, pp.132-133. SP, Vol.2, pp.229-230. Thomson, pp.92-93). (59) (ALHTS, vol.10, pp. xxxii-vvviv. SCML, 7th Oct, 1552, CCXLIII, pp.360-361). (60) (ALHTS, vol.10, pp. xxxii-vvviv. RPCS, Dec 6th, 1552, (221, 222). (61) (RPCS, April 22nd, 1552, 126, Oct 19th, 1552, 128). (62) (Thomson, p.261). (63) (RPCS, November 30th, 1552, 217, 218). (64) (RPCS, Dec 12th, 1552, 223, 224). (65) (RPCS, Dec 13th, 1552, 225. (66) (CSP, Spain, December 1552, Volume 10, pp. 596-607). (67) (CP, Volume 1, pp. 94-106). (68) (ODNB, vol.48, 409-410). (69) (ODNB, vol.16, 616-620). (70) (CSPS, Cornille Scepperus to the Queen Dowager, Jan 16th 1553). (71) (RPCS, May 16th, 1553, 231). (72) (CSP, Spain: May 1553, Vol.11, pp. 37-48). (72) (RPCS, August 29th, 1553, 233, 234). (73) (RPCS, Sept 18th, 1553, 238, 239, 240, 241). (74) (Hume-Brown, vol.2, pp. 36-37. ODNB, vol.52, 729-733). (75) (CSPF, November 1553, pp. 22-34). (76) (CSP, Spain: January 1554, 11-20, pp. 20-36). (77) (CSPF, December 1553, pp. 34-44. CSPF, January 1554, pp. 44-54. CSP, Spain: December 1553, Volume 11, pp. 439-446). (78) (CP, Spain, pp. 1-20. RPCS, Jan 11th,

1554, (242)). (79) (ODNB, vol.16, pp.616-620). (80) (SCML, 20th Nov, 1552, CCXLIV, pp.362-363), (81) (SCML, 12th Nov, 1553, CCL, pp.368-369). (82) (CSPF, February 1554, pp.55-69). (83) (CSP, Spain: April 1554, pp. 181-206). (84) (Thomson, pp.92-93). (85) (Thomson, pp.92-93). (86) (ODNB, vol.24, pp.862-864). (87) (Herkless & Hannay, pp.68-79). (88) (APS, April 12th, 1554. Holinshed, pp.549-555.Thomson, pp.92-93)

Chapter Eight

The rascal multitude

Chatelherault had played hard to get the best arrangement for himself and family. He was made Lieutenant-General of Scotland in place of D'Osell, a position which could be passed to his son. He was made exempt from the crown deficit of £30,000 acquired during his term as governor. He was made governor of Dumbarton Castle for 19 years. On April 12th a procession of nobles and prelates rode from the Palace of Holyroodhouse to the Parliament with the Honors of Scotland, the sword, scepter and crown. When the Queen Mother arrived a little later, Chatelherault resigned, and D'Osell crowned the Queen Mother, and handed her sword and scepter. She was now Queen Regent of Scotland.[1]

The Queen Regent began to form a new government and D'Osell was appointed her chief adviser. Bartholomew

Villemore was made Comptroller. Huntley was retained as Chancellor, with Roubay granted responsibility for the Great Seal and seconded to Huntley. The Earl of Cassilis was appointed Lord Treasurer, James MacGill became clerk register, and the Abbot of Coupar kept the Privy Seal, while Bonet was made Baillie of the Orkneys.[2] Her trusted adherent Lord Erskine was given custody of Edinburgh Castle.[3]

In July 1554 Queen Mary Tudor married Philip of Spain. This was a powerful alliance of two Catholic monarchs with powerful resources. It also boded badly for Protestants in England, many of whom would flee to Scotland as religious oppression intensified. However, the Queen Regent of Scotland continued to follow a more lenient attitude towards Protestants, a tactic which took into consideration the Continental rivalries between France and Spain and the potential for war between Scotland and England. She would need to ensure she did not offend the Protestants of Scotland in the event of hostilities breaking out.[4]

The Queen Regent was beset by rebellions in the Orkneys and Western Isles. In June she sent Huntley to the north to deal with John Moidart in the Highlands, whilst Argyll was provided with ships to endeavour against MacLeod of Lewis and Donald, heir of Sleat, both feuding with the MacKenzies. At Dunstaffage Argyll prepared to join with James of Dunyvaig and MacLean, and was provided with a company of harquebusiers led by Sartabous, captain of Dunbar. There is no account of Argyll's expedition.

Huntley led a mixed force of Highlanders and Lowland horsemen. As they approached hills and valleys it was difficult for the horse to advance and Huntley did not want to advance alone with the Highlanders as there was hostility amongst the ranks due to his execution of Macintosh a few years before. The army disbanded and the Lowlanders and Huntley returned to the south.[5]

The Queen regent and the French considered Huntley's failure an act of treason and had him imprisoned.[6] The Earl of Cassilis and other lords would intervene on Huntley's behalf, fearing that this charge of treason, if successfully pushed, could act as a precedent which the French could use against the Scottish nobility. The charge was dropped, yet harsh measures were laid against Huntley. He was deprived of administration of the earldoms of Moray and Mar, and from the governorship of Orkney and Shetland. He was to be banished for five years to France, but this was remitted. The attack against Huntley was extreme, considering past services to the Queen Regent, nevertheless Huntley was very powerful in the north and possibly the accusations were an excuse to cut his power. It alerted the nobility to the danger of such regal attacks being made against their own power and honor.

Further north in Sutherland and Ross a commission was granted in Edinburgh on August 17th to Sir Hugh Kennedy of Girvan Mains to pursue 'Y McKy rebelle'. This campaign resulted in the siege and destruction of the Castle of Borwe in Sutherland. During the early months of her governorship the Queen Regent displayed determination and ruthlessness in setting out to quell lawlessness and insurrection.[7]

There were also many reports of French troops planning to land in Scotland. The Duke of Guise, the Queen Regent's brother, was reported to be going to Scotland, with 3,000 troops, including those Scots who had already served with France. French ships were being prepared, but there was a fear that Calais, still in English hands might be the real aim.[8] Reports abounded that French troops were to sail in 17 ships for Scotland, the numbers said to as large as 15,000. Their aim was seemingly to strengthen the borders. The French ambassador in England complained that the Earl of Lennox was causing mischief with claims that he had had letters signed by the Queen Regent, where she promises to marry the Earl of Bothwell. These letters were said to have been written six years before, although this may be a mistake and may relate to 1543, when Bothwell and Lennox openly competed unsuccessfully for her hand in marriage.[9]

The Queen Regent was an energetic ruler, consistently attending parliament during 1555 in efforts to impose strong centralized government and to regulate trade and commerce. Strong administration of justice was also a concern of hers, and she would attend Justice Ayres in the north of Scotland. On the borders she attended trials against accused thieves and reivers.[10] The growing power and influence of the French in her administration and cabinet would build up resentment amongst the Scots. To counter a possible groundswell against the French, she had an Act of Parliament passed offering severe penalties for anyone insulting Frenchmen, or stirring up trouble against them.[11]

She would also counter anti-French sentiment by a seeming tolerance towards those of a reformed mind. Cassilis was Lord Treasurer, and as advisers she drew close her stepson Lord James Stewart, who was openly sympathetic to Protestant ideas. The Protestant Earl of Glencairn and

Andrew, 1st Lord Ochiltree were also trusted, as was Archibald Campbell, 4th Earl of Campbell, an enthusiastic supporter of reformation, as was his son Lord Archibald of Lorne. Lorne had also married Lady Jane Stewart, natural daughter of James V, making him brother-in-law to Queen Mary of Scots.[12] The Queen Regent may have been conciliatory towards them because she needed their support, but they were also using her conciliation to gradually open Scotland to further reformation.[13] It was in this environment of conciliation that John Knox would arrive in Scotland from Geneva during the autumn of 1555.[14]

Having been released from French captivity after a few years as a galley slave, John Knox travelled to England, where the Privy Council employed him as a preacher in Berwick-upon-Tweed from the spring of 1549. Knox enjoyed a good reputation with his oratory, attracting large congregations amongst the locals and gentry. Whilst his doctrine, influenced by Ulrich Zwingli, was at odds with the Anglican Church, his appointment was more aimed at inspiring religious and political dissent within Scotland, and large numbers of Scots would slip across the borders to see him preach.[15]

With the arrival of Mary Tudor as Queen of England and her strict legislation against Protestants, Knox had to flee to the Continent in 1554. After a brief stay at Dieppe he travelled to the Protestant city-state of Geneva and had an audience with John Calvin, the head of a religious reformation as important as that of Martin Luther.[16] His next important position was in Frankfurt, preaching to a large congregation of English who had fled the rule of Queen Mary Tudor. After being expelled from Frankfurt for entering into potentially dangerous theological arguments with other Protestants, he went to Geneva.[17] Letters from Scotland would invite him to come and preach. From Dieppe he arrived in Edinburgh at the end of autumn and was lodged at the house of James Sym.[18] Knox would be further invited to reside with important nobles, and also to suppers and dinner parties which were covers for private ministries. He received support from several powerful men inspired by reformed religion; John Erskine of Dun, John Lord Erskine, Captain of Edinburgh Castle, the Earl Marishal, the Earl of Glencairn, Sir James Stewart, stepson of the Queen Regent, William Maitland of Lethington and many other influential nobles and gentlemen.[19]

Knox was asked to preach publicly in Edinburgh, which he did with success, and was then invited to preach publicly in Forfar and Ayr. In doing so he built up large followings. In May 1556 the church authorities of Edinburgh summoned him.[20] John Hamilton, the Archbishop of St Andrews, decided that his efforts had to be stopped and ordered him to Blackfriars Church for May 15th to hear charges of heresy. Knox arrived with a large number of people, including Erskine of Dun, and the charges were dropped, whether through 'informality in their proceedings' or 'feared danger'.[21] The Queen Regent is said to have stopped the proceedings because of the threat of violence, and Knox took advantage of this climbdown and continued to preach within the city of Edinburgh.[22]

Glencairn and the Earl Marishal asked Knox to compose a writing to the Queen Regent called "The letter to the Queen Dowager', an invitation to see him preach and a plea for toleration. Having read it she apparently jokingly discarded it by passing it to the Archbishop of Glasgow with a request to write a 'lampoon' upon it.[23] Knox was apparently surprised by this report, believing no doubt from his sponsors that she would be open to discussion. Her attitude seems uncharacteristic to her usually pragmatic approach. Insulting Knox would have insulted the Protestant lords and it seems unlikely she would have wanted to do this. It is possible the report of her disdain was an exaggeration coming from the Archbishop of Glasgow and other clergy to sow dissent between the Queen Regent and the Protestants. Her actions during that summer would back up that view, since she invited the laird of Brunstane, Kirkcaldy of Grange, and Sir Henry Balnaves to return to Scotland and through an Act of Parliament have their lands and titles restored to them. This is remarkable, since the three were implicated in treason plots against Scotland and the latter two were directly involved in the assassination of Cardinal Beaton. In a bid to appease the Protestants she banned certain festivals that offended them, such as the Elections of Robin Hood, the Abbots of Unreason, and Queens of the May. She was drawing to herself the Protestants in Scotland in an effort to stop them allying with England,[24] and across the water in Paris the news of the revocation brought thanks from the influential and admired Balnaves.[25] During July 1556, John Knox left for Geneva, where an English kirk requested him to be their pastor. His leaving surprised the Scottish Protestants and delighted the bishops, who burned an effigy of him at the Cross at Edinburgh.[26]

There was a truce between France and Spain, which the French King hoped would lead to a final peace. Elsewhere

Scots were raiding Ireland again, although there is no evidence of direct involvement of the Scottish Government. The matter was discussed with the French King, who promised a English ambassador that he would write to the Queen Regent and request that she put a stop to the raids if she could.[27]

One measure that drew opposition from all classes and religions in Scotland was her intention to establish a standing army. The estates of the Kingdom were surveyed and tax was to be imposed which would be used to hired troops. This would replace the ancient practice of the feudal muster and diminish the power of the feudal lords. This was seen as an insult to the Scots, who had always seen it as their duty to defend Scotland; in fact monarchs were responsible for defending the Scottish people during times of peace and war, and could not levy new taxes for raising armies. Three hundred barons gathered at Edinburgh to protest this measure of the Queen Regent and her French advisers. They appointed Sir James Sandilands and John Wemys to represent their views. To her credit the Queen Regent considered their points of view and dropped the plans to create a standing army.[28]

Godscroft claimed that the Earl of Angus had helped compose the speech that Wemys and Sandilands presented to the Queen Regent. He also backed the speech with a show of force. When the barons made their way to Edinburgh to remonstrate, a proclamation was put out ordering that no baron will bring a number larger than his household. Angus decided to show fully encased in armour, with 1,000 men. The Queen Regent scolded him for wearing a coat of mail and for bringing so many men. She ordered him to ward himself in Edinburgh prison and handed him a warrant. Upon reaching the prison gates and handing over the warrant, which allowed Angus four attendants, the gatekeeper could not admit Angus because instead of only four being admitted to serve Angus a large throng of followers tried to get inside. Angus turned and went back. This demonstration showed the Queen Regent that the barons were capable of raising enough strong and loyal men to lead into war without the need of a mercenary army.[29]

The Earl of Angus would die in January 1557 at Tantallon Castle; Godscroft says by erysipelas. The French were not sorry as he was a critic and opponent of their steady encroachment into Scotland, once complaining that they would bring 'French laws and they be sharp'. He was proud of the *Order of St Michael* he received from France, but his relationship with the Queen Regent was rocky. Once when she was trying to gain control of Tantallon Castle he commented whilst feeding a goshawk, 'Confound this greedy gled, she can never have enough', which was a reference that the Queen Regent did not catch. Although Angus's relationship with Scotland could be ambiguous, he did consider that he had done good service to his nation country. When the Queen Regent considered making Huntley a Duke, Angus replied 'If he be a duke(duck) then I be a drake,' and he also implied a threat that if Huntley was awarded Angus would not easily lose his place in the hierarchy, which he claimed his ancestors had won through service to the crown. The Queen Regent took this hint and thought it better not to award Huntley a dukedom.[30]

Under Angus and his brother George, the Red Douglas family was one of the most powerful and infamous families in Scotland, such that both France and England thought it necessary to win them to their side during any struggle. Their political and military actions had profound effects on the development of politics, whether during the reign of James V or during the minority of Queen Mary. Angus was buried in his ancestral home at Abernethy. Unlike his brother Sir George Douglas, who was a Protestant, Angus, despite his long association with the Protestant party, seems to have kept to the Catholic faith. He died in his bed grasping a crucifix.[31]

With Angus gone another kind of warrior would emerge, this one less inclined towards bloody warfare and more towards fiery evangelical oratory. John Knox had been preaching in Geneva when he received a letter, dated March 10th 1557, inviting him to return to Scotland and spread the Calvinist doctrine. The letter was signed by the Earl of Glencairn, Lord Lorne, Erskine of Dun and Lord James Stewart. In the letter they stated that the Friars were in 'less estimation' with 'the Queen's grace and the rest of the nobility'. The Protestants who signed the letter represented a significant power block within Scotland, and inviting Knox was of religious significance. It was also politically important as it set out to challenge the pro-Catholic French power block within Scotland. The four were also close to the Queen Regent and the letter implied that through her disapproval of the established church it might be open to further reforms.[32] Knox consulted with John Calvin before setting off in the autumn.[33]

Matters on the Continent would have a direct effect on Scottish/English relations. France was defeated by Spain at the battle of St Quentin, August 10th 1557, and King Henry called on the Queen Regent to declare war on England and divert the English soldiery away from the Continent. At that time English and Scottish commissioners were at Carlisle in non-hostile negotiations. She called a council meeting at Newbattle asking for a declaration of war, a plea which was refused,[34] and not getting approval from the council to declare war, she decided on some arbitrary action to provoke hostilities from the English. D'Osell led French and Scots from Dunbar and captured Fort Desmond or Eyemouth, near Berwick, which over the next few months was refortified and provisioned to the sum of £1861.17s. Cannon and food supplies were transported by oxen indicating a large garrison. The whole exercise was a breach of the Treaty of Norham.

Skirmishing ensued around Berwick, and the commissioners were recalled from Carlisle. To add to this two 'bastard sons' of James V and a 'gentleman' from near the borders, who may have been Lord Hume, led 3,000 into England, burned some villages and returned with a great number of livestock. There was a English counter-raid, led by Northumberland, which by account left them 'satisfied with their progress'; they had lifted some 4,000 livestock and prisoners. It was reported that whilst the Scots were testing and wearing out the border defences, the real aim was the capture of Berwick. The King of Spain was asked to send ships from Flanders and the Low Countries and cut all economic ties with the Scots. Philip sent an ambassador to find out if the Scots sought war; if they did he would declare war against them. The Spanish were also wary of security on the seas. Whilst they had a fleet of ships patrolling northern seas and defending against Scots pirates, there were concerns about reports that the French were outfitting 20-30 ships which could be used in the north.⁽³⁵⁾

Philip, King of Spain and King of England, sent his ambassador D'Assonleville to visit Queen Mary and learn the reasons why the Scots were raiding the border. He was also to remind the Scots of the danger of disrupting economic relations with Flanders and the Low Countries. He also intended to visit Scotland, and met with the Queen Regent and her council to discuss the latest hostilities. D'Assonleville also had licence to treat with the Duke of Chatelherault and to deliver some letters, and to emphasize that Philip believed that the French were stirring up conflict for their own ends. By meeting the Duke he would be attempting to gain a sympathetic ear from Chatelherault, and possibly turn him against the French. He was also to assess the feelings of the civic authorities, the nobility and the people with regard to the breakout of warfare, and gather knowledge about the divisions and factions within Scotland.⁽³⁶⁾

During September the fighting on the borders intensified. Huntley and D'Osell returned to Eyemouth and endeavoured to fortify it whilst fighting off English attacks. In one encounter 500 English were slain, and in another against the Earl of Northumberland's light horse the lord's standard was captured. In a raid against Berwick the stores of hay were burned, depriving the town of much-needed supplies. In Tweedsdale another 500 English were defeated. Overall nearly 2,000 men were killed or made prisoners. The English got the better of Lord Hume when he led a raid across the border, defeated him at Blackbrey. The mutual hostilities made a mockery of any peace treaties and the Queen Regent declared war and ordered a muster to invade England.[37]

The army met at Kelso on October 11th 1557. Chatelherault as Lieutenant-General was put in command. However there was reluctance in the Scottish nobility to cross over the border. They argued that they were prepared to defend the country but not to invade England and thereby be perceived as the aggressor. The nobles speaking against invasion were Chatelherault, Cassilis, Huntley and Argyll. D'Osell would later claim that he was certain he had gained the Archbishop of St Andrew's support in waging war against England and there was a hope that he could convince Chatelherault. He would later learn that for whatever reasons the Archbishop would change his position and side with his brother in opposing the invasions.[38]

Chatelherault would discuss with Sir Henry Percy a few years later the reasons for not advancing towards Wark, even though it was 'not provided nor furnished' against attack. The reason given was that the top nobility did not support the wars instigated by the Queen Regent, the 'French and Scottish flatterers who wanted to enrich themselves'. It is difficult to believe that the above nobility, with extensive experience of warfare, would decline an opportunity to invade, as their forces were stronger than the English. Huntley had already invaded alongside D'Osell, so his reluctance does not ring true. There is no evidence that D'Assonleville, the Spanish envoy, succeeded in his mission and made contact with Chatelherault, although if he did then it is not outside the realms of possibility that gold was offered to halt a Scottish invasion.[39]

With the bulk of the Scottish army refusing to cross the border the Queen Regent in disgust sent D'Osell with an artillery train to besiege Wark. This he did, whilst the nobility on the borders demanded his recall. To emphasize their determination they threatened to disband the army. D'Osell was recalled by the Queen Regent and as he withdrew he was attacked by the borderers and the Wark garrison,[40] and it was this humiliation by the Scottish nobles that sharpened the division between them and the Queen Regent and her French cohorts. Chatelherault, Argyll, Cassilis and Huntley had positioned themselves as opposition to the Queen Regent.[41]

Up to late 1557 the Protestant faith in Scotland continued to survive through the efforts of Harlow, Willock, and others. By late September John Knox was at Dieppe, preparing to travel to Scotland under invitation from Glencairn, Lorne, Erskine of Duns and Lord James Stewart. However he received a letter from the lords stating that the time was not right for his return. 'Confounded' and 'with sorrow and anguish', Knox sent a letter to the Scottish nobles expressing his disappointment whilst encouraging them to continue to follow the 'Reformation of Religion'. His words seem to have spurred the lords to give a written commitment in support of reformation.

On December the 3rd 1557 five lords put signatures to bonds and covenants giving their oath to establish the reformed religion in Scotland. They were the Earl of Argyll, his son Lord Lorne, Erskine and Glencairn, and they were joined by James Douglas, Earl of Morton, the son of Sir George.[42] Their religion was not Lutheran or that of Anglican church, it was Calvinist, and similar to that of the

Huguenots, who were also presenting a problem to France. They made their proposals in the form of a petition, which James Sandilands of Calder presented to the Queen Regent early in 1558.

The petitioners became known as the Lords of the Congregation. They were opposed to the corrupt practices of prelates and the church, and they wanted public and private freedom of worship in their native language, which would bring better understanding of the scriptures to the people.[43] Sir James Melville wrote that the Queen Regent had been able to appease or manipulate the powerful Protestants, 'ingratiating herself with them' and turning a blind eye to 'their secret preaching'. Yet whilst the Protestant religion began to spread and become better organized through the work of the Lord of the Congregation and the preachers, the Queen Regent may have realised that this was a phenomenon that could be controlled or contained and she now considered taking harsher measures against religious dissent. With her authority having been challenged in the recent warfare, she would be in danger of being perceived as weak. However, she had to be cautious, since with the future marriage of her daughter to the Dauphin she would need the conditions of marriage to be ratified by parliament so that France could take a stronger hold on Scotland.[44]

With respect to the resistance of Scottish nobles to invade England on behalf of France, Henry II felt it was necessary to bind Scotland closer to France. A letter was presented to the Scottish Parliament from Henry II, King of France, on December 14th 1557, urging the finalization of the marriage between Queen Mary of Scotland and the

Dauphin. Eight commissioners were chosen to go to France and negotiate the terms of the marriage treaty. James Beaton, Archbishop of Glasgow, Robert Reid, Bishop of Orkney and James Stewart, Prior of St Andrews, represented the church. George Lesley, Earl of Rothes, the Earl of Cassilis and Lord Fleming represented the lords. The provosts of Edinburgh and Montrose represented the commoners. They were to ensure that the final treaty protected the ancient rights, laws and independence of Scotland.

After a stormy journey with two ships and some lives lost, the commissioners arrived in France and were escorted to the French court. The negotiations led to an agreement in which the Dauphin would be recognised as King of Scotland, and the arms of Scotland and France would be combined. The eldest son of the marriage would become King of Scotland and France. If there were no sons and only daughters, the eldest daughter would become Queen of Scotland, but future marriages would be decided by the three Estates of Scotland and the King of France. These conditions and more were satisfactory to the commissioners.[45]

War did continue on the borders, and Holinshed gives an exhausting account of the campaigning and some brutal battles and skirmishing. From around Christmas French troops and Scots receiving French pay would raid England and burn settlements and lift livestock, and the English border captains would retaliate in equally brutal fashion. The Earl of Bothwell as lieutenant, Lord Keith and the Laird of Grange were some of the prominent Scots lords in these campaigns. On the side of the English were the Earls of

Northumberland and Westmoreland and Lord Talbot. Sea raids were conducted in the Orkneys, whilst the Earl of Sussex, Lord Deputy of Ireland, wasted Arran, Cumbrae, Kintyre and other isles on the western coasts.[46] Thomson wrote that because of this fighting many English lords had left the Continent to defend their lands against the Scots and in doing so the defence of Calais was weakened, so it was easily recaptured by the Duke of Guise on January 8th 1558. The fighting on the borders would drag on into late 1558, and severe taxes were raised to pay the French troops, who did not always get paid from France. A sum of £24,790 was raised over a period of five months prior to October 1558.[47]

The Lords of the Congregation seemingly took no part in this fighting. Possibly with so many French troops on the borders this was an opportunity to pursue their agenda of religious reform within Scotland. Individuals such as the Earl of Argyll and other Protestant nobles and gentry encouraged more public preaching. The Archbishop of St Andrews entered into a correspondence with the Earl of Argyll. He was critical that Argyll was employing a pastor called John Douglas whom he identified as following heretical practices. He offered to send a teacher to instruct Argyll on proper doctrine. Argyll defended Douglas as well as defending his own position, stating that Douglas was preaching against the same vices that Christians should oppose, such as corruption, fornication and idolatry, and in some way it was a criticism of a church associated with these attributes. The correspondence between them was done in a courteous and thoughtful manner, yet Argyll warned about the dangers of Scots becoming divided on the issue of religion and how certain Houses within Scotland would benefit from civil strife. Argyll was too powerful to be persecuted, but the church within Scotland continued to attack those without material power.[48]

There was another invitation to John Knox to return. The clergy were alarmed and called this resistance to their authority as acts of treason. In their opinion the Lords of the Congregation were a political party using religious dissent to gain public support. They sought to use petitions and the threat of rebellion to command legislation. Yet the Queen Regent had to be cautious, not wishing to alienate or antagonize the Protestants whilst important negotiations were going on in France.[49]

The church authorities were on the other hand prepared to act. On 28th April 1558, an elderly preacher called Walter Mill was executed for heresy. He preached around Angus, and had at one time when younger been a guest of Cardinal Beaton at St Andrews until escaping and hiding out in Scotland. With the apparent tolerance of the Queen Regent he began to openly preach again but was arrested on heresy charges. He was taken to St Andrews, tried and burned at the stake. This act did not discourage the reformed religion, but it made people more determined to defy church and state authorities. The Lords of the Congregation demanded an audience with the Queen Regent, who denied involvement with the act, and this may be true, as the execution had been speedily carried through.[50]

Besides Harlow preaching and teaching in Edinburgh, John Douglas now began preaching in Leith and Paul Methven in Dundee. The Queen Regent was pressured by the clergy to exert her authority; these preachers were blatantly challenging the crown and church authorities. She issued a proclamation calling on the preachers to appear in Edinburgh on July 19th, but another great gathering converged on the city. Armed men surrounded her palace, their grievances articulated by a baron called Chambers of Gathgirth. They placed no blame on the Queen Regent, implying that they believed she was being manipulated by the clergy. He stated that they were prepared to fight for the preachers, and placed 'steel caps' on their heads to emphasize their determination to oppose the clergy. The Queen Regent stated that she meant no harm to the preachers and she postponed the summons.[51]

The protestors were heartened by this success. The date for the trial before ecclesiastical judges was the day of the St Giles Festival. During the Sacred Procession of St Giles a Protestant crowd rioted, the image was vandalized and the ceremony halted. The arranged trial was also postponed.[52] There followed a fruitless hunt for the rioters, afterwards the Queen Regent continued the course of toleration. She also persuaded the clergy to modify their hatred for the Protestants and to enter into debates instead of conflicts. A proposal to meet in open discussion was initially accepted by the clergy and then refused when the Protestants insisted that scripture alone would be the basis for argument, disarming the Catholics of council decrees and canon law to quote from.

There were attempts at compromise, but here the Protestants rejected the Catholic proposals, which in return for tolerance the Protestants were to accept the idea of purgatory, the mass, and prayers to images and saints. This the Protestants would not do. The Queen Regent attempted to buy time by listening to applications from the

Protestants. She agreed to review the proposals for reform at the next parliament once the commissioners returned from France, and in return for this commitment the Protestants agreed not to hold any more assemblies or public preaching in cities and towns. The Lords of the Congregation asked John Douglas to withdraw from public preaching in Leith.[53]

Whilst the Queen Regent used diplomacy to slow down religious dissent in Scotland, in France a secret diplomacy was adopted by King Henry II and the young Queen of Scotland's uncles. They presented the fifteen-year-old Mary with three papers to sign. This was done without the knowledge of the Scottish commissioners. She was to agree that in the event of her dying without heirs the Kingdom of Scotland would pass to the King of France as a free gift, and if the Scots opposed this the King of France was to be reimbursed of the amount spent on Queen Mary's education and maintenance in France.[54] The third paper would testify that Queen Mary was of sound mind when signing these agreements, and overall the three papers would supersede any other treaties.[55]

The marriage was concluded on April 11th 1558 with Queen Mary and François betrothed in the Great Hall of the Louvre Palace in Paris. On April 24th the actual royal wedding took place in Notre Dame Cathedral, followed by celebrations across Paris and France as throngs of people entered the city to witness the grand occasion. When news reached Scotland celebrations were organized during June and July across the country in the form of processions and ceremonies. Whilst both King and Queen were young, François being 14 and Mary 15, they were a contrasting couple. François being small, was described as not attractive, shy, moody and lacking people skills, whilst she was tall, elegant, outgoing and attractive. Yet they were apparently close and affectionate playmates, and she was caring and defensive of her 'sweetheart and friend'.[56]

Four days after the marriage the commissioners were asked to return to Scotland and bring to France the Crown-Matrimonial and royal regalia of Scotland and present them to the Dauphin. The Commissioners stated that this was beyond the duties and responsibilities assigned to them and they would need to first consult the Scottish parliament.[57]

As the commissioners set off for Scotland, four of the nine became ill and died. Robert Reid, the Bishop of Orkney became sick and died on September 6th, and the Earl of Cassilis and the Earl of Rothes followed several days later.[58] The three had been in Dieppe at the time. Sir James Stewart, also at Dieppe, was also struck by illness, yet managed to survive and return to Scotland. In Paris Lord Fleming also became ill and died. Many of their attendants also suffered illness and death,[59] and as there was no disease prevalent in France, it was suspected that poison was used against the commissioners. Poison was a common method attributed to the Guise family, and if they were the culprits it implies that the four victims and Sir James Stewart were leading obstacles to French designs.[60]

As to the manner of their deaths, Knox points the finger of suspicion at the Continental foods that all victims had feasted from, and to a Frenchman who prepared the foods. Upon arriving back in Scotland the Queen Regent was reportedly surprised on learning of the deaths, yet she called them 'beasts', and stated that 'God is not with them, neither with that which they enterprise'. What this 'enterprise' entailed was not revealed, although it may be support of the reformation. Knox called them the 'patrons of papistry', a statement of irony since Cassilis, Fleming, Rothes and Stewart were openly Protestant or sympathetically minded, whilst Reid was the only Catholic among the victims.[61]

On the mainland other prelates would pass on. Andrew Durie. Bishop of Galloway died on October 1st 1558 and was replaced by Alexander Gordon, Bishop of Athens and brother of the Earl of Huntley. Knox attributed Durie's death to the shock of the Edinburgh riots on St Giles Day, September 1st.[62] David Paniter would suffer a 'lingering death' at Stirling, also on October 1st, and his replacement, Henry Sinclair, would be nominated by the Queen Regent.[63] James Stewart, another illegitimate son of James V and Commendator of the Abbeys of Kelso and Melrose, died a youth in 1558, and the Queen Regent passed the Commendatorship to her brother the Cardinal of Lorraine.[64] 1558 was a year when several prominent prelates and nobles met their deaths.

Fraser does not attribute the deaths in France to poison as she argues that the Scots when returning home did not call for an inquiry. This is true, yet possibly this was a tactical decision as they did not have the evidence. There also may have been reluctance at that time to openly challenge the French in Scotland, and it should be remembered the Queen Regent had introduced an Act of Parliament in 1555 not to insult or slander Frenchmen or stir up trouble against them. Accusing the French King or the Queen Mother's brothers of poison without proof would constitute a severe criminal offence,[65] although in later years there would be many stories of poisoning committed by the Guise family.

Why the French king or the Guise family would poison the commissioners is hard to explain. They had achieved through diplomacy the marriage treaty. As five were poisoned and four survived it may be that the former were opposed to the handing over the crown and royal regalia, important symbols that would effectively make François King of Scotland and enable the French to argue that they ruled Scotland. The poisonings would also be an example of Guise power and their ability to intimidate potential opponents and enemies. During the reign of Queen Elizabeth of England poison plots by the Guise family would cause a measure of panic and paranoia, which was in many cases the purpose of the reports. Whatever stories of poisonings were spreading across Scotland, the Lords of the Congregation would not use them politically against the regime of Mary of Guise.

The Lords had a plan; they would approach the Queen Regent and ask her to support their reformation, or at least give them protection against church oppression. Their demands would be forwarded in a solemn and moderate manner. A parliament was assembled during November in Edinburgh. The Protestants presented a petition which they asked the Queen Regent to present to the Three Estates. They requested that until a European conference was assembled that would consider the disputes between reformed religions and the Catholic religion, then no churchmen should be given the power to try or punish reformers, and that clergymen could not sit as judges.

Anyone accused of heresy should be allowed to be tried by judicial authorities and the question of their guilt or innocence should be determined by the laws inscribed within the Bible. The Queen Regent did not put the petition before the Three Estates, claiming that the pressing business of parliament and the nation had to take priority. She promised that on a later date their petition would be fully considered. The Protestants were satisfied with her answer.

From the four surviving commissioners the Three Estates gained an account of the terms of the marriage agreement. With the Protestants joining the Catholics the terms were ratified. They also agreed to send the Crown Regalia to France, and François and Mary would be known as King and Queen of Scotland.[66] Argyll and Lord James Stewart, both having sympathy with reformed religions, were asked to take the items to the Dauphin.[67] Argyll refused to perform this task.[68] The Archbishop of St Andrews was also reportedly against sending these items; he still considered the possibility of the young Queen Mary dying without heirs and his own House of Hamilton succeeding to the crown, and it would be easier to crown Chatelherault with the Regalia if it was in Scotland. He could not openly oppose the French proposals, but he, like many others in the country, was wearying of their domination.[69]

Chatelherault put forward a claim that his interests as heir to the succession were still secure, and the Archbishop and the new Earl of Cassilis acted as witnesses. The Duke was still a dangerous rival to the ambitions of the Queen Regent, and it appears that during 1558 he was proposing the marriage of Henry VIII's daughter Elizabeth to his son, James, 3rd Earl of Arran. This marriage would have linked Hamilton dynastic ambitions with that of the crown of England and forward the prospect of a union of the crowns. It was a prospect that would seriously rival that of the French marriage. Unfortunately Elizabeth's thoughts on this proposal are not known, although the Bishop of Salisbury was supportive, as was John Knox. Chatelherault may have contemplated this move, as the French King's promise to find his son a bride had not been fulfilled. Henry II had offered the hands of several noble ladies, none of which for various reasons led to marriage. In 1557 Chatelherault had approved of a match with Henry's illegitimate daughter Mademoiselle de Bouillon, daughter of Diane de Poitiers, but this too failed to materialize. There were also reports that Arran had converted to the reformed religion, a fact which made him an unfavourable prospect for the French noble families. Chatelherault, a powerful foe to the Queen Regent, lacked the alliances to fully challenge her, and appears to have been waiting for circumstances to change in his favour.[70]

During these parliamentary sessions the Lords of Congregation produced another petition, called the 'Protestation', requesting from the Three Estates that the people be allowed freedom of worship and reformation of religion. They also wanted to debate with the Catholic Church on who was the true representative of God. There was also a commitment not to introduce a violent reformation. Their intention was to follow a legal path to reformation, and they asked for protection from the 'sacred authorities', being the Queen Regent and the parliament.

The Queen Regent listened to their proposals, which the Three Estates refused to register in the parliamentary records.[71] She assured the Lords that she would consider their views and would only act on matters of religion 'that now be in controversy'. The Lords were content with this response, although it did not satisfy the general public, who sought immediate attention to their grievances.[72]

On November 17th 1558 Queen Mary Tudor died and her half-sister Elizabeth, daughter of Henry VIII, became Queen. The Lords of the Congregation and the Protestants had fought their campaign alone without any international help. Now, with the Protestant Elizabeth on the throne of Protestant England, that might change. With Mary Tudor dead this was an opportunity for the Guise family to exert themselves in Scotland and then prepare for deposing Elizabeth of England. Elizabeth was the daughter of Anne Boleyn, Henry's second wife, and as the Papacy did not sanction Henry's divorce of his first wife Katherine of Aragon, Elizabeth was considered illegitimate with no legal right to the throne. The Catholic League of Pope, Spain and Emperor was determined on the destruction of the reformation, and the Guise family was enthusiastic supporters of this.

The Cardinal of Lorraine would persuade the King to send Monsieur Bettancourt, Master of the Household to Scotland, to meet the Queen Regent and desire her to join the League and focus her efforts in crushing the reformed religions.[73] The Queen Regent had been reluctant to join the League as it would put her on a collision course with the strong Protestant party, with which she had long sought an understanding. Yet the meeting with Bettancourt had a profound effect. She was expected not only to follow the wishes of the King of France and her brothers, but also the Catholic League. Such pressures were immense and she would eventually bow to them as the reformation grew stronger.

The Guises would also insist that Mary Queen of Scots should also be titled Queen of England and Ireland and join the symbols of England with those of Scotland and France.[74] This meant Elizabeth's reign would in the future be threatened by France and the claims of the Guise-sponsored Mary Queen of Scots, so it would be natural that in time she would need Scottish allies.

Another Protestant manifesto made an appearance in January 1st 1559, called the 'Beggar's Summons', and numerous religious establishments across Scotland had placards carrying the manifesto nailed to doors and attached to gates. It accused the churches of misappropriating funds meant for the poor, the blind, the lame, children, widows and orphans. The accusers were to cease their corrupt practice of 'stealing' from those that could not fend for themselves, or else be expelled by force. On March 1st the Queen Regent called a provincial council of the church as a means to address the grievances of the Protestants. Although some measures introduced were reform-minded it was possibly too late to appease the Protestants, who no longer sought reform of the church, instead wanting to replace it with their own style of worship.[75]

By the end of March unauthorized preaching had been prohibited, and the church interpretation of Easter had to be followed. On behalf of those Protestant supporters of the preachers, the Earl of Glencairn and Sir Hew Campbell, the Sheriff of Ayr visited the Queen Regent, and despite the tense atmosphere she agreed to halt her action. Yet her authority was challenged across Scotland, and in Dundee, Perth and Montrose the preachers were given the right by civic authorities to halt rallies and congregations. She ordered all preachers to gather in Stirling for May 10th. Erskine of Dun was sent to speak to her.[76] Once more she agreed not to prosecute the preachers. Once Erskine had left her, and perhaps by the encouragement of the Archbishop of St Andrews, she changed her mind and declared the preachers outlaws for not showing at Stirling.[77]

Large sections across Scotland began to challenge the authority of the Queen Regent's government and her Frenchmen by building up a well-orchestrated and popular movement for religious reform. Rumours of how the commissioners met their deaths may have also served their cause, because of the Guise family's reputation for dispatching enemies through poison.[78] At Perth, where John Knox was preaching, having returned from France on May 2nd 1559, there were riots where churches and monasteries were vandalized. Iconoclastic behaviour was now a characteristic of the 'rascal multitude', as Knox called the rioters.

The Queen Regent called levies from Clydesdale, Stirlingshire and the Lothians to gather at Stirling for May 24th. She also had her experienced French troops under D'Osell,[79] and would later be accused of being conciliatory to the Protestants in order to win their favour until French power was fully established in Scotland and the Crown Matrimonial had been claimed. There may be a measure of truth in this, but whilst she was accused of 'Guisian practices' by Knox and others, her history of associations with Protestants suggest that she may have been open to the idea of tolerance. Unfortunately there were powerful forces to contend with; the French and her anti-reformation Guise kin, and the Catholic Church in Scotland, which were pressuring her away from conciliation. It would have been difficult to balance these opposing forces so as to avoid civil conflict. With the rioting and the breakdown of public order, she would now be forced to sideline arbitration and adopt a harder and more oppressive attitude.[80]

D'Osell gathered 8,000 French and Scots and advanced to Auchterarder, 12 miles from Perth. The walls of Perth had been strengthened by the Protestants. Calling themselves the Faithful Congregation of Christ Jesus in Scotland, they responded in a letter dated May 22nd stating that they wanted freedom of worship and were prepared to 'take the sword of just defence' to uphold this right. Whilst Argyll was a Lord of the Congregation, and Lord James Stewart sympathetic to reformation, they were sent to Perth by the Queen Regent to find out what the people of Perth wanted. Once again they claimed freedom of worship was what they sought, whilst the Queen Regent would argue that what they were engaging in was rebellion. The Queen Regent sent a proclamation by the Lyon King of Arms that they should surrender under 'pain of treason'. The Earl of Glencairn arrived with 2,500 Ayrshire men, and once more the Queen Regent had to negotiate. She granted freedom of worship, and also agreed that no French troops would enter Perth.

On May 29th the Queen Regent marched into Perth along with Chatelherault, the Archbishop and several nobles and prelates. She was angered by the destruction of church property. She began to replace the provost and lawful magistrates, and authorized 400 troops to defend the churches and suppress the reformers. This was a breach of the promise not to impose French soldiers. Although she would argue that they were Scottish troops they were technically waged by France, and she reportedly said she would not honor promises to heretics.[81] With Perth seemingly secure, the Queen Regent marched to Falkland.

Argyll and Lord James Stewart, weary of this double-dealing and of what Knox called 'mere tyranny and falsehood', openly joined the Lords of the Congregations. They called a muster for St Andrews on June 3rd for the purpose of marching to Perth and supporting the Protestants. They were joined near Cupar by the Lord Ruthven, the Earl of Menteith and Murray of Tullibardine. They bound themselves faithfully to support each other and promote the cause of reformation. John Knox was intending to hold a sermon in St Andrews and received a warning from the Archbishop, who entered the town with 100 spears, that Knox would be praised with guns if he attempted to speak from the pulpit. Knox decided to give a sermon on June 11th despite the threat and advice of friends, and related the account of Jesus throwing the moneylenders and traders out of the Temple of Jerusalem. Whilst Knox would condemn the wanton violence of the 'rascal multitude' his words would inspire his audience to destroy religious buildings, smashing religious icons and images.[82] The Archbishop fled out of St Andrews to Falkland, and pleaded that the Queen Regent should punish the rioters. After some advice she proposed first capturing Cupar.[83] D'Osell and Chatelherault, the Lieutenant-general of the Scottish army, marched to Cupar to prepare for an assault on St Andrews.

Initially leading a small force of around 100 horse and foot, Argyll and Lord James would be joined by Lothian Lairds from Ormiston, Calder, Halton, Restalrig and Colstoun, and from Fife new recruits would arrive, adding up to around 3,000 men by June 13th. They positioned themselves at Cupar Muir and were arrayed with such military skill that their true numbers were concealed, and passages leading to them were strictly guarded.[84] The artillery was positioned in such a way as to defend all sides. More and more people from far and wide would join the congregation as if 'men had rained from the clouds'. D'Osell and Chatelherault did not have enough men to be certain of victory, and amongst their ranks there were French Huguenots who might be sympathetic with the Scots. According to Melville, who visited the Queen Mother at this time, she was 'offended' at this failure to engage militarily with the Congregation. The Queen Regent agreed a truce for eight days, with the Protestants demanding that the French army leave Fife .[85]

There was hope that a peaceful settlement could be reached, and commissioners were arranged by both sides to meet at St Andrews. The Protestants restated their aims of demanding freedom from oppression and being allowed to worship in peace according to their consciences. The Queen Regent used the lull in fighting to ship French troops and artillery across the Firth of Forth. The Lords of the Congregation, realising that they were being tricked, marched to Perth. The Queen Regent had imposed as provost her own choice of the Laird of Kinfaun. As the Protestants laid siege to Perth they demanded that Kinfaun open the gates, but he refused. Once more the Queen Regent attempted to negotiate, and this time the Lords attacked Perth. On June 24th the Lord Ruthven assaulted the west of the town with cannon whilst the forces from Dundee advanced from the east. The garrison surrendered and were allowed to march out with full honors on June 25th.[86]

A mob of Dundee Protestants marched from Perth to the Abbey of Scone to confront Patrick Hepburn, Bishop of Moray, who was responsible for the burning of Walter Mill. The Abbey was demolished and burned, despite the Lords and John Knox trying to stop them. An elderly women praised the destruction, comparing the Abbey to a 'den of whoredom' and expressed her hatred for a bishop who she accused of corruption and immoral behaviour.[87] As the Queen Regent sought to garrison Stirling, Lord James Stewart and Argyll pre-empted her by occupying it first. They found that prior to their capture of Stirling the people had risen up and destroyed churches and monasteries. The Lords were clearly having problems controlling the violent riots that were occurring, and in Linlithgow similar destruction ensued.

In Edinburgh there was potential for mob violence, and in a surprising move the Queen Regent moved her forces away from the capital to Dunbar. This allowed the Lords an opportunity to occupy Edinburgh. From June 26th they had taken Stirling, and on June 29th they took Edinburgh with a small group of nobles and retainers.[88] The Laird of Kirkcaldy wrote to Sir Henry Percy at Berwick, stating that their aim was to persuade the Queen Regent to support the reformation in Scotland. They would still give her allegiance if she did this, and would allow the crown the revenues of the abbeys and monasteries. There would be no peace if she rejected it. John Knox would also write to Percy outlining the reformers' purpose as freedom of worship. He insisted that this was not rebellion against a just monarch, but implied that if the Queen Regent was not checked then victory for the French would cause the Scots to 'mourn and smart', yet 'England will not escape worse trouble'. Knox was saying that it was in England's national interests to help the Scottish Protestants. A Catholic victory, in his opinion, would turn Scotland into a French stepping-stone into Protestant England.

At Dunbar the Queen Regent began a propaganda campaign against the reformers. She targeted her half-brother Sir James Stewart, stating that reformation of religion was not his goal and he sought the Crown of Scotland, despite being illegitimate. She made a proclamation in the name of King Francois and Queen Mary ordering the Lords to leave Edinburgh within six hours, and accused them of appropriating the irons of the mint. The Lords declined and once more asked for a peaceful settlement, sending several delegations to the Queen Regent with a request that matter should be discussed before parliament. Finally a conference was arranged for Preston on July 12th, with both sides sending eight commissioners and accompanied by 100 men. The Duke of Chatelherault and Huntley were chief amongst the Queen Regent's party, and Moray and Argyll were chief amongst the reformers. The preachers wanted to use the parliament to debate with the bishops on the subject of scripture interpretation. Despite these intentions the Queen Regent was once more playing for time.

The feudal array called by the Lords would soon reach the 40-day limit and the troops would be allowed to dismiss themselves and return home. The power of the Lords would then diminish and they would have to rely on their own retinue and paid troops, which would further strain their resources. The Queen Regent, on the other hand, had a contracted army of French and Scots, paid for with French coin. Based at Dunbar, she would receive supplies from France, and the treaty with England would ensure no interference with transport routes.

News then reached the Queen Regent that made her determined to crush the reformation as quickly as possible. In July Henry II of France was killed during a jousting tournament, when a splinter from a lance pierced his head above the eye. He died ten days later, on July 10th..[89] Soon to be Queen of France, Mary's youth was practically over as she would now be thrown into the forefront of Renaissance politics.

With the Lords of the Congregation weakened by loss of troops, the Queen Regent sent her own army towards Edinburgh. The Lords arrayed themselves at Craigend Gate, preparing to fight.[90] D'Osell and Chatelherault had entered Leith and were preparing to attack. Chatelherault's true opinion at that time is difficult to gauge. Events in France would have a bearing on the political and religious path he would follow. During the month of June Queen Mary had taken seriously ill, and with Chatelherault's son now close to the succession Henry II had ordered him to be arrested. It appears also that the Earl of Arran had openly adopted the Protestant religion, setting up a congregation in Chatelherault and employing a Pastor from Poitiers.

Arran's religious convictions, if he was allowed freedom, would encourage the Protestants in Scotland and had already attracted the attention of the English.

Arran fled to hide in the woods near Chatelherault, and making contact with English agents was assisted in escaping to Switzerland. Lord Cecil of England would cite the example of Arran and how he had been treated in France in a letter composed on July 28th to the Lord of the Congregation. He would also note the fate of Chatelherault's second son David, cruelly imprisoned by the French, and how Queen Mary had vowed to wipe out the house of Hamilton. Cecil advised the Lords of the Congregation to empathize with the Duke: 'God open his heart according to his knowledge'.[91]

When about to face the army of the congregation, representing a religion that he himself had been sympathetic to, and was now adopted by his refugee son, Chatelherault would have faced a personal dilemma. The Queen Regent, possibly recognising the danger of fully relying on Chatelherault with his son Arran considered an enemy of France, decided to resort to negotiations. Chatelherault, D'Osell and Huntley put their signatures to a truce agreed to run from July 24th to January 1st 1560. During this period religious freedom was to be granted to both sides. The clergy would not be impeded on church business and there would be no more destruction of church property. The Queen Regent was allowed access to royal houses and establishments. There would be no garrison placed in Edinburgh. The Lords retired their forces to Stirling and endeavoured to stay united, realising that there would be attempts to undermine their cause. Fresh bonds were entered into, and they vowed not to communicate with the Queen Regent or any of her people without the knowledge of the other Lords.

The Lords also sent correspondence to Sir William Cecil, the Queen's secretary in England, requesting money and aid. They repeated their aims, seeking freedom of worship, liberty from oppression, and the eviction of French troops. They offered friendship with England, and would preserve this friendship with their lives and until their deaths. Elizabeth began to see the consequences to England if the Scottish Protestants were to fail. However she could not openly support them due to the treaty with France.[92]

There was a common belief that Chatelherault would join the Protestants once his son returned from the Continent, where the English spy network was hoping to pass him into England, then Scotland. It was expected that as second person of the realm he would lead the Lords of the Congregation. Knox noted how in Edinburgh Chatelherault attended a sermon by John Willock at St Giles Church. The Queen Regent and her closest advisers reminded Chatelherault of the dangers of going to these sermons as he would be associated with the Lords of the Congregation. Chatelherault had already begun to introduce a few conditions on the Queen Regent to give him an excuse to defect, such as opposition to French troops entering Edinburgh. This was Chatelherault's convenient opt-out, if he chose to use it.[93]

John Knox was sent to Berwick in early August to negotiate support from the English. In a secret interview with Sir James Croft, the Governor, he requested that the English supply money and arms, so that the Lords of the

Congregation could seize Stirling, and also asked for naval assistance in taking Dundee, Perth and Broughty Craig. He suggested that the English capture the border fort of Eyemouth, and wanted the English to encourage those border clans under their sway to support the reformers. Knox received a letter from Elizabeth's secretary Sir William Cecil, in which there was an offer of money if needed; however there could be no open support due to the recent treaty of Cateau-Cambresis agreed in April, and with the English population two thirds Catholic, assisting rebellion in another country might encourage them to rebel in England. He suggested that the Scots should acquire the wealth of the Church, as the English Reformation had. The Earl of Moray replied to these points. Whereas the English and Danish reformations had been established from the top down, he pointed out 'we have against us the established authority', and explained that 'without support we cannot bring [the churches] to such obedience as we desire'. Queen Elizabeth would finally authorize £3,000 to be distributed to the Scots through Ralph Sadler, the former ambassador and veteran of Scottish politics, who was also tasked with causing dissent between Scots and French.

Knox may have also been informed about the activities of James Hamilton, Earl of Arran, since Croft was part of the scheme to bring him into Scotland. Arran had been smuggled into England and met with Queen Elizabeth in the gardens of Hampton Palace. The meeting was supposedly 'accidental', but in truth it was an arranged meeting which involved some negotiations and promises, the details unknown. Arran next travelled to Berwick, where Croft arranged for him to safely get to Teviotdale, and by September 10th he had reached Stirling and joined the congregation as a leader. The Lords then passed to Hamilton Palace, where they met with the Duke. Father and son joined each other for the first time in years. Within a day the son had persuaded the father to join the reformation.[94]

Francois was crowned King of France at Reims Cathedral on September 18th. The Guise family was now more powerful than ever, although they would enter into a bitter struggle with the widowed Queen Mother, Catherine de Medici. The Queen Regent would write to her son-in-law for an army and money, explaining the dire straits she was in and the lack of victuals and supplies. During the truce she would receive fresh troops from France. She was also getting messages from her brothers, the Duke of Guise and the Cardinal of Lorraine, encouraging her to become more active and crush the reformation.[95]

In response the Queen Regent began to refortify Leith and garrison with French troops, a clear breach of the truce. The Lords from Hamilton send a message on September 29th insisting that she halt this. The Queen Regent continued the building work and military occupation of Leith. The Lords called a muster for October 15th at Stirling. The Queen Regent would claim she had fortified Leith so as to protect herself against the Congregation, who besides opening correspondence with England, had taken command of the Castle of Broughty. The Lords would respond that Broughty had been taken to stop it being taken by France and threatening Dundee and Perth. They also argued that the occupation was done after the fortification of Leith.[96]

On October 16th the Lords of the Congregation marched

on Edinburgh. They were joined by Chatelherault, alongside his son the Earl of Arran. This defection of Chatelherault was used by the Queen Regent to accuse him in terms similar to those used against her stepson James, that he sought the Crown of Scotland. Chatelherault would claim that he and his son had joined the Lords to further the cause of religion and ensure the nation's independence. On October 19th he published a proclamation on the market cross to this effect. The Queen Regent employed the Lyon-King-at-Arms to send a message to the Congregation, calling them to disband and to remind Chatelherault of the vow he had made not to join the Congregation.[97] The Archbishop of St Andrews tried and failed to persuade his brother Chatelherault away from the Protestants.[98]

The nobles, barons, lairds and burgesses assembled at Edinburgh on October and demanded that the Queen Regent should end the fortification of Leith, and expel all French and foreign soldiers.[99] Lord Ruthven would explain that in deposing a tyrannical ruler who had rejected and disregarded a petition from the nobles and opposed the will of the people in following their chosen religion, they were entirely within their right. John Willock made a speech regarding the moral and spiritual rightness of the course they followed. This was followed by a vote. The assembly reiterated its allegiance to King Francois and Queen Mary, but decided to suspend the authority of the Queen Regent. They gave her 24 hours to leave Leith.[100]

The Congregation prepared to lay siege to Leith. They had 12,000 poorly-equipped or provisioned troops. Scaling ladders were made in the High Church of St Giles, much to the complaint of preachers and ministers, who had to work over the sound of constant hammering. At Linlithgow contracted troops threatened to mutiny over lack of pay and joined the Queen Regent. Nobles brought family plate into the mint so as to make coin and pay them, but the coining instruments were gone. Elizabeth, recognising that the success of the reformers depended on money, authorized a convoy from England carrying 4,000 crowns. It was intercepted by the Earl of Bothwell, who had rejected his supposed protestant sympathies to support the Queen Regent.[101]

The first assault against Leith, on October 31st, was repulsed. A French sally out of the town captured artillery placed on a hill above, and they chased the troops into Edinburgh. There were a series of skirmishes, the Congregation getting the worst of it. On November 5th French troops, whilst intercepting a convoy set for Edinburgh, came close to capturing the city gates but were pushed back by the Earl of Moray and the Earl of Arran. Moray and Arran become constrained around Restalrig Park, allowing the French to regroup and counter-attack, inflicting heavy losses on the Scots. When the French were pillaging houses from Edinburgh Castle Lord Erskine fired on them, despite his neutrality.[102] These setbacks were demoralizing the Edinburgh contingent, and there was talk of breaking up the siege and retiring to Stirling.

Maitland of Lethington, the former Queen's secretary, had recently joined them, and along with Chatelherault, Lord James Stewart, he tried to convince them to stay the course. However on November 7th, the Lords of the Congregation withdrew to Stirling. They were demoralized and Knox used his oratory and words to inspire them out of the gloom. He particularly focused some attention on Chatelherault, scolding him for his hesitancy in joining the reformation, yet reminded all that although the Duke had been one of the enemy who 'with their blind fury pursued us', shedding blood 'through his default' Knox acknowledged that he had repented. Knox was reminding his audience that although the Duke was a great and powerful man he was but a man, and ultimately the congregation would need to remember that when they had begun this struggle they 'had only God as their protector', and oppressed as they might be 'they must in the end be triumphant'. Inspired by his oratory and faith, the Congregation sent Maitland to England to represent the Congregation and request further aid and money. The nobility were using their own resources to fund the fighting. Lord James was said to have spent 13,000 crowns from May 10th.[103]

The Queen Regent learned from informants about the travels to England of her former secretary Maitland. He had a meeting with Queen Elizabeth during which he stated that if she did not help then 'she herself will be ruined'. His pleadings seem to have worked, with Elizabeth and the Council deciding to enter into a league with the Congregation. Dispatches were sent out across the country to raise money and support. Fourteen vessels were outfitted and made ready to sail to Berwick under the admiralship of Winter. Making the excuse that the increase in French forces could threaten the borders, Elizabeth sent an army under the Duke of Norfolk to Berwick. In addition she provided a commission to gentlemen of the borders instructing them to raise as many armed men as possible, whether horse or foot, and then to muster at Newcastle under the command of Norfolk.[104]

The Congregation divided into two armies, one based at Glasgow led by Chatelherault and one at Fife under Lord James Stewart. The French entered Edinburgh and quartered themselves on the citizens, and generally behaved oppressively. The Queen Regent demanded the surrender of Edinburgh Castle, held by Lord Erskine, who throughout the conflict remained neutral. As noted above, only once did he fire the castle cannons, when French troops were pillaging houses. He refused to surrender to either Queen Regent or Congregation.[105] Not being able to get control of Edinburgh Castle, the French decided to surprise the assembly at Stirling on December 16th but the Congregation learned of their approach and dispersed.

In December Fife was invaded by the French. They fortified St Andrews and Burnisland, and captured Kinghorn. During January the Dingwall Pursuivant was given letters authorizing him to 'charge the sheriff, provost, and Bailles of Stirling and Stirlingshire' to provide food and drink supplies for the French. Similar letters were sent to Newbottle, Dalkeith, Musselburgh, Fisharrow, Tranent and Prestonpans. Boatmen were ordered to Leith so that these supplies could be transported to Fife. From this region the French raided and devastated the lands of the Protestants. There ensued a series of skirmishes and small engagements which compelled the Protestants to withdraw to Cupar, reorganize and reassess their tactics. The French had 4,000 troops, but Lord James Stewart and the Earl of Arran gathered 500 horse and 100 foot. The Scots began to skirmish effectively against the French, attacking small attachments and cutting off supplies until the French were pushed to the coastline. Supplies begin to run down and a sea transport of provisions was captured and taken to Dundee.[106]

Upon hearing of the fighting in Fife, Norfolk suggested sending the English fleet under Winter to the Firth of Forth for the 'impeachment of the French succours' or blocking of supplies. To do so and not breach the truce with the French was the main problem.[107] Queen Elizabeth also agreed with sending the fleet into Scottish waters and wanted to aid the Scots with 500 harquebusiers who would sail with the ships and be prepared to land wherever Winter thoughts best. The fleet was not able to travel out of Berwick at that time due to the weather, but the French fleet was even less fortunate, part being blown back to Dieppe and the rest diverted to Denmark and Zeeland with 1,000 troops. The Queen Regent, no doubt aware of the mustering of English forces at the border, sent messengers on the 20th January to the lairds and barons of Lothian, calling on them to assemble at Edinburgh on January 24th. A further summons was posted on the market crosses of Linlithgow and Stirling calling all able men to mobilize at Edinburgh on February 2nd, whilst proclamations were made in Dunbar, Haddington, North Berwick, Langton, Lauder and Coldingham calling on all to be ready to deprive an approaching English army of food and supplies.[108]

During this period a letter emerged which was claimed to be from Chatelherault and dated January 25th, addressed to the King of France and seeking pardon and forgiveness for joining the reformation. The letter would be found to be a forgery, for which the Queen Regent would later admit responsibility. With Chatelherault's history of changing sides she must have thought such a fabricated letter would help sow seeds of dissolution amongst her opponents.[109] There are other reports of conspiracies from the House of Hamilton; an informant related how the Earl of Arran, when in England, had entered into a secret compact with Elizabeth in which, in return for helping him drive out the French and become crowned King of Scotland, he would acknowledge that he held it for her, and would grant her four important Scottish castles. There is no other evidence for this story, but the writer seemed to believe it was true, although he admitted the Scots would likely oppose such an agreement.[110]

Not to be undone in this conspiracy, the Earl of Lennox sent a Mr Nesbitt to Sir William Cecil, secretary of the Privy Council, with Lennox's request for permission to involve himself in Scottish intrigues in the form of safe conducts for agents to travel to and from Scotland. His brother, the Bishop of Caithness, had advised him to enact his claim as second person of the realm and negotiate with the Queen Regent. Lennox appeared to be seeking support from England, yet such an act would alienate his enemy Chatelherault, who was now on the side of the Protestants. It was also learned that Nesbitt, on behalf of Lennox, had approached the French Ambassador in London and asked him to write to the Queen Regent as well as ensuring that the French were kept informed of Lennox's schemes.

The council believed Lennox had received English safe conducts, and this became common knowledge. It was part of a French scheme whereby the Earl was set up to create a 'quarrelsome offence' that would sow seeds of suspicion within Chatelherault's camp and create friction with the English. The council ordered that Nesbit should be housed in the Tower of London so that they could learn more about the intrigues.[111] The aim of the scheme might have been to send Lennox's son Henry, Lord Darnley, to Scotland to stir things up, and he may have been one of the agents sent to the Queen Regent. During the crowning of François in September 1559 at Reims, Lennox had sent the 12-year-old Lord Darnley to petition for a restoration of the lands in Scotland. He was refused but received a gift of 1,000 crowns.[112]

On January 23rd 1560 a fleet was spotted off the coast. Unfortunately for the French, instead of being the anticipated supplies from Dieppe it turned out to be 14 English men-at-arms, who under the pretext of chasing pirates took control of the Firth of Forth. The French, who had been preparing for a march to St Andrews, were hemmed into a narrow stretch of coast by the hit-and-run tactics of Moray and Arran. Short of supplies and threatened by sea and land, the French turned back to Leith. The arrival of this fleet was due to the successful embassy of Maitland to Elizabeth, and the fleet would remain on Scottish waters to prevent supplies reaching the French. A commission led by Lord Ruthven would go to Berwick and with the Duke of Norfolk negotiate the Treaty of Berwick, February 1560.[113] In writing to Norfolk Elizabeth made it clear that England needed to support the Lords of the Congregation in repulsing the French out of Scotland. She feared that a French victory would lead to a French invasion of England.[114]

The Duke of Guise and the Cardinal of Lorraine would write to their sister in a letter that was seen and copied by an English spy and sent to Lord Cecil. They admitted the difficulty of sending supplies, as instead of 14 ships there were now 30 English ships reported and eight Scots ships blocking the Firth of Forth. The ships were said to have 6-7000 troops. The letter suggested that with the threat of attack from the English at Leith the Queen Regent was advised to make some kind of arrangement with the Protestants by offering tolerance in return for their continued allegiance to the King and Queen of France. They also asked her to spread 'little libels' to the effect that the English also agreed that the Scots should re-enter into allegiance with their sovereigns.[115]

The Treaty of Berwick was agreed on February 27th by the Duke of Norfolk, representing the English, and Lord James Stewart, Sir William Maitland, Sir John Maxwell of Terrigle, John Wishart and Henry Balnaves. An army of 8,000 English was offered to help the Congregation to drive the French out of Scotland. Chatelherault and the Earl of Arran were recognised as presidents of the Congregation, whilst the father was recognised as heir-apparent. The Scots would consider any enemy of England their enemy, and if the French attacked England they would provide in assistance 2,000 horse and 1,000 foot. Chatelherault managed to impose his authority on the treaty and ensured that any castles or forts captured by the English were either demolished or handed over to the Scots. His experience of past dealings with the English enabled them to draft a treaty that was fair and balanced and truly focused on mutual aid. He also ensured that whilst opposed to French occupation and the Queen Regent, the Scots would recognise Mary and François as sovereigns of Scotland, and the English commissioners supported this.[116]

Whilst preparations were being made for the armies of Scots and English to join up, the Duke of Chatelherault was the victim of rumours that he had written to the King of France seeking forgiveness. A letter was handed to the Ambassador, apparently from Chatelherault, accusing him of reporting this allegation to the Queen of England and issuing the challenge that once Mr de Secure resigned from his position as Ambassador he would match 100 of his men against a 100 of de Secure's in mortal combat. The French ambassador denied the charge, and although he wrote to Chatelherault he disputed the authenticity of the letter handed to him, since the bearer was not a servant of the Duke. He also stated that when his functions as ambassador were over he would accept any challenge from Chatelherault's party. The letter may have been a French concoction, an attempt to keep the question of Chatelherault's true loyalties debated in London.[117]

Queen Elizabeth made a proclamation that her English armed forces were mustering in Scotland to counter the designs of the Guise family, who were now governing France and challenging the rights of the Queen of England by having the Queen of Scots carry the arms of England and Ireland. She would not allow a French army in Scotland to endanger England, so her national security was tied in with supporting the Scottish Protestants. Taking into consideration the ages of François and Mary, she did not blame them, but pointed the finger at the manipulations of the House of Guise. She outlined a determination to assist the people of Scotland to expel the French soldiers out the isles.[118]

Whilst the Scottish army was preparing to muster, they

learned that four ensigns of the French were making their way to Glasgow to disrupt the place of assembly. However nothing of importance was reported and the Scots made their way south.[119] On April 2nd Lord Grey led 8,000 English into Scotland and joined with a similar number of Scots. On April 6th the joint army advanced to Restalrig. Reportedly the French had 3,500 men plus 500 Scots behind the walls of Leith. Once the joint army had advanced to the walls of the town the French sallied out with 900 harquebusiers and there was a savage six-hour battle with firearms, until a contingent of Scottish horse beat them back.

The joint army dug trenches, and raised mounds with fixed artillery so as to blast the walls or fire over the walls and into the town. On the field with Lord Grey's army were the Earls of Argyll, Arran, Morton and Glencairn, Lord James Stewart and Lords Boyd and Lord Ogilvy. Chatelherault housed himself in the splendor of Holyrood. The Queen Regent, with the approval of Lord Erskine, who sought to act as a mediator, was allowed to reside in Edinburgh Castle. Chatelherault's brother, the Archbishop of St Andrews, stayed with the Queen Regent, along with the Bishop of Dunkeld and the Earl Marshal. The walls of the castle allowed her to watch the fighting.[120] The Queen of England made a decision that there should be no English attempt on Edinburgh, so as not to offend the Scots.

During the month of April Elizabeth met with a Baptista de Favoury, another English agent, who brought a ciphered letter which revealed an apparent plot by the Guise family to poison the Queen of England. The plot was intricate and involved an Italian engineer who was to infiltrate Elizabeth's confidence by offering his services. The plot was collaborated by the Bishop of Aquila, a pensioner of the French King, who passed the information to Elizabeth's continental agent, Throckmorton. The envoy also reported that the King of Spain could not assist the French as he was 15,000,000 crowns in debt and his troops were involved in the siege of Tripoli. But it also stated that troops that were stationed at Zeeland and now sent to Tripoli were to have been sent to Scotland, so there was a real danger of the conflict escalating.[121]

It was also reported that the French in Leith had only three weeks' victuals. Whilst the joint Scots/English army lacked the professionalism and experience of the French, they had the advantage of the English fleet, which was able to prevent supplies getting in but also able to target the artillery positions of the French, such as when the ordinance on St Anthony's Stipple was bombarded. The siege would tighten, and there would be resolute defence from the French each time the Scots and English tried to force through a gap or a breach.[122] At one point new trenches were dug on the south and south-west corners, new artillery mounds allowed a concentrated bombardment of the walls and a passable breach was forced. On May 7th Scots and English used scaling ladders to surmount the walls whilst other troops engaged through the breach. Whilst they came close to succeeding, the French defenders were assisted by Scottish women who loaded firearms and threw solid objects and fuel down on the attackers until they were driven out. The French taunted the attackers by laying their dead on the walls for several days, exposed to the sun. The besiegers built more mounds and gave a constant bombardment into Leith, destroying houses and buildings. The French would send out raiding parties and sharp fighting would occur in the trenches, with more dead and wounded.[123]

The fighting was hard and the English and Scots suffered throughout the months of April and into May, with both enduring up to 8,000 dead and wounded. Elizabeth, realising the dangers of losing, provided more resources. Despite the inconclusive skirmishing the siege was taking a toll of the French, and they resorted to eating horses. The Duke of Norfolk made arrangements to send another 2,000 men to Scotland. But what determined the conflict was the news that the Queen Regent was dying, reportedly of dropsy.

The Queen Regent sent for the Lords of the Congregation. The Earl of Argyll, the Earl of Glencairn, The Earl Marishal and Lord James Stewart were allowed to visit her in the Castle. Initially they suspected a 'Guisian practice', but once they overcame their suspicions they were greeted by a weakened individual who would admit her faults and accept blame for wrong decisions, especially those decisions that had forced them to request help from England. She regretted not using the Preston Convention to address grievances and reach a settlement. The Scots nobles who had opposed Mary of Guise were said to have wept at her bedside when she asked them to forgive her. John Willock would meet with her and explain his interpretation of scripture and faith, to which she listened. She died on June 11th 1560, and her body was encased in lead. On October 19th it would be shipped to France and interned in Reims, at the church of the convent of Saint-Pierre-les-Dames.[124]

Her death ended the war. The French, without Mary of Guise, viewed her family's grand scheme of monarchical union of France, Scotland, England and Ireland as stalled for the present. The English now sought peace and security on their northern borders.[125] The Treaty of Edinburgh was signed on July 6th 1560 by French and English representatives, and approved by the Lords of the Congregation. It was a peace treaty that covered military activities not just in Scotland but in Ireland, England and France. The King and Queen of Scotland and France were to stop using the arms of England and Ireland. The Scots would acknowledge the two as their sovereign monarchs, whilst they were to treat the people and nobles with 'mercy and grace'. The French armies were to leave Scotland along with English naval and land forces, and neither François nor Mary was to introduce new troops. A parliament was to be formed in which a council of governance made up of 24 individuals would be short-listed, and 12 from that group picked to administer state affairs whilst their majesties were absent in France.[126]

This Parliament that was assembled in August would change Scotland's political structure and herald a religious revolution. The Three Estates voted onto the statute the abolition of papal authority, to be replaced by a system of reformed religion. The Act for approving the Confession of Faith was put to the vote and passed on August 25th, and so began the Reformation in Scotland. Recognising the recent alliance with England the Parliament was also to support a marriage between James, 3rd Earl of Arran, and Queen Elizabeth. Such a binding held out the possibility of Chatelherault having a grandchild ruling England, a prospect that would have potentially made the Hamiltons one of the most powerful families in Britain. *The Book of Discipline*, commissioned by the government and introduced in its final form in January 1561, gave the Lords of the Congregation the recommendations on how to proceed with the setting up of the new religious structure.[127] Scotland was now a Protestant nation.

References: (1) (Marshall, pp78-80. ODNB, vol.37, pp.71-77). (2) (Hume-Brown, pp.31-32. Marshal, pp.79-81). (3) (Calderwood, p.282). (4) (Hume-Brown, pp.37-38). (5) (Gregory, pp.183-185. Mary of Lorraine: 12th August, 1554, CCLIX, pp.388-389. Spain: August 1554, 1-15, Calendar of State Papers, Spain, Volume 13: 1554-1558 (1954), pp. 13-30). (6) (Mary: January 1555, Calendar of State Papers Foreign, Mary: 1553-1558 (1861), pp. 149-152). (7) (ER, vol.9, pp. lxxi-lxxiii, p.572. Thomson, pp. 93-96). (8) (Mary: December 1554, Calendar of State Papers Foreign, Mary: 1553-1558 (1861), pp.142-149). (9) (Spain: February 1555, Calendar of State Papers, Spain, Volume 13: 1554-1558 (1954), pp. 137-143). (10) (ODNB, vol.37, pp.71-77). (11) (Hume-Brown, p.32). (12) (ODNB, vol.9, pp.699-703). (13) (ODNB, vol.37, pp.71-77. Marshal, pp.72-74. Knox, 100-101). (14) (Knox, p.111). (15) (Marshal, Hume-Brown, pp.29-34). (16) (Knox, pp.98-100. Thomson, pp.96-97). (17) (Knox,p.98-100). (18) (Knox, p.111). (19) (Hume-Brown, pp.38-39, Knox, pp.111-115). (20) (Knox, pp.111-115). (21) (Knox, pp.116-120). (22) (Knox, pp.118-119. Thomson, pp.97-98). (23) (Knox, pp.118-119). (24) (Thomson, pp. 93-96). (25) (Mary of Lorraine: 9th August, 1555, CCLXX). (26) (Knox, pp. 119-120). (27) (Mary: March 1556, Calendar of State Papers Foreign, Mary: 1553-1558 (1861), pp. 214-220). (28) (Thomson, pp.93-96). (29) (Fraser, pp.250-252). (30) (Mary: March 1557, Calendar of State Papers Foreign, Mary: 1553-1558 (1861), pp. 290-292. Fraser, pp. 254-255). (32) (Knox, pp.128-130). (33) (Knox, p.130). (34) (Hume-Brown, pp.33-34). (35) (ALHTS, vol.10, pp. lxxi-lxxii, pp.421-431. MacDonald Fraser, pp. 283-285. Spain: August 1557, Calendar of State Papers, Spain, Volume 13: 1554-1558 (1954), pp. 308-318. Thomson, pp.94-95). (36) (Mary: September 1557', Calendar of State Papers Foreign, Mary: 1553-1558 (1861), pp. 332-339). (37) (Spain: October 1557, Calendar of State Papers, Spain, Volume 13: 1554-1558 (1954), pp. 320). (38) (Herkless & Hannay, pp.86-87. Tytler, vol.6, pp.65-67). (39) (Elizabeth: January 1559, 21-30, Calendar of State Papers Foreign, Elizabeth, Volume 1: 1558-1559 (1863), pp. 96-110). (40) (MacDonald Fraser, pp.284-285). (41) (Tytler, pp.67-68). (42) (Knox, pp.129-134). (43) (Knox, pp.129-134). (44) (Hume-Brown, pp.38-39. Melville, pp.50-51. Thomson, pp.98-99). (45) (Thomson, pp.95-96). (46) (Holinshed, pp.583-587). (47) (ALHTS, vol.10, pp. lxxvi-lxxix. Thomson, pp.95). (48) (Herkless & Hannay, pp.89-94). (49) (Tytler, pp. 86-87). (50) (Tytler, 87-89). (51) (Tytler, pp. 81-83). (52) (Hume-Brown, pp.38-39.Thomson,pp. 100-101). (53) (Thomson, p.101). (54) (Thomson, pp.95-96). (55) (Hume-Brown, pp.34-35). (56) (ALHTS, vol.10, pp. lxxiv-lxxvi. Weir, pp.12-18). (57) (Thomson, pp.95-96). (58) (Tytler, pp.70-72). (59) (Hume-Brown, pp. 35-36. Knox, pp.126-127). (60) (SP, vol.2, pp.470-471.Tytler, pp.70-72). (61) (Knox, pp.126-127). (62) (Dowden, pp.373-374). (63) (Gordon, vol.1, pp.236-237). (64) (Gordon, vol.1, pp.485-486). (65) (Hume-Brown, pp.32). (66) (Tytler, pp.71-72). (67) (Hume-Brown, pp.35-36). (68) (SP, vol.1, pp.340-341). (69) (Herkless & Hannay, pp.88-89). (70) (ODNB, Vol.24, pp.833-835. Herkless & Hannay, p.99). (71) (Hume-Brown, pp.39). (72) (Thomson, pp.101-102). (73) (Melville, pp.50-52. Weir, pp.17-18). (74) (Thomson, vol.3, p.106). (75) (Hume-Brown, pp. 41-42, Knox, pp.136-139). (76) (Hume-Brown, pp.3-44). (77) (Hume-Brown, pp.44-45). (78) (Thomson, vol.3, pp.96). (79) (Hume-Brown, pp.44-45). (80) (Herkless & Hannay, pp.105-106). (81) (Calderwood, vol.1, pp.444-460. Herkless & Hannay, pp. 106-107. Hume-Brown, pp.46-47. Knox, pp.170-173). (82) (Knox, p.172-178. Thomson, p.110). (83) (Herkless & Hannay, pp.108-109. Knox, pp.177-178. Tytler, vol.6, pp.108-110). (84) (Thomson, p.110), (85) (Calderwood, pp.464-467. Hume-Brown, pp.46-47. Knox, pp.177-179. Melville, pp.54-55). (86) (Thomson, p.110). (87) (Knox, pp.179-180. Thomson, pp.110-111). (88) (Thomson, pp.111-112. Tytler, vol.6, pp.117-119). (89) (Knox, pp.181-182. Thomson, pp.112-113. Tytler, vol.6, pp.116-121). (90) (Thomson, pp.112-113). (91) (Herkless & Hannay, pp.110-111. Tytler, vol.6, pp.123-125). (92) (Thomson, p.114-115). (93) (Herkless & Hannay, pp.110-113. Knox, pp.182-184). (94) (Hume-Brown, vol.2, pp.50-51. Knox, pp.210-216. ODNB, vol.24, pp.833-835. Tytler, vol.6, pp.126-128). (95) (Marshal, p.90.Thomson, p.116. Weir, p.19).

(96) (Thomson, pp.116-117). (97) (Thomson, pp.116-117). (98) (Herkless & Hannay, pp.113-114). (99) (CP, October 1559, 'The Lords of the Congregation to the Queen Dowager', October 19th 1560. Thomson, pp.116-117). (100) (Thomson, pp. 117-119). (101) (Thomson, pp.118-119). (102) (Thomson, p.119. Tytler, vol.6, pp.148-150). (103) (Thomson, pp.119-120. Tytler, vo.6, pp.218-221). (104) (CP, 1559, 'Noailles to the Queen Dowager', 1559, Dec 21st). (105) (Thomson, pp.119-120). (106) (ALHTS, vol.11, pp.6-7.Knox, pp.213-214. Thomson, p.120.). (107) (CP, January 1560, 'The Duke of Norfolk to Sir W. Cecil' January 10th, 1560). (108) (ALHTS, vol.11, pp.8-9.CP, January 1560, 'The Queen to the Duke of Norfolk', January 11th, 1560). (109) (SP, vol.4, pp.367-368). (110) (CP, 1559, 'Noailles to the Queen Dowager', 1559, Dec. 21st). (111) (CP. 'Mathieu Earl of Lennox to Sir Wm. Cecil'. 1559, Dec. 14th, 1559. CP, January 1560, 'The Lords of the Council to the Duke of Norfolk', 1559/60, Jan. [13]). (112) (Weir, p.19). (113) (Thomson, p.121). (114) (CP, February, 1560, 'The Queen to Duke of Norfolk', 1559/60, Feb. 15th). (115) (CSP, Elizabeth Vol 2, 1559-1560, (1865), pp.378-394). (116) (CP, February 1560, 'Articles agreed upon at Berwick.', February 27th, 1560). (117) ('James, Duke of Châtelherault to M. de Seurre, the French Ambassador in England.' 1559/60, March 21st. 'M de Seurre to the Duke of Chastleherault'. 1560, March 28th). (118) ('The Queen's Proclamation concerning peace', March 24th, 1560). (119) ('The Duke of Norfolk and his council to Sir W Cecil', March 21st, 1560). (120) (Holinshed, pp.599-601). (121) (CSP, Elizabeth, vol 2, April 1560, pp.21-25). (122) (Thomson, vol.3, pp.122-123). (123) (Holinshed, pp.600-602. Thomson, vol.3, pp.122-123). (124) (Thomson, pp.123-124). (125) (Thomson. Pp.123-124). (126) (SHD, Treaty of Edinburgh, pp.120). (127) (Knox, pp.224-233. SHD, First Book of Discipline, pp.126).

Epilogue

Mary Queen of Scots would arrive in Scotland on August 14th 1561, with her companions the Four Maries, her household friends and servants and three uncles. She lacked a king and husband, as Francois had died on December 5th 1560. Whilst she was a devout Catholic, the country she was invited to rule was Protestant. Mary did not give regal approval to those acts of the Reformation parliament, so there was uncertainty in respect of the legality of the legislation introduced. Yet the Lords would argue that they had won the rights to the parliament through force of arms and by the common consent of the people.[1]

The nobles and politicians she would need to work with, or against, were formidable. Her illegitimate half-brother John Stewart, Earl of Moray and Archibald Campbell, fifth Earl of Argyll had given leadership to the Scottish

Reformation. Around them were equally talented and resourceful figures such as James Douglas, Earl of Morton and second son of George Douglas of Pittendreich, William Maitland of Lethington, Sir William Kirkcaldy of Grange, a participant in the slaying of Cardinal Beaton, John Erskine, Earl of Mar, and John Knox, who would use his considerable oratory skills to remind Mary that she was now in a Protestant nation.[2]

However the Scotland she now ruled was also a nation-state that had developed through the leadership of her mother Mary of Guise and Chatelherault. Her mother Mary had been a French patriot who whilst in Scotland had fought vigorously for Scottish survival and French interests. Her outlook was European and she saw the Scottish/French alliance as vital to challenging the alliance between England, Spain and the Habsburg Empire. Scotland also gave France good seaports with close access to Scandinavia, and the potential for mischief in Ireland. Mary was an astute politician, and tactically minded. She outplayed Chatelherault in 1543, and showed how ruthless she could be by exploiting his rivalry with Lennox. She also had an uneasy partnership with Chatelherault, and after the invasions and raids of 1544 she managed to oppose Chatelherault and Cardinal Beaton successfully by siding with the disaffected Scots, including the Protestants. This was politics at the sharp end, where one mistake could spell disaster considering the dangerous rivalries amongst the Scots. But she saw it through, and when an uneasy coalition was formed in 1544/45 the Scots began to win back territory against the English. Nevertheless, being the mother of a future Queen Mary made her a target for many conspiracies, not just from the English but the Scots. In context we can view her career as that of a mother protecting a daughter, and to do so she employed the same ruthless and duplicitous techniques as her rivals.

Up until 1547 she supported more French involvement whilst opposed by those powerful Scots who were wary of foreign encroachment in Scottish affairs. Chatelherault probably had the upper hand until Pinkie changed the game and gave Mary the open door to invite more French involvement in the defence of Scotland and the expelling of the English. Bringing the French in with more money and men allowed her to slowly but surely pull power away from Chatelherault, until in 1554 he finally resigned the governorship. Mary clearly wanted Scotland as a satellite of France and a launch pad into England. She also believed that the influence of France would transform Scotland into a modern European state. Religion and the reformation hampered this design. Whilst she appeared to be tolerant to Protestants, it is unclear whether she would have continued this policy whilst her brothers in France became the major powers following the death of Henry II. Possibly she would have granted tolerance if she had been allowed to. In an interview reported by Sir James Melville, James Stewart, Earl of Moray and the future Regent of Scotland, claimed that Mary of Guise would have granted 'liberty of conscience' if done secretly. This changed when she was visited in 1558/59 by Bettancourt, an envoy from the King of France and an associate of the Guises, asking her to join the Catholic League and crush the reformation in Scotland.[3] The religious revolts in Scotland forced her to act; she could not ignore these occurrences, which she saw as rebellions. In confronting them she became duplicitous, and this did not serve her cause. What should have been contained spiralled into a full Scottish revolution against the Catholic religion, structures and symbolism. Mary became a victim of powerful events that shaped Scotland and ended in her defeat.

Mary of Guise had incredible courage, with a mentality suited to military pursuits. She understood military strategy and tactics, and she could inspire her troops, as she did before the storming of the Isle of Inchkeith in 1550. She was resolute during warfare, as when she sought to invade England to wage war against Philip of Spain and Mary Tudor in support of France. Her life was constantly at risk, as when she narrowly missed death when St Mary's church in Haddington was bombarded, yet such harrowing events did not stop her from taking the field, and during the war against the Congregation she was at the forefront in military and political decisions. She proved herself resolute in her war against the English, and determined in her struggle against Chatelherault for power. She was also an assured diplomat and could be conciliatory and appeasing if need be, yet ruthless and dangerous if the occasion warranted. She was defeated only by her own death, and this event itself determined the course of Scottish history, allowing the Protestants to take power, reject the historic alliance with France and enter into friendship with England.

Mathew Stewart, the deposed Earl of Lennox, whilst enjoying favour with Queen Mary of England, was imprisoned by Queen Elizabeth in 1559, and placed alongside his wife in the Tower of London. Their son

Darnley was a great-grandson of Henry VII, and therefore a potential royal rival to Elizabeth. Lennox and his wife would be released in 1563, and he and his son would play significant roles in Scottish politics. Lennox was a unique figure in Scottish history, born of feud and bloodshed. His energies and aggression were harnessed in continental warfare and let loose in Scotland. Whilst initially a Scots patriot with immense French backing, he is credited with saving Mary of Guise and her daughter from Chatelherault. Yet he was used and manipulated by Beaton and Mary of Guise. Believing his honor and royal ambitions betrayed, he sought revenge through joining Henry VIII. Lennox was a relentless soldier, brutal and cruel during the Rough Wooing, even making up detailed maps of Scotland that made it all the easier for the English and their mercenaries to raid into Scotland.

His main rival Chatelherault during the reformation is described by Knox as 'inconstant'. Yet Knox had the luxury of making judgments from an absolutist position , which could not take into context the political pressures that men like Chatelherault endured during times of religious and political change and turmoil. Chatelherault managed to outmanoeuvre and outsmart many experienced politicians. This cannot be down to luck, more down to determination and an ability to navigate through political uncertainty.

After he resigned his commission as Lord Governor in 1554 he apparently lived a lazy life of leisurely pursuits. He enjoyed hunting on his vast Hamilton estates, and kept a large stable of horses. He enjoyed music, gambling and entertaining friends with lavish amounts of food and drink. During that period his main political aims were to find an important wife for his son James and further the Hamilton family's dynastic ambitions. Perhaps he felt politically shackled, through his sons James and David being guests or hostages to France, reliant on the goodwill of the French king. Yet it was the activities of his eldest, James, Earl of Arran that forced Chatelherault to once more enter the political and military arena, and make the decisions which would shape Scottish history.

There can be no doubt that he loved and admired his son, the perpetual hostage who embraced the reformation whilst living in Catholic France. It was his son who persuaded him to return to the Reformation, and it was Chatelherault who became head of the Congregation. His resources and manpower allowed them to continue the fight, and offered time to convince the English that this fight was also their fight, for if Scotland fell then England could be next. The Treaty of Berwick, whereby Scotland and England entered into an alliance against France, is a remarkable document and an indication of the powerful personality of the Duke, in that he was recognised as the second person of the realm, thereby giving royal legitimacy to his leadership. It was also Chatelherault's grand revenge against France and the way his sons and he had been treated. Whilst recognising the sovereignty of Queen Mary and King François, the Treaty effectively ended the Auld Alliance, with the promise to support England militarily against France in the event of the latter invading.

Chatelherault's brother John, Archbishop of St Andrews, followed another path. He stayed loyal to Mary of Guise to the end, and during the Reformation Parliament, whilst supporting a measure of church reform, he refused to vote for the Confession of Faith. It was said by Chatelherault's enemies and critics that his half-brother dominated his policies, yet it would be fairer to say that Chatelherault followed advice when it suited him, or when the circumstances were right. Chatelherault continued to be a major political player in Scotland up to his death in 1575. He never realised the dream of his son James becoming a crowned head of state. Elizabeth of England would reject him, as would Mary, Queen of Scots after the death of her husband François. The story of James, 3rd Earl of Arran is one of tragedy, and not to be told in this work.

Whilst they were political rivals, Mary of Guise and Chatelherault in their own ways were very similar. Their tools were diplomacy heavily laced with duplicity, yet they were no different from the rulers, kings and nobles of Renaissance Europe.[4]

References: (1) (SHD, Acts of Reformation Parliament, pp.124). (2) ODNB, vol.32, pp.15-30.ODNB, vol.52, pp.684-685. ODNB, vol.16, pp.667-673.ODNB, vol.9, pp.699-703. SP, vol.5, pp.590-636. (3) (Melville, pp55-56. ODNB, vol.37, pp.71-77) (4) (ODNB, vol.24, pp.827-833.ODNB, vol.24, pp. 862-864).

Biblography

Primary Sources

(ALHTS) Accounts of the Lord High Treasurer of Scotland, 13 volumes, Paul, J.B. (ed.),(1904), H.M. General Register House, Edinburgh.

Buchanan, George, The History of Scotland. Aikman, J, (ed.) (1827), Glasgow.

(CP) Calendar of the Cecil Papers in Hatfield House, Vol.1, 1306-1571

(CSPF) Calendar of State Papers Foreign. Edward 1547-1553. Mary 1553-1558. Elizabeth 1558-1561, Volumes 1-3.

(CSPS) Calendar of State Papers, Spain, Volumes 6-13.

(CSPSS) Calendar of State Papers, Spain (Simancas), Volume 1.

(CSPV) Calendar of State Papers relating to English affairs in the Archives of Venice, Volume 5-7.

(CSPVA) Calendar of State Papers relating to English affairs in the Vatican Archives, Volume 1.

Dickinson, C. (ed.), Two missions of Jacques De la Brosse, an account of the affairs of Scotland in the year 1543 (1942), Scottish History Society.

(ER) The Exchequer Rolls of Scotland, vol.9, 10. McNeil, G.P. (ed.), (1898), H.M. General Register House, Edinburgh.

(HP) Hamilton Papers, Vol.1, Vol.2. Bain, J. (ed.) (1890), H.M. General Register House, Edinburgh.

Holinshed, Ralph. Holinshed's Chronicles of England, Scotland and Ireland (ed.) Vernon, F. Snow, (1965) New York, AMS.

Knox, John. The Reformation in Scotland. (ed.) Guthrie, G.J. (1898). The Banner of Truth Trust, Edinburgh & Pennsylvania.

Lesley, John, Bishop of Ross, The History of Scotland. (1829) Bannatyne Club, Edinburgh.

(LP) Letters and Papers, Foreign and Domestic, Henry VIII, Volumes 17-21.

Melville, Sir James : Memoirs of Sir James Melville of Halhill 1535-1617. Thomson, Thomas. (ed.) (1827), Bannatyne Club, Edinburgh.

Pitscottie, Robert Lindsay of, The History and Chronicles of Scotland,vol.1, vol.2 (1814), G Ramsay and Company.

(RPCS) Register of the Privy Council of Scotland, vol.1. (ed.) Burton, J.H. (1877), H.M. General Register House, Edinburgh.

(RPS) The Records of the Parliaments of Scotland to 1707 (RPS) www.rps.ac.uk/

(SCML) Scottish Correspondence of Mary of Lorraine, (ed.) Dunlop, A. I. (1927), Scottish History Society.

(SHD) Scottish Historical Documents. (ed.) Donaldson, Prof. G. (1974 edition with corrections), Neil Wilson Publishing, Glasgow.

Secondary Sources

Bellesheim, Alphons, History of the Catholic Church of Scotland, vol.2, vol.3, William Blackwood & Sons, Edinburgh & London

Bindoff, S.T. (1950), Tudor England ,Penguin Books, Middlesex.

Byrne, K. (1997), Colkitta, House of Lochar, Argyll

Calderwood, Mr David, History of the Kirk of Scotland, (ed.) Rev. Thompson, Thomas, Vol.1, Woodrow Society, Edinburgh.

Cameron, J. (1998), James V: The Personal Rule, 1528-1542. Tuckwell Press, East Linton.

Cathcart, A, (Oct, 2012), Scottish Historical Review, Vol XCI, 2:, no 232, pp.239-264

David M., 'Henry VIII's Scottish Policy', in Scottish Historical Review, vol. 61 no. 171 (April 1982).

Dowden (1912), Bishops of Scotland, James Maclehose & Sons, Glasgow

Eddington, Alexander, (1926) Castles and Historic Homes of the Border, Oliver and Boyd, Edinburgh

Fraser, A. (1969) Mary, Queen of Scots , Phoenix, London.

Fraser, W. (1885), The Douglas Book, Edinburgh.

Gordon, Rev. J.F.S. Monasticon, Vol.3, Gordon John Tweed, Glasgow.

Gregory, Donald (1881), History of the Western Highlands and Islands of Scotland from A.D. 1493 to A.D. 1625, T.D. Morison Publisher.

Grub, George, 1861, 'Ecclesiastical History of Scotland, pp.28-29

Herkless, J, & Hannay, R. Kerr, The Archbishops of St Andrews (1915), Vol.5, William Blackwood & Sons, Edinburgh & London.

Herkless, J. Cardinal Beaton, William Blackwood & Sons, Edinburgh & London.

Hume-Brown, P. (1911) History of Scotland. Cambridge: at the University Press.

Luckoch, D.D. The Church in Scotland. (ed.) Herbert Mortimer, Dean of Lichfield (1893), Wells, Gardner, Darton & Co, London.

McCulloch, D. Reformation: Europe's House Divided 1490-1700 (2003), Penguin Books, London.

MacDougall, N, (2001), An Antidote to the English: The Auld Alliance, 1295-1560. Tuckwell Press, East Lothian.

MacDonald-Fraser, The Steel Bonnets, (1971), Harper Collins,

MacFarlane, Angus, Clan MacFarlane, A History. (2001), House of Lochar, Argyll.

MacLean-Bristol, N. Warriors and Priests: The History of the Clan Maclean, 1300-1570. Tuckwell Press, East Linton.

Marshall, R. (2001), Mary of Guise, NMS Publishing, Edinburgh.

Maxwell, Sir H. (1902) A History of the House of Douglas. Freemantle.

Merriman, M. (2000), The Rough Wooings: Mary Queen of Scots, 1542-1551. Tuckwell Press, East Linton.

Paterson, R.C. (1997), My Wound is Deep: a History of the Later Anglo-Scots Wars 1380-1560. John MacDonald Publishers Ltd, Edinburgh.

Reid, David, David Hume of Godscroft's History of the House of Angus, Two volumes (2005)

(ODNB) Oxford Dictionary of National Biography (2004), Oxford University Press, Oxford.

Scott, W, History of Scotland, vol.1, vol.2. (1830) Longman, Rees, Orme, Brown & Green. London.

Somerset Fry, P & F. (1982). The History Of Scotland. Routledge, London & New York.

(SP) Scots Peerage, vols 1-9, (1904) (ed.), Paul. J, B. David Douglas, Edinburgh.

Spottiswood, J. History of the Church of Scotland, by John Spottiswood, (ed.) Russell, M. & Napier, M. (1851), Spottiswood Society.

(SSP), Sadler, State Papers. The State Papers and Letters of Sir Ralph Sadler, (1809) Chifford, A. (ed.), Edinburgh.

Thomson, Rev. T. A History of the Scottish People. vol 3. Blackie & Son, Limited, London, Glasgow, Edinburgh, and Dublin.

Tytler, Patrick, Fraser. (1828) History of Scotland, Vol.5, Vol.6, William Tait, Edinburgh.

Weir, A. (2003), Mary Queen of Scots and the murder of Lord Darnley. Jonathan Cape, London.

Williams, R. (1997 edition) The Lord of the Isles, House of Lochar, Argyll.

Index

Aberdeen 15, 45, 63, 169, 265-266, 350

Albany, John Stewart (Stuart), Governor of Scotland, Duke of 5-6, 12, 14, 38, 40, 49

Ancrum 231, battle of 152-154

Angus, Archibald Douglas, 6th Earl of 5-8, 16-17, 28-29, 33, 35-36, 39-46, 49, 57-58, 61-62, 67, 70-72, 74-76, 84-86, 89, 92, 98-104, 106-109, 112, 115-121, 128-130, 132, 135-141, 145, 148, 151, 153-154, 157, 160, 165-168, 170-172, 178, 183-186, 189, 198, 203-205, 207, 213, 218-220, 222, 231, 235, 257, 267, 271, 275, 292-294

'Appointment' (The truce between Arran, Lord Governor and 'Castilians' 1546-47) 193- 195

Aquileia, Marco Grimani, Patriarch of 65, 97, 118

Argyll, Archibald Campbell, 4th Earl of (Died November 1558) 8, 26, 29-30, 33, 35-36, 41, 47-51, 57, 61, 63, 67, 70-71, 77, 80-82, 84-87, 97, 108-109, 113, 121, 128, 130-131, 133-134, 155-156, 160-162, 171-172, 174, 177, 187, 189, 213, 219, 214-215, 266, 268, 275, 286, 297-398, 301-303

Argyll, Archibald Campbell, 5th Earl of (Formerly Lord of Lorne. Succeeded as earl on November 1558) 298, 308, 313-317, 332, 334

LET THE WOLVES DEVOUR

Arran, James Hamilton, Earl of 6-7, 13

Arran, James Hamilton, Lord Governor of Scotland and 2nd Earl of (Subsequently; Duke of Chatelherault) 27, 30-37, 42-48, 50-58, 60-67, 69-71, 73-74, 93-118, 121, 123, 125-129, 132-133, 135-140, 142, 144, 151, 153-154, 156-157, 160, 164-165,168-170, 172-175, 179-180, 182-183, 185, 187-197, 201-202, 208, 210, 221, 224 (also Duke of Chatelherault) 225,227-228, 230-234, 243-244, 251-254, 257-261, 263-268, 270-277, 279-282, 285, 296-298, 308-309, 313-315, 317-320, 323-324, 326-328, 331-332, 335, 340-345

Arran, James Hamilton, 3rd Earl of 86, 94, 104, 106, 142, 172-174, 187, 225, 257, 309, 318-319, 321, 323-324, 326, 328-330, 332, 335, 344-345

Aubigni John Stewart, Lord of (Brother of Earl of Lennox)118, 261

Bale warning system 199

Balfour, Henry (accused of forging the will of James) 30

Balnaves, Master Henry (Secretary of State) 46, 52, 56, 74, 105, 194, 291, 330

Barton, John (Scottish merchant and privateer) 101, 149

Beaton, Cardinal David (Also Archbishop of St Andrews, Bishop of Mirepoix, Chancellor of Scotland) 10, 12, 14-15, 21, 23, 26-27, 29-33, 35-40, 42-47, 49-51, 53-56, 58- 86, 93-99, 101, 103-107, 109-111, 113-117, 119-121, 123, 126, 128-129, 132, 138-139, 141-143, 148, 157-161, 164-165, 169, 172-175, 179-183, 185-186, 193, 196, 200-201, 250, 257, 280-281, 291, 302, 340, 343

Beaton, James (Archbishop of Glasgow, uncle of David) 4, 7-10

Beaton, James (Archbishop of Glasgow, nephew of David) 300

Berwick 8, 26, 33, 43, 103, 106, 119, 122-123, 138-140, 150, 164, 194, 220-223, 228, 242, 258, 260, 289, 295-296, 320-321, 325, 327, 329-331, 344

Bishop, Thomas (Secretary of the Earl of Lennox) 115, 119, 134

Blackness Castle 55, 71, 85, 116, 118, 123, 245, 259

Book of Discipline (1561) 335

Bothwell, Patrick Hepburn, Earl of 8, 34, 46, 50-51, 55, 57, 70, 74, 77, 80, 82, 85, 111, 121-122, 135-137, 139-140, 160, 170, 181-182, 263, 276, 288, 300, 324,

Boyd, Lord 126, 207, 332

Broughty Craig Castle 42, 209, 214-215, 235, 239, 244-245, 259, 321-322

Brosse, Jacque de la (French ambassador to Scotland) 97, 99-100, 108

Brunstane, Alexander Crichton Laird of 37-38, 69, 72, 82, 102-105, 119-120, 157, 180, 220, 291

Buccleuch, Walter Scott Laird of 8, 55, 105,124, 151, 153, 165-166, 210, 220, 223, 230-231, 267-268

Caerlaverock Castle 24, 168, 174

Caithness, Bishop of (See Robert Stewart)

Calvin, John 31 289 295

Calvinism 294, 298

Cameron, Ewan Allanson (Leader of the Camerons of Locheil) 130

Camerons 130, 266

Carlisle 21, 42, 119, 125, 141, 154, 175, 220, 259, 295

Carpi, Cardinal 60, 142

Carrickfergus (Irish town and seaport) 162, 171

Cassilis, Gilbert Kennedy, 3rd Earl of 35-36, 39-40, 57, 64, 67, 69, 76, 81, 97, 108-110, 112, 128, 130, 137, 139, 156, 165, 180-181, 185, 207, 235, 245, 254, 258, 268-269, 271, 286-288,297- 398, 300, 305-306, 308

Castlemilk 206

Castilians (The besieged within St Andrews Castle, 1546-47) 188-190, 193, 196-197, 201, 224, 250-251, 258, 282

Catherine de Medici of France, Queen Mother 227, 322

Cecil, Sir William (English secretary) 319-321, 328-329

Chambers of Gathgirth 303

Chapelle, Seigneur (French commander) 212, 214-215

Charles V (Habsburg Emperor) 36, 47, 149, 264, 269

Clinton, Lord (English naval commander) 230

Cochrane, John (Privateer) 194

Coldingham 227

Coldingham, Fortified Abbey of 5, 135, 138-142, 151, 165, 241-242

Convention of Clergy at St Andrews (1543) 51, 63

Crichton, Robert (nominee for Bishop of Dunkeld) 59-60, 179

Cupar 314-315, 326

Dalkeith 45, 59, 85, 96-97, 103, 135, 152, 157, 205, 221-222, 231, 326

Darce, Lord 21

Darnley, Henry, Lord 261, 329, 343

D'Assonleville (Spanish ambassador) 296-297

David I, King of Scotland (1124-53) 2

D'Esse, Andre de Montallembert, Sire de (French commander) 224, 228, 230, 232-234, 237, 240-241

Donlanark, Laird of 109

D'Osell (French ambassador to Scotland) 196, 210-211, 259, 270-271, 274, 285, 295, 297-298, 312-315, 318-319

Douglas, Sir Archibald (see Angus, Earl of)

Douglas, of Pittendriech, Sir George 6, 8, 17, 26, 28-29, 33, 35-37, 44, 46, 51, 53-57, 63-64, 66-67, 69, 72-73, 75-77, 79, 81-82, 84-85, 96, 98, 102-103, 106-107, 111-112, 114, 116, 118, 121, 123-124, 128-130, 133, 135-137, 139-140, 142, 149, 151, 157, 165-166, 170, 172, 180, 183-184, 188-189, 198-199, 203, 207-208, 221-223, 231, 243, 254, 257-258, 266, 294, 340

Douglas. George (Postulate of Arbroath, natural son of the Earl of Angus) 189

Douglas, John (Pastor of the Earl of Argyll) 301-302, 304

Douglas, Margaret (Countess and wife of the Earl of Arran) 45, 79

Douglas, Lady Margaret (Daughter of the Earl of Angus) 95, 98, 109, 261

Douglas Bond, The 85, 101, 108, 282

Douglas Castle 101

Drogheda 176

Drumlanrig, Battle of 218-219

Drumlanrig, James Douglas, Laird of 198, 213-214, 218-220

Dryburgh, Abbot of, (John Erskine) 196

Dryburgh, Thomas Erskine, Commendator of (Son of Lord Erskine) 170

Dublin 162, 176

Dumfries 115, 157, 174, 213, 220, 267

Dumfries Castle 174

Dunbar 5, 124, 139-140, 199, 231, 239, 259, 316-318, 327

Dunbar Castle 55, 59, 80, 82, 209, 213, 224, 230, 245, 252, 281, 286, 295

Dunoon Castle 133-134

Dumbarton 38, 43, 50, 60, 62, 94, 97-98, 100, 117, 125-127, 133, 163, 174-176, 189, 211, 224, 227, 241, 252, 285

Dundee 15, 42, 69, 83, 105, 120, 180, 209, 214, 259, 267, 302, 332, 316, 321-322, 327

Edinburgh 5-7, 11, 15, 20, 27, 30-33, 36-39, 44, 49, 51, 57-59, 62, 66, 71, 74-75, 77-84, 96-99, 101, 106, 110-111, 116-118, 121-123, 127, 129, 132, 135-139, 141-142, 149-150, 156, 160, 164, 167, 169, 174, 179-182, 185-186, 199-200, 202, 205-209, 213, 220, 223-224, 229-234, 236, 238, 240, 243-245, 251-252, 254, 259-260, 263-264, 267-269, 275, 279, 281, 286-287, 290-293, 300, 302-303, 306-307, 316-320, 323-324, 326-327, 332, 335

Elgin 49, 266

Elizabeth, Queen of England 63, 73, 239, 307, 309-311, 320-321, 324-325, 327-329, 331-332, 334-335, 342-343, 345

Ellenarne, Isle of (Election of Lordship of Isles:1545) 161

Erskine, John (of Dun) 69, 290, 294, 296, 312, 324, 326, 332

Erskine, John, 5th Lord of 74, 93, 158-159, 160, 163, 208, 227, 286, (Earl of Mar) 340

Erskine, Master of (Slain at Pinkie) 206

Eure, Lord Ralph 82, 84, 122-125, 135, 138, 148, 151-154

Eyemouth 244, 295-296, 321

Falkland Castle 24, 27, 185, 314

Faunrig Muir 164

Fast Castle 199, 244

Favoury, Baptista de (English Agent) 332

'Field of Shirts', (Highland battle) 131

Fitzgerald, Gerald (claimant of Earldom of Kildare) 161

Fleming, Lord 35, 95, 139, 206, 227, 255, 300, 305-306

Foster, John (English envoy) 157-158

Flodden, Battle of (1513) 1, 5, 29

Francis I, King of France 24-26, 47, 50, 52, 59, 72-73, 77, 129, 181, 208

Francois (Francis), Dauphin of France, King of France (Husband of Mary Queen of Scots) 239, 268, 316-317, 319-320, 341-343, 347, 356

Gamba, Pedro de (Spanish mercenary commander) 216, 238, 240

Gayton, Leonard (Alleged poison plot against Henry VIII) 206-207

Geneva 9, 301-303, 306

Chapuys, (Imperial Ambassador to England) 34, 45, 112

Glamis, Lady Jane (Sister of the earl of Angus) 23, 91

Glasgow 111, 121-122, 124, 127-129, 132, 138-139, 145, 172, 194, 200, 279, 338, 344

Glasgow, battle of Muir of (March 1544) 138-139

Glencairn, Cuthbert Cunningham, 2nd Earl of (Died 1541) 47-48, 52

Glencairn, William Cunningham, 3rd Earl of (Died 1548) 52-53, 69, 75, 81, 84, 87, 92-93, 109-111, 121-122, 124, 131-133, 137-139, 145-146, 149, 151, 172, 177, 197, 201, 219, 225-226

Glencairn, Alexander Cunningham, Master of (Subsequently 4th Earl of Glencairn 1548) 137-139, 226, 263, 270, 280, 283, 300-302, 306, 310, 324-325, 344, 346

Gray, 4th Lord of (Patrick Gray) 47, 54, 116-117, 132, 177, 219, 221, 226

Grange, James Kirkcaldy, Lord Treasurer, Laird of 16, 30, 59, 85, 105, 119, 183, 185, 190

Grange, William Kirkcaldy, Laird of 258, 291, 300, 340

Green, John (Scottish Privateer 265

Grey, Lord (of Wilton) 207, 216, 227, 232-235, 240, 243, 253, 344

Guillaume, Thomas (Black Friar) 58, 86

Guise, Claude, 1st Duke of (Died 1550) 24-25, 59, 173

Guise, Francis, 2nd Duke of 173, 267-268, 272, 281, 289, 299, 313, 317, 319, 322-325, 341, 343-344

Hadden Rigg, battle of 17, 52

Haddington, 21, 110, 124, 169, 180-181, 220-222, 327, 342

Haddington, siege of, 224-226, 228-235, 239, 241-243, 259, 281

Hamilton, Gavin 209

Hamilton, Sir James (See Earl of Arran)

Hamilton, of Finnart, James 30, 41, 43, 108

Hamilton, Abbot of Paisley, John (Also Lord Treasurer, Bishop of Dunkeld, Archbishop of St Andrews) 58-60, 67, 73, 82-83, 95-96, 101-102, 105, 107, 109, 121, 150, 159, 179, 186, 188, 190, 197, 202, 220,222, 236, 243, 250, 252, 263, 265, 270, 278, 290, 301, 308, 312, 323, 332, 344

Hamilton, of Clydesdale, John 150

Hamilton, Patrick (Reformer) 9, 39

Hamilton, of Sanquhar, Sir William 52, 56

'Hamilton's catechism', 265

Harlow, William (Reformer) 274

Hay, Alexander (Privateer) 194

Hay, John (Scots envoy to France) 196

Hay, Nicholas (Privateer) 149

Haverton, John (Scottish pirate based in English South coasts) 253

Henderson, James (Reveals poison plot against Queen Mary of Scots) 261

Henry II, King of France 196, 200, 224, 227, 234-235, 241-242, 249-250, 255-257, 260-261, 264, 267, 272, 294-295, 299, 304, 309, 318, 341

Henry VII 343

Henry VIII, King of England 1-2, 6-8, 11, 15-18, 20, 27-30, 33-35, 37, 42, 44-47, 51-56, 58, 62-68, 70, 72-73, 75-76, 78, 80-81, 84-86, 94-103, 106, 108-109, 112-120, 125-127, 129, 132, 134, 137-141, 148, 150, 152, 154, 156-158, 161-163, 168, 171, 173, 176, 187-190, 193-196, 200, 212, 246, 279-280, 282, 309-310, 343

Hepburn, Bishop of Moray, Patrick 10, 316

Hepburn, Patrick (See Bothwell, Earl of)

Huguenots, 256-257, 299, 315

Hume Castle, 69, 168, 221, 235, 242

Hume, George, Lord of 8, 33, 69, 72, 122, 124, 164, 168, 170, 202, 221

Huntley, George Gordon 4th Earl of 17, 26, 29-30, 33, 35, 42, 48-51, 57, 71, 75, 77, 80, 82, 85, 109, 121, 128, 130-131, 142, 155-157, 160, 162, 165, 174-175, 186, 203-207, 223, 251, 254-255, 257, 266, 269, 271, 286-287, 293, 296-298, 306, 317, 319

Inchkeith, Isle of 240, 245, 259, 342

James IV, King of Scotland 1, 48

James V, King of Scotland 1-45

Knox, John (Reformer) 26, 46, 58, 69, 73, 78, 120, 180-183, 197, 201, 204, 225, 251, 258, 280, 289-291, 294, 298, 302, 305-306, 309, 312-314, 316-317, 320-321, 324-325, 340, 343

Langholm 200, 259

Layton, Sir Brian 148, 152, 154

Leith 9, 76, 110-111, 118, 121-123, 149, 180, 206, 208, 213, 224, 227, 240, 252, 302, 304, 318, 322, 326

Leith, siege of 323-324, 326, 329-330, 332-335

Lennox, Matthew Stewart, 4th Earl of 42-43, 47, 60-62, 64-65, 67, 70-71, 74-75, 77, 80, 82, 87, 93-95, 97-100, 106, 109-112, 113-117, 119, 121, 125-127, 132-134, 137, 141-143, 154, 156, 160-163, 167, 171-172, 174, 176, 206, 213, 218-220, 222, 261, 273, 277, 282, 288, 328-329, 340, 342-343

Lennox, John Stewart, 3rd earl of 7, 40-41

Leslie, John 182

Leslie, John (see Rothes, Master of) 185-186

Leslie, Norman (See Rothes, Laird of)

Lindsay, Sir David 46, 74, 182

Linlithgow 1, 7, 24, 30, 40-41, 43-45, , 52, 54, 57, 59, 61, 65-66, 71, 74, 77, 83, 107, 110, 112, 117, 125, 132, 158, 163, 169-170, 199, 229, 275, 316, 324, 327

Lochmaben Castle 21, 102, 168, 174-175, 198, 264

Longueville, Louis, Duke of (first husband of Mary de Guise) 12, 255

Lords of the Congregation 299, 301-302, 304, 307, 310, 314-315, 318-320, 322, 324, 329, 334-336

Lorges, Jacques de Montgomery, Sieur de 65, 159-161, 164, 193

Lorne, Archibald Campbell, lord of (See Argyll, Archbald Campbell, 5th Earl of)

Louis XII, King of France 2, 13

Lorraine, Charles, Cardinal of 173, 267-268, 289, 317, 319, 322-325, 341, 343-344

Lovat, Lord Fraser of 130-131, 163

Luther, Martin 9, 31, 198, 289

Lutherans 13, 23, 34, 39, 272, 298

MacDonald, Donald Dubh, Lord of the Isles (see Ross, Earl of),

MacDonald, James of Dunivay, of Islay and the Glens of Antrim 156, 187

Madeleine of Scotland, Queen 11, 27

MacLean, Alain 176

MacLean, Hector Mor 86-87, 133, 156, 162-163, 171-172, 286

Maclean, Patrick 156, 161-162

MacLean, Rory 162

Maitland, William of Lethington,

Margaret Tudor, Queen 1-2, 5-8, 16, 38

Marshal, Sir William Keith, Earl 48, 69, 83, 255, 332

Mary of Guise, Queen (Also Queen Mother, and subsequently Queen Regent) 9, 24-25, 27, 29, 38-39, 41-45, 47-48, 50-52, 55-57, 59-61, 63, 64-67, 69-70, 72-75, 77-78, 80, 82-83, 86, 89-90, 93- 101, 105-106-109, 111, 114, 117, 125, 127-130, 132-133, 135-138, 141-142, 149, 152, 156, 158-161, 165-166, 170, 172-174, 178-179, 184, 187, 189, 192, 194-197, 205-206, 208, 210, 213, 222-223, 225-226, 233-235, 238-240, 243, 245, 249-250, 252-280, 285-299, 302-320, 321-330, 332, 334 346, 352-357

Mary of Scots, Queen 24, 27-28, 30-36, 38, 40, 52, 55, 66, 72-75, 95, 97, 100, 126, 138, 141, 158-159, 161, 170, 173, 183, 196, 201, 208, 211, 214, 223, 225-227, 235, 255-257, 260-261, 273-275, 277, 279, 289, 294, 296, 299-300, 304, 308, 310, 317-319, 323, 340, 344

Mary Tudor of England, Queen 273-274, 277, 286, 289,310, 342

Mason, John (English ambassador in France) 258

Maxwell, John, Master of (Subsequently Lord Herries) 175,218-219, 330

Maxwell, Robert, 5th Lord of (Died 1546) 38

Maxwell, Robert, Master of (Subsequently Lord Maxwell) 102, 254,

Melrose , Battle of (July 20th, 1526) 7

Melville, Sir James 183, 185, 189, 263, 299, 341

Menage, Jules de (French ambassador to Scotland) 97

Methven, Henry Stewart, Lord of 137-138, 206

Methven, Paul (Reformer) 302

Mill, Walter (Reformer) 302, 316

Moidart, of Benbecula, John 130-131, 163, 266, 286

Montalembert, Andre de (French commander) 224

Montrose, 69, 180,244, 300, 312

Moore, John (Surgeon and English spy) 98

Moray, James Stewart, Earl of (illegitimate son of James IV) 7-8, 10, 18, 21, 26, 29-30, 33, 35, 48-51, 57, 63, 70, 85, 96, 108-109, 128

Moray, James Stewart, Earl of (illegitimate son of James V and Janet Kennedy) 273, 288, 290, 294, 298, 300, 305-306, 317, 321, 324, 329, 339, 341

Morton, James Douglas, 3rd Earl of 45-46

Morton, James Douglas, Master of (Subsequently 4th Earl of Morton) 75, 96, 103, 118-120, 222, 257, 267, 298, 332, 340

Musgrave, Sir William 21-22

Musselburgh 111, 123, 203, 222, 233, 236, 326

Nesbit, Mr (Envoy for Earl of Lennox) 328

Nith River, Skirmish at (1547) 213-214

Ormiston, John Cockburn, Laird of 69, 180-181, 210, 220, 250-251, 315

Paget, Sir William 116

Paniter, David (Scottish Ambassador) 59, 67, 73, 82-83, 96, 105, 118, 154, 188, 190, 196, 211, 235, 258, 306

Paris, Charles,(Irish envoy to French) 271

Paul III, Pope 58, 60

Penningham, Simon (King's servant and Sir George Douglas's spy) 26

Percy, Sir Henry 297, 316-317

Perth 9, 15, 50, 69, 104-105, 113, 115, 209, 266-267, 271, 312-316, 321-322

Pinkie, Battle of (1547) 203-208, 268, 280, 341

Philip, King (Spain) 274, 277, 286, 295-296, 342

Portugal 124

Pringle, Sandy 85

Quarry Holes (Duelling areas in Edinburgh) 269

Isabella, Queen-Dowager (Of Hungary) 154, 191, 207, 253, 269-271

Raith, John Melville, Laird of 250

Reformation Parliament (1560) 339, 344

Reid, Bishop of Orkney, Robert 51, 159, 300, 305

Rhinegrave, The 224, 233-235

Roberts, Andrew (Scottish Privateer) 194

Ross, Donald Dubh MacDonald, Lord of the Isles and Earl of 49-50, 81, 87, 131, 155-156, 161-163, 171-172, 176

Rothes, George, Earl of 257, 300, 305-306

Rothes, John Leslie, Master of 153, 185-186

Rothes, Norman Leslie, Laird of 104-105, 119, 160, 188, 194

Rough, John (A Dominion Friar) 46, 197

Roxburgh 210, 231, 235, 237, 239, 244

Ruthven, Patrick, 3rd Lord of 52, 104, 139, 188-189, 269, 271, 314, 316, 323, 329

Rutlin, Lord 242-243

St Andrews Castle, siege of (1546-1547) 188-201

St Giles Festival 303

St Monans, battle at (1548) 191

Sadler, Sir Ralph (English ambassador) 15,37-38, 51, 53-56, 59, 64-66, 68, 75-78, 81-84, 86, 95-96, 98, 100-106, 321

Sandilands, of Calder, Sir James 292, 299

Sandilands, of Calder, John 103, 180

Scot, of Dieppe, Gilbert (Scottish privateer) 155

Seton, George, 6th Lord of 55-56, 123-124, 136, 139, 165

Seymour, Sir Edward (Earl of Hereford, 1st Duke of Somerset, Lord Protector) (119, 121-125, 127, 130, 132, 137, 142, 149, 152, 158, 162-165, 168-171, 174, 180, 183,194-195, 199-204, 206-208, 210-211, 215, 222, 227, 229,236-237-240, 244, 246, 279-280

Shaw, of Easter and Wester Sauchie, Alexander 172

Shrewsbury, Earl of 140, 229

Sinclair, Sir Oliver 16, 21-22, 24

Solway Moss, Battle of (1542) 21-24, 27, 32, 34, 39-42, 49, 66, 68, 259

Somerville, Hugh, 4th Lord of 35-36, 41, 75-76, 85, 101-102, 107-108, 123, 128, 139, 189

Somerville, John 172-173

Stewart, James (Captain of the Scots Guards in France) 65, 77, 97-98

Stewart, Robert (Captain in Scots Guard in France, involved in plot to poison Queen Mary)

Stewart, Robert (Bishop of Caithness. Caithness, Brother of the Earl of Lennox) 126, 142, 167, 174- 175, 255, 273, 328

Stirling 5-8, 57, 70-71, 74-76, 80-86, 93, 97-100, 109-111, 114-117, 127-128, 130, 132-133, 135-136, 156, 160, 162, 169-170, 173-175, 179, 186, 191, 205, 208-210, 213, 224, 229, , 266, 281, 306, 312, 316, 319, 321-322, 324, 326-327

Stirling of Glorat 133

Strozzi, Leone (Commander of fleet besieging St Andrews Castle; 1547) 200, 213, 252

Suffolk, Earl of 103

Tantallon Castle 5, 10, 55, 80, 102-104, 115, 118-121, 135, 189, 205, 231, 293

Thermes, Peter de (French commander) 240-242, 252,

Throckmorton (English agent) 333,

Treaty of Ardrossan (1546) 187

Treaty of Berwick (1560) 328-329

Treaty of Boulogne (1550) 244-245

Treaty of Campi (1546) 187-188

Treaty of Crepi (1544) 149-150

Treaty of Edinburgh (1560) 335-336

Treaty 'The enterprise of Paris' (1543) 47

Treaty, Greenwich (1543) 66-68

Treaty, 'Greneside Agreement' (1544) 111-112

Treaty of Norham (1551) 244-245

Treaty of Perpetual Peace (1502) 1

Tyndale, William (Welsh reformer and translator of the bible) 31

Umbaldino, Captain (Italian engineer) 230

Vonar, David 64-65

Wallace, Adam (Reformer) 251, 255

Zucculo, Hironimo (Venetian Secretary) 39

Printed in Great Britain
by Amazon